The Radical Rhetoric
of the English Deists

Studies in Rhetoric/Communication
Thomas W. Benson, *Series Editor*

The Radical Rhetoric
of the English Deists
The Discourse of Skepticism, 1680–1750

James A. Herrick

UNIVERSITY OF SOUTH CAROLINA PRESS

© 1997 University of South Carolina

Published in Columbia, South Carolina, by the
University of South Carolina Press

Manufactured in the United States of America

01 00 99 98 97   5 4 3 2 1

Library of Congress Cataloging-in-Publication Data

Herrick, James A.
  The radical rhetoric of the English Deists : the discourse of
skepticism, 1680–1750 / James A. Herrick.
    p. cm. — (Studies in rhetoric/communication)
  Includes bibliographical references and index.
  ISBN 1-57003-166-5
  1. Deism—Great Britain—History. I. Title. II. Series.
BL2765.G7H47 1997
211'.5'0941—dc21   97–4864

Contents

Editor's Preface

In *The Radical Rhetoric of the English Deists,* James Herrick of Hope College presents the first full length rhetorical study of a remarkable group of controversialists. The English Deists of the seventeenth and eighteenth century engaged in a heated, high-stakes public debate with defenders of traditional religious doctrines. Herrick demonstrates that the doctrines of the Deists, though highly varied, are best understood as rhetoric—that is, as addressed to readers in a particular historical circumstance and in the context of a bitter public controversy.

The Deists argued that religion must be based on free, critical rationality and that any doctrine that could not hold up to rational inspection was untenable. From the advocacy of rationality in religious reflection, the Deists concluded that religious thinking must be free of coercion, intolerance, and violence. If all true religion is based on what is evident to common reason, then it follows, argued the Deists, that any religion, and not exclusively Christianity, has a claim to spiritual truth. The Deists typically rejected the Bible, which they regarded as exclusive and restricted. Priests and priestcraft were rejected as self-serving mystification. Miracles were rejected as incompatible with reason and experience. An important cultural legacy of the Deists is their early work in biblical criticism, which, according to Herrick, is in itself a considerable achievement, but an invention that is more strategic and rhetorical than scholarly.

The radical English Deists were indefatigable arguers, using a powerful arsenal of reason and ridicule to attack established religion. They were met by a sustained counterattack from the defenders of religion. Professor Herrick engages in a detailed analysis of the rhetorics of leaders and debaters on both sides. The form and consequences of Deism were part of a larger social upheaval in which the power of a conservative class was under challenge. Because they were in a position of genuine risk, the Deists, according to Herrick, typically disguised or outright lied about their own religious views, pretending, for strategic reasons, to loyalty to a Christianity in which they did not actually believe. Because of the class antagonisms that were an inseparable part of the Deist controversy, the debate over religion spilled over into a more general political debate.

In this account of the rhetoric of the English Deists and their orthodox opponents, Professor Herrick illuminates English public life in the period 1680–1760 and illustrates the origins of cultural assumptions that are part of the common sense of our own time.

Acknowledgments

I am indebted to a number of people for their help and encouragement with this project. Professor Lloyd Bitzer of the University of Wisconsin originally suggested to me that the Deists would be a fruitful topic of study. I owe him my thanks for that suggestion and for his assistance with my early explorations into the Deists' arguments against revelation and miracle. I would also like to thank the staffs of the British Library, the Bancroft Library at the University of California, the Huntington Library, the University of Michigan Libraries, the Newberry Library, and the Harvard University Libraries for their consideration and assistance with archival research. My thanks are due also to Hope College, the Knight Foundation, the University of Wisconsin Alumni Research Foundation, the Lilly Foundation, Mr. and Mrs. Peter Northrup, and the National Endowment for the Humanities for their financial support of my research and travel. Finally, I wish to thank my colleagues at Hope College and my family for their consistent support, encouragement, and interest.

Thomas W. Benson

Chapter One

The Social and Religious Context of the Deist Controversy

> The religion of nature, and therefore of the God of nature, is simple and plain; it tells us nothing which our reason is unable to comprehend, and much less anything which is repugnant to it. Natural religion and reason are always agreed, they are always the same.
>
> Henry St. John Viscount Bolingbroke, c. 1730

> The Father of Lies never had more Hands at Work in advancing his Interest, by venting Errors and Heresies of every kind, than in these latter Ages wherein our Lot is cast. . . .
>
> *Shaftesbury's Ghost Conjur'd*, 1738.

John Evelyn wrote in his journal in May 1690 of "our threatening Calamitie provided from men's Vices and for want of stable, christian and Moral principles. . . ." The deplorable moral state of England resulted from "an universal atheistical, or sceptical, humor overspreading the nation" (quoted in Holmes, p. 186). Evelyn had reason for concern. Religious skepticism was evident in every segment of British society. From the artisan's clandestine lodge and the literary hack's coffee house to the courts of royalty, the works of "atheistical" writers were read voraciously and debated vigorously. Surely "errors and heresies of every kind" could be found anywhere one cared to look for them in late-seventeenth-century England.

The causes and background conditions of skepticism, freethinking, and religious unrest in this period are complex, and no single factor accounts for the massive change taking place in British religious thought and life. Increased tolerance likely encouraged religious exploration toward the end of the century. Whereas in 1682 "so many Norwich Quakers were in prison that their Monthly Meeting had to be held in Norwich gaol," by decade's end Dissenters and other religious dissidents found England a considerably freer setting (Watts, p. 254). The Catholic King James took measures in middecade to stop anti-Catholic activities. Moderate Anglican clerics were so tolerant of liberal theologies that they were accused by conservatives of encouraging heresy (Morais, p. 32).

In March of 1686 James pardoned many imprisoned for their religious convictions, freeing in the process more than twelve hundred Quakers.[1] In 1689, the Earl of Nottingham introduced the Toleration Act into the House of Lords. The act, which suspended much of the Clarendon Code, did not end religious persecution, but it did go a long way toward making the open practice of religion according to conscience possible in England under William of Orange (Watts, p. 259). Freedom of religious expression increased markedly, while the act also "dramatically reduced attendance in Anglican churches, which in turn reduced the authority of parish priests over the morals and religious practices of parishioners" (Holmes, p. 192).[2]

Corresponding with this period of relative religious freedom was an era of unusual political and social stability in England. Though revolution and political intrigue had characterized the seventeenth century, from 1688 to 1722 the political scene in England stabilized remarkably, and even relations with other nations were less hostile than they had been for a century. Under George I, who took the throne in 1714, England was a "lightly governed society . . . in a state of relative control and equilibrium" (Rack, p. 7). This period of calm in English social and political life encouraged religious speculation and provided the leisure and security that made possible a serious and lasting religious debate. England also experienced at this time an unusual growth in trade, rapid economic change, civic development, and a general increase in prosperity. All of these factors provided impetus for challenging old structures and beliefs.

Social factors such as the Glorious Revolution, improved access to the Continent, and gradual urbanization also played their parts in the massive religious revolution taking shape from the middle to the end of the century. William Stephens noted in the 1690s that "this Revolution . . . has wonderfully encreased Mens Prejudices against the *Clergy*" (p. 10). Increased travel is an often overlooked factor in the rise of British skepticism in the seventeenth century. Early in the century it became fashionable for gentlemen and their sons to make "the grand tour" of the Continent. James Force calls the tour a "crash course in comparative religion" which left many of the tourists suspicious, even contemptuous of clergy and dogmatism (p. v). Clerics in the 1680s were openly mocked, as in these verses from *A Satyr on the Parsons:*

> Religion's a Politick Law,
> Devis'd by the Priggs of the Schools;
> To keep the Rabble in awe
> And amuse poor Bigotted Fools.
>
> And they, for good vitualls and Bubb,
> Will bellow their Nonsense aloud,
> And rant out a Tale of a Tub,
> To {fright} the ignorant Croude.
>
> (quoted in Gillian, p. 155)

A generally negative impression of Catholicism was often brought back from Europe and colored perceptions of the Anglican Church. An ugly debate between the Church of England and its opponents in the Church of Scotland did not help matters. And were the officers of the Inquisition worse than the elders of the Church of Scotland who executed Edinburgh University student Thomas Aikenhead for blasphemy in 1697 at the tender age of nineteen years? Nor did the flamboyant rhetoric of Presbyterian leader Mungo Craig improve the public image of the clergy when he affirmed that Aikenhead's writings were "a compleat Aggregate of all the Blasphemies that ever were vented, maintained, or excogitated by all the *Atheistical* ministers of Satan in all ages." Young Aikenhead is "the General Generalissimo of Sophisters" and "surpasses the most malevolent of all the Devils in everything except knowledge . . ." (M. Craig, pp. a2, 12).

Though England was largely a rural nation in 1700, London already had half a million residents out of a total English population of just over five million. The city's rapid growth provoked concern that there would not be enough churches to accommodate the city's new residents. "In 1711," notes Henry Rack, "government money was offered to build fifty new churches (only ten were actually erected) . . ." (Rack, p. 2). Between 1700 and 1750, the population of Bristol doubled from about 22,000 people to more than 50,000. Cities such as Birmingham and Newcastle were also growing rapidly. Whereas the countryside and village remained largely free of religious ferment, a new urban population provided a fertile field for religious doubt and theological experimentation. By 1700, William Talbot, Lord Bishop of Oxford, felt compelled to preach against the publications of the notorious Deist Charles Blount in his Easter Monday sermon for the Lord Mayor and other dignitaries gathered at St. Bridget's Church in London.

The press, including book printers, assumed a more significant role in British religious life toward the end of the century. The Licensing Act lapsed in 1695, and an active Opposition Press challenged the established government. Printers in London published and sold the works of radical "atheists" such as Blount and John Toland. In 1678, a year before the death of Hobbes at age ninety-one and two years after the birth of the Deist Anthony Collins, Blount noted that his *Anima Mundi* was condemned as "a Atheistical Heretical Pamphlet" (preface). In turn, such authors kept up a constant polemic in favor of freedom of the press. Some printers themselves played leading roles in London skeptical societies or "clubs" and were also vocal advocates of press freedoms. Christianity's opponents became increasingly bold. By 1708 the author of *Letter Concerning Enthusiasm* freely mocked the "good Christian, who . . . thinks he can never believe enough" and whose faith encompasses "not only all Scriptural and Traditional Miracles, but a solid System of old Wives Storys" (Cooper 1708, p. 9).

By the end of the seventeenth century, anti-trinitarian theologies such as Arianism and Socinianism were frequently advocated in books and tracts. By 1695, anti-trinitarianism seriously challenged the Church of England, which sought to defend orthodox theology by rhetorical and legislative means. So threatening was the combined skeptical and Unitarian challenge that the Blasphemy Act was passed in 1697 "for the effectual suppressing of blasphemy and profaneness." The act targeted those who would "deny any one of the persons in the holy Trinity to be God, or . . . assert or maintain there are more Gods than one, or . . . deny the Christian religion to be true, or the holy Scriptures of the Old and New Testament to be of divine authority" (Berman 1988b, p. 5). A three-year prison term was mandated for these crimes.[3]

Denying Christ's divinity was "the prevailing heresy of the early eighteenth century," and social class or position were not protections against prosecution. William Whiston, professor of mathematics at Cambridge, lost his position for the Arianism of his *Primitive Christianity Revived*. As respected a figure as Samuel Clarke, rector of St. James's, Westminster, "in attempting to explain *The Scripture-doctrine of the Trinity*, also came to conclusions which his critics branded as Arian" (Watts, p. 373). Even Archbishop John Tillotson, the greatest preacher of the age, advocated positions that smacked of unitarianism and that his critics labeled unorthodox. Tillotson was attacked in print by the powerful polemicist Charles Leslie. The anonymous author of *Blasphemia Detestanda: or a Caution Against the Diabolism of Arius* affirmed in 1719 that Arianism "certainly was trumpt up by the *Devil,* and his faln, or Infidel *Angels.*" This writer longed for a return to the days when blasphemers were properly punished, as was Bartholomew Legat a mere century earlier. Authorities "burnt him at Smithfield, at *London, March 18, 1611*" (pp. 3, 4).

Intellectual life at the end of the seventeenth century in England was dominated by Hobbes, Newton, and Locke. Hobbes's *Leviathan* (1651) affirmed that all willful human acts were motivated by self-interest, a claim that launched the whole school of British moral philosophy as a response. There was for Hobbes, the Monster of Malmesbury, "nothing simply and absolutely so; nor any common rule of good and evil. . . ." What one took to be good or evil was an expression of one's individual desire. Hobbes was deeply skeptical that any proposition in religion could be demonstrated.

Newton's *Principia* was first published in 1687, only three years before Locke's *Essay;* the former made the natural world less mysterious, the latter the world of the mind. For all of Locke's professed beneficence toward Christianity and reticence about his own religious views, astute readers saw "in Locke's thought a challenge to every old orthodoxy." Locke "condemned ideas not derived from the sense, or from rational reflection on the evidence of the senses, as 'rubbish'" (Edwards, p. 394). Thus, revelation as a source of rational ideas was implicitly rejected. Several early Deists were greatly influenced by Locke, and at least two— Toland and Collins—considered themselves disciples. Whereas Locke distanced himself from the former, he was a close friend of the latter.[4]

Sir Isaac Newton was, in Addison's memorable phrase, "the Miracle of the Present age." Though Newton advocated Christian faith, and though science and religion achieved a "holy alliance" around this time, Newton's work emboldened those wishing to push back the curtain of mystery which had for nearly two millennia hung over the entrance to the Church (Gasciogne, pp. 2–3). "Science gave new freedom and new hope, as if mental and stellar horizons were expanding together," writes James Sambrook. "The sudden and huge growth of ordered and apparently certain knowledge seemed greatly to enlarge the possibilities of the intellectual, moral, and practical improvements" (p. 1).

Unyielding rational scrutiny of religious ideas and biblical texts engendered skepticism in the seventeenth century. The English tradition of biblical criticism extended back at least to Sir Walter Raleigh's *History of the World* (1603–1616) and was more fully developed in Lord Herbert of Cherbury's *De Religioni Laici* (1645) and Sir Thomas Browne's *Religio Medici* (1643), wherein Browne challenged such rudimentary biblical doctrines as the Fall and the curse on Adam and Eve. Rene Descartes's *Discourse de la Methode* (1637), which promoted systematic doubt as a criterion for testing propositional truth, was having its influence in England as elsewhere by mid-century. Spinoza's *Tractatus Theologico-Politicus* (1670) was translated into English in 1689.

Spinoza affirmed the supremacy of reason to revelation and was determined to "examine the Bible afresh in a careful, impartial, and unfettered spirit, making no assumptions concerning it, and attributing to it no doctrines, which I do not find clearly set down therein" (quoted in Cameron, p. 16). Noting the implausible nature of many biblical stories, Spinoza urged that "whatsoever is contrary to nature is also contrary to reason, and whatsoever is contrary to reason is absurd, and *ipso facto*, to be rejected" (quoted in Cameron, p. 14). He suggested "naturalistic interpretations of miracles" and questioned traditional attributions of biblical authorship. The Pentateuch "was written by Ezra, with its author being given the name Moses simply because Moses was the name of its principal character" (Hurlbutt, p. 69). On the foundation provided by Hobbes, Locke, Newton, Raleigh, Herbert, Descartes, and Spinoza, hard-edged critical approaches to revelation were erected.

By 1680, the virulent skeptical movement known as Deism asserted itself in British cities and universities. Blount's *Oracles of Reason* (1693) advanced a critical apparatus that drew on ancient sources as well as on the religious documents of Islam, Hinduism, and Zoroastrianism in attacking Christianity. Blount "collected Hobbes' statements favoring Deistic notions, and translated Spinoza's *Tractatus* chapter which gives a naturalistic explanation of miracles" (Hurlbutt, p. 70). He searched classical and contemporary sources for material to support his unorthodox religious views, drawing upon Philostratus, Porphyry, Celsus, Lucian, Seneca, Cicero, Averroes, Pomparatius, Erasmus, Montaigne, Bacon, Spinoza, Hobbes, and Locke. Blount provided any interested readers a catalogue of skepticism and inspired later and more caustic Deists such as Thomas Woolston and Peter Annet.[5]

The Bible's supernatural accounts were consistently under assault by the century's end, and ridicule was emerging as a favorite tactic of skeptics. William Stephens, a chronicler of skepticism's progress in the period, wrote in 1696 that, "having read *Spinoza* and *Hobbes*, and been taught to laugh at the story of *Balaam's* Ass, and *Sampson's* Locks," the skeptics then "proceed to laugh at all *Miracle* and *Revelation*." Ridicule was the rule in skeptic societies where, as Stephens put it, "a witty Jest and t'other Glass puts an end to all further consideration" of biblical accounts (Stephens, p. 5). Orthodox writers lamented that ridicule was the most characteristic element in the new skeptical writers.

By the turn of the century, the social and intellectual ground in Britain was fertile for the growth of heresy and skepticism.[6] Free thought was fashionable, and Deists like Toland popularized a "religion of reason" which required neither clergy nor revelation.[7] Rationalist theology was gaining ground even inside the church. Miracles and revelation were the subjects of raging controversies. Anti-trinitarian books by Socinian refugees to Holland were finding their way into England and having their effect. The situation was serious for the English Church as traditional Christian views and practices were everywhere under assault. Thomas Stackhouse, an ardent opponent of the skeptics, urged his English readers "to remember, that *Infidelity* is not properly the *natural* product of our Country, but an *exotic* Weed" that, though it might "thrive beyond the *Alps*," had no "fix'd Rooting in this cold Climate, till the Heat of our *civil Distractions* gave room for the *Leviathin* to bring it in, and, in Process of time, for the *Oracles of Reason* to make it grow" (1733, preface). Cromwell plowed the field, Hobbes planted, Blount watered, and the imported weeds of skepticism, Arianism, and atheism flourished in England's Christian garden.

Religious Controversy and Persecution

As the eighteenth century opened, the British religious scene was greatly unsettled. Toland's popular *Christianity Not Mysterious* (1696) made Deism the subject of intense public debate. His books were burned by the common hangman in his homeland of Ireland, an action initiated in the English Parliament, and Toland fled for safety to the Netherlands. But Toland's writing catalyzed an already explosive situation. Christian revelation was subjected to a unceasing criticism, careers and fortunes were staked on the outcome of theological debate, and the public's interest in the topics and characters involved was insatiable.

When arguments did not suffice to silence the most extreme critics of the faith, prosecutions were pursued. Edmund Gibson (1669–1748), the Bishop of Oxford, threatened many writers with prosecution under the Blasphemy Act and was angered by the popularity and influence of the University's arch-Deist, Matthew Tindal. Though no one was executed for religious crimes in Britain in the eighteenth century—Aikenhead was the last to die for such an offense—there were three trials for blasphemy between 1729 and 1770, all of Deists and all resulting in conviction. Gibson, elevated to the powerful position of Bishop of London in 1720, had not changed his views on how to deal with blasphemers. He was personally responsible for the first successful blasphemy trial of a Deist in the eighteenth century—Woolston, in 1729.

Interest in religious controversy ran high as the new century dawned, and polemical documents abounded. Public interest was evident also in works on illicit topics related to religion such as speculative theology, sexual mores, occult practices, magic, and secret organizations. Always a keen student of public tastes, Daniel Defoe scandalized readers with accounts of immorality and ritual occultism in books such as *The Perjur'd Free Mason Detected* and *The Free Masons; an Hudibrastic POEM*. In his sensational *A System of Magic or, a History of the Black Art,* (1727) Defoe traced the history of magic from "the darkest Ages of the World, when Miracle, and something Wonderful, was expected to confirm every advanc'd notion; and," he adds, "when the wise Men, having rack'd their invention to the utmost, call'd in the Devil to their Assistance, for want of better Help" (preface). In *The Secrets of the Invisible World Disclos'd or, an Universal History of Apparitions* Defoe catalogued popular and obscure ghost stories, miracle accounts, and strange tales.

A vein of public interest in religious experiment and exploration, sacrilegious and heretical allegation, strange and frightening spiritual narrative, and exotic theology provided subjects for other writers as well. Jacob Ilive speculated about the possibility of space travel and life on other planets, apparently a theme in Aikenhead's heresy as well. Toland's *Letters to Serena* and Blount's *Anima Mundi* introduced British readers to the religions of the Near and Far East and advanced their authors' derived pantheistic schemes. Woolston mocked Christ and reinterpreted biblical miracles as allegory in his *Six Discourses*. Blount and Ilive discovered and translated "lost" biblical texts which, they claimed, overturned cherished Christian beliefs. Stephens and Woolston both suggested that Christ deserved crucifixion. Virtually no aspect of the moral or theological structure of the day passed unchallenged, and no rhetorical tactic was ruled out in efforts to establish a new religious vocabulary and social order.

A radical social agenda sometimes attended exhilarating forays into uncharted religious territories, suggesting that spiritual and social revolution were linked. Ilive argued strenuously for penal reform based on his own experiences in British jails. Annet advanced a case for liberalized divorce laws, again based largely on personal experience. Collins, Annet, Ilive, Thomas Chubb and other Deists pleaded incessantly for greater freedom of expression and of the press. All of the Deists advocated religious tolerance, and many affirmed an openness to the teachings of various faiths. Deists and Freemasons were typically Whigs, and the lodges and societies of the freethinking sort often functioned as cells for the discussion of liberal political ideas and for criticism of the social conservativism and political power of the Anglican Church. Pierre Manent has argued that political liberalism itself developed in part as the result of "the natural desire to escape from the political power of revealed religion . . ." (p. 116).

Of course, theological and social conservatives inside and outside the church were not silent in the face of affronts to faith and tradition. And it is James Sambrook's view that the paganism and irreligiosity of eighteenth-century Britain has been exaggerated in recent scholarship. "Eighteenth-century England was a Christian country," he writes. "Most educated laymen were greatly concerned about religion." He adds, "most of the Anglican clergy were not the venal and torpid time-servers of legend," though he admits that "reform of their ecclesiastical organization was very slow." Anglicans and Dissenters cooperated in establishing both "the Society for the Propogation of Christian Knowledge (1696) and the Society for the Propogation of the Gospel in Foreign Parts (1701), as well as in the many local societies for the reformation of manners set up from 1695 onwards" (p. 25). The well-organized and damaging Sacheverell riots on the night of March 1–2, 1710, touched off by Henry Sacheverell's sermon "The Perils of False Brethren," further revealed the strength of Anglican conservatism at the very height of Deistic and Dissenting activity.[8] Moreover, Deists and atheists were answered in hundreds of pamphlets, sermons, pastoral letters, broadsides, and books from 1685 on for a century. Church and State employed stocks, fines, imprisonment, and censure against the skeptics to silence them. Toland's *Christianity Not Mysterious* was burned, many periodicals such as Annet's

Free Inquirer were banned, and some print shops daring to publish Deist literature were closed.

The Deists

At the center of the ferment in England were those writers known as the Deists.[9] At their head were religious radicals such as the polyglot Toland, whose *Christianity Not Mysterious* marked a turning point in an already longstanding dispute between skeptics and the clergy. Toland affirmed provocatively that we embrace religious doctrines "not for any convincing evidence in them, but because they serve our ends better than the truth; and because other contradictions we are not willing to quit are better defended by their means" (pp. 36–37). Robert Rees Evans calls Toland's book "the boldest use of the press since Milton and Sir Roger L'Estrange" (p. 5). Toland suggested, among other things, that the supernatural elements of Christianity—prophecies and miracles— were propagated for political motives and rested on irrational and even non-Christian presuppositions. The mysteries of faith should be jettisoned, and a new religion of reason built from what remained. The formula was simple, as was the new criterion of canonicity: "all the doctrines and precepts of the New Testament must . . . agree with *Natural Reason, and our ordinary ideas*" (p. 46).

Toland's claims threatened an orthodoxy wed to revelation, mysteries, prophecies, and miracles. More dangerous still was the fact that, persuasively presented by several talented writers, "rational religion" attracted many adherents. Collins and Tindal refined the arguments of Blount and Toland. By 1720 Deism was widespread in British cities, posing a serious threat to social and religious stability.[10] Bishop George Berkeley was sufficiently exercised by Collins's *Discourse of Free Thinking* (1713) to write his lengthy and carefully reasoned refutation, *Alciphron, or The Minute Philosopher* (1731). When Woolston blasphemously denounced both Jesus and his miracles in his *Six Discourses on the Miracles of our Savior* (1727–29), Bishop Thomas Sherlock responded with his enormously popular *Tryal of the Witness to the Resurrection of Jesus Christ* (1729). William Law and Joseph Butler answered Tindal's *Christianity as Old as Creation* (1730), a work which received more than a hundred replies. Law's brilliant *The Case of Reason* (1731) is among the most astute apologies for Christianity ever penned, while Butler's *Analogy* (1736) remains a classic of religious philosophy. The long controversy produced a massive literature on both sides. "Around the 1720's," writes R. M. Burns, "the debate had received enormous attention; so much so that almost every English theologian, philosopher, or even simply man of letters of the period made some contribution to it" (p. 10). Even Defoe's Robinson Crusoe mused on his desert island about the possibility of miracles (pp. 110–11, 127).

"The whole question of the reasonableness of Christian belief" rested on the extraordinary foundation of miracles (Tennant, p. 69). Though "equally reasonable persons" may have "entertained opposite views" regarding miracles, does this observation support F. R. Tennant's conclusion that "the whole matter is thus psychological" (p. 87)? Such reductionism ignores a range of important rhetorical issues energizing this debate. Though psychological commitments mark the controversy, as they do all public debates, they are insufficient by themselves to account for the strikingly different positions taken by "equally reasonable persons" on revelation, miracles, and related issues. Nor does psychology alone account for the duration, energy, and venom that characterized this contest. Powerful human motives, including the desire for rational freedom and the opposed insistence upon religious tradition and social order, inaugurated the Deist controversy. The extraordinary rhetorical prowess of many of its chief figures animated the contest. A massive struggle for social and political power served as an engine propelling the debate for most of a century. Finally, deep personal animosities also played a role in lending this dispute a singular energy. Deists affirmed that "we have a right to test revelation by reason, and need not accept it untested," and Christian writers "moved to meet this attack with great confidence" (Stromberg, p. 60).

Failure to account for the debate's rhetorical impulses has led to incomplete interpretations of some of its most paradoxical literature. Norman Torrey, for instance, concludes of Woolston's strange works that he appeals to "the wildest fancy he can invent to support his thesis" (p. 65). But Torrey thus misses the rhetorical cunning of Woolston's "wild fancy" which rendered his attacks on the miracles the greatest threat to Christianity in the middle decades of the eighteenth century. Woolston's assault was rhetorically adept and persuasive to many readers. Similarly, Ernest Mossner has written that "Orthodoxy now driven to its last defenses, clung desperately to probability and the external evidences" (p. 145). But "desperate clinging" hardly captures the rhetorical brilliance of Butler's *Analogy*, Berkeley's *Alciphron*, or Sherlock's *Tryal*. These and other similar works brought popular Christian apologetic to its highest point of sophistication and force. Probability, argument, and historical evidence were employed by orthodox writers for reasons not accounted for by the explanation of rhetorical desperation. While Torrey and Mossner draw our attention to the rhetorical choices energizing this controversy, they fail to explicate the controversy's most fascinating components.

Rhetorical controversies always inhabit historical space as private convictions are driven into the public realm by human motives, where such convictions, now having taken the shape of arguments, are often altered by force of impact with rival arguments. The rhetorical history of the Deist controversy, that is, its history as an account of the invention, articulation, and collision of arguments in the service of human motives, is the subject of this study. The consequences of the enormous efforts expended on both sides in this long polemical struggle are only fully understood from a rhetorical perspective, a perspective attentive to writers' personal motives, discursive goals, and argumentative strategies and to the profound shaping influence exerted on the development of cases by the presence of an adjudicating audience. I will emphasize the work of several important but lesser-known Deists whose rhetorical careers were, I will argue, more consequential than has so far been suggested by historians and whose rhetoric exhibits the radically controversial spirit and willingness to absorb enormous personal risks that made the Deist controversy so intriguing and consequential. Throughout I have sought to set texts in their contexts, to interpret arguments as both statements of philosophies but also as responses to controversial emergencies, and to present personalities in personal conflict. I hope by these means to illuminate the major discursive battlefields of the Deist controversy as rhetorical war was waged for the religious mind of Britain and eventually of Europe and the Colonies.

Early-eighteenth-century Deism influenced scholarly criticism of the Bible as well as the approach taken to the Christian scriptures by many ordinary readers. Deism also shaped subsequent discourse about religion generally, particularly in its advocacy of a universal and fundamentally univocal religion of reason and tolerance. Moreover, English Deists contributed importantly to eighteenth-century discussions of freedom of religion, speech, and the press. The Deists were also ardent though often unsuccessful advocates of a number of progressive social reforms, such as liberalizing divorce laws, humanizing penal practices, and eliminating blasphemy prosecutions. Thus, in a number of important ways we yet live with the victories and defeats of English Deism in our religious, literary, and social practice.

Historical Antecedents of Deism

The Deists were the inheritors and popularizers of a skeptical tradition with a complex history. Before undertaking a more detailed overview of the Deist controversy, it will be helpful to sketch out the Deists' line of historical descent. "At the beginning of the Renaissance," George T. Buckley writes, "the classics began to be read once more as literature." As a result "the Humanists soon discovered that in Seneca and Plutarch there was a system of morals worthy to be compared with the Christian . . ." (p. 17).

Indeed, many ancient sources were translated into English and French in the sixteenth and seventeenth centuries, and works such as Cicero's *Academica* and Sextus Empiricus's *Pyrrhonian Hypotyposes* greatly influenced European thought in the period.[11] "The recovery and the reassimilation of the ancient writings," notes C. B. Schmitt, "were the primary factors in the evolution of the modern sceptical attitude" (p. 228). Schmitt places particular emphasis on the role of Cicero in the development of modern skepticism. Similarly, Richard Popkin notes that "Sextus, a recently discovered oddity, metamorphosed into 'le divin Sexte' who, by the end of the seventeenth century, was regarded as the father of modern philosophy" (p. 19). George Buckley as well draws attention to skeptical tracts which were influential in sixteenth-century England, works such as Cicero's *De Amicitia*. There were also numerous reprints of Marcus Aurelius, Dionysius Cato, Epictetus, Plutarch, and Seneca between 1481 and 1600. By contrast there was nothing of Homer's in English before 1580, no Plato before 1598 (Buckley, pp. 17–18).

Many readers of these ancient sources noted that pagan systems of morals were often "closely related to Christianity, urging the same moral virtues." Thus, Stoicism, writes Buckley, "was advanced by its apologists as an aid to Christianity, and the churchmen, unable to condemn it because of its lofty sentiments, saw little to which they could object. Thus in a way Stoicism actually enjoyed the protection of the church" (p. 19). The secularization of morals is clearly evident in works such as Sir Thomas Elyat's *The Governour*, published in 1531.

More recent developments on the Continent also contributed to skeptical movements in England. Harold Hutcheson finds "the main immediate source of Deism" in the "widespread scepticism in the Italian academies of the second quarter of the sixteenth century" (p. 60). Gian Francesco Pico della Mirandola was among the early-sixteenth-century Italian writers who, interestingly, employed skepticism to defend Christianity (Schmitt, p. 236). By revealing the weaknesses in Aristotelian sense-based epistemology, Mirandola hoped to show the scriptures to be the only source of true knowledge. Other Christian authors in the late fifteenth and early sixteenth centuries, such as Henricus Cornelius Agrippa, provided skeptical grounding for Christian piety. Rejecting the humanistic ideas of pagan antiquity, the Christian would live by a simple faith in God. "The end result was not supposed to be that all would be in doubt, but rather that one would turn from philosophy as a source of knowledge, to the only guide men had in this 'vale of tears,' the Christian Revelation" (Popkin, p. 20).

The skeptical orientation was also clearly evident in Montaigne's "Apologie de Raimond Sebond" (1575–76). Reason provided inadequate ground for knowledge. Thus, "the things that come to us from heaven have alone the right and authority for persuasion, alone the stamp of truth . . ." (quoted in Popkin, p. 49). Fear of Protestant rationalism led Jean-Pierre Camus to "undermine . . . human rational pretensions" and take refuge in "a fideistic defense of Catholicism" (Popkin, p. 63).

Deism could also trace its roots to some unlikely European ancestry a century and a half before Montaigne wrote. Richard Popkin argues that the Reformation aided the project of biblical criticism by its endorsement of private interpretation. Luther's "new criterion of religious knowledge" was that "what conscience is compelled to believe on reading Scripture is true." "The Pandora's box that Luther opened at Leipzig," writes Popkin, "was to have the most far-reaching consequences, not just in theology but throughout man's entire intellectual realm" (Popkin, p. 4). Similarly, Roscoe Pound argues that "private interpretation of the Bible . . . involved a claim of primacy for the individual reason" (p. 30). And S. G. Hefelbower affirms that freedom of interpretation was "a logical deduction from the right of private judgment, which was a basal principle of the Reformation" (p. 3). Erasmus was more skeptical about rational approaches to religious faith. "All the machinery of these scholastic minds had missed the essential point, the simple Christian attitude" (Popkin, p. 6). But Luther held that faith was founded on certainties ascertained by the rational believer. "The Holy Ghost is not a Sceptic," he warned Erasmus (quoted in Popkin, p. 7). "The rule of faith of the Reformers thus appears to have been subjective certainty, the compulsion of one's conscience. But," adds Popkin, "the world is full of people convinced of the oddest views" (pp. 7–8).

The question of the proper grounds for religious knowledge persisted from the fifteenth through the seventeenth centuries. Sebastian

Castellio of Basel, a defender of the heretic Servetus burned by Calvin, "tried [in *De Haereticis*] to destroy the grounds for Calvin's complete assurance of the truth of his religious beliefs, without at the same time destroying the possibility of religious knowledge" (Popkin, p. 10). Like the later Deists he sought a principle for judging religious truth that would "be so manifest, so well recognized by all, that no force in the universe, that no probability, can ever make the alternative possible." Popkin notes that for Castellio "this principle . . . is the human capacity of sense and intelligence, the instrument of judgment on which we must rely" (Popkin, p. 12).

Reason again emerges as the criterion of religious truth. Even Jesus Christ, Castellio pointed out, resolved questions by using his senses and his reason (Popkin, p. 12). Thus, the evidence of sense and the operations of reason are sufficient for resolving questions in religion. Castellio writes like a Deist. In response to "those authors who wish us to believe . . . certain things in contradiction to the senses," he wants to know "if they came to these views . . . without judgment." If, on the other hand, "they base their views on judgment and reason, they are inconsistent when they persuade by their judgment to renounce ours" (quoted in Popkin, p. 12). There were problems, of course, in the Protestant position. To claim a "self-validating or self-evident criterion" meant that "one would never be able to tell with absolute certainty what book was Scripture, how to interpret it, what to do about it, unless one were willing to substitute a doctrine of personal infallibility for the acceptance of Church infallibility" (Popkin, p. 15).

Deist rejection of authority eventuated in a rejection of all "revealed" texts. Reason, the light of nature, was their sole criterion of rationality, operationalized as Locke's clear and distinct ideas or Herbert's *notitiae communes*, ideas common to all normal human minds. Deist skepticism about authority drew sustenance from writers such as Cicero and Sextus Empiricus, from Stoicism and Pyrrhonianism, especially as interpreted by Montaigne in the sixteenth and seventeenth centuries, and even from Luther. "Even in the Middle Ages the church had been willing to call reason and conscience to the aid of revelation and authority." Writers such as Erasmus, Vives, and Bude' "wished to bring back pagan culture with Christianity added . . ." (Buckley, p. 17). Erasmus, for instance, wrote, "remain good Christians, but profit by ancient wisdom" (quoted in Buckley, p. 17).

Such thinking encouraged the comparison of Christianity with other moral systems. The intellectual movement, according to Buckley, "could only suggest that Christianity had no monopoly on morality." He adds that it "encouraged a comparison of religions, and it made for the secularization of morality by declaring it to be the province of reason rather than that of the church (Buckley, p. 17). An Oxford scholar turned recusant priest, William Chillingworth urged in *The Religion of Protestants*, according to David Edwards, that "schismatics, heretics, even heathen Turks, could find that their good lives led them to salvation" (Edwards, p. 367). Later, Toland and Blount pursued a systematic comparison of religions to find an irreducible core of common elements, the elements of a natural religion.

Thus, Buckley finds Stoicism to have been a major encouragement to rationalistic approaches to religion. It "laicized morals," by "remov[ing] them from the church and plac[ing] them in the sphere of reason." He adds that "Stoicism taught that Fate or Destiny ruled the world, that man's struggles were useless, and thus tended to lessen the moral responsibility of the individual." However, "more important than either of these, [Stoicism] drew men's minds to other religious systems and suggested a comparison not always unfavorable to the non-Christian creeds" (p. 19). Toland and Blount, like many Stoics, concluded that "all creeds have many points in common . . ." (Buckley, p. 19). Moreover, "the attempt to discover and reconstruct the original belief from which the separate religions were supposed to have varied" would yield the true, rational religion of the human race. Buckley, thus, traces a straight line from the ancient Stoics to "the deism of Lord Herbert of Cherbury" (p. 19).

Study of the classics during the sixteenth century presented orthodoxy with other, more specific problems. Miracles were reported in many ancient writers, and thus Christian writers "found themselves in a difficult position in defending one set of miracles, while rejecting others as unreasonable."[12] The universality of rational faith also posed a problem. Bushell points out that eighteenth-century thinkers are concerned "to give to Christianity a more universal justification than it was thought at the time to possess" (p. 85).

Deists were "re-shaping for fresh usage certain ancient beliefs while discarding others as neither credible nor useful to the modern mind." Or, perhaps they were shaping the modern mind by deciding which ideas were credible or useful according to their own rational standards. The Deists' goal was "a renovation of religious belief" (Bushell, p. 86). But this renovation required the demolition of the existing structure, rather than its modification. Deists advocated a "religion of humanism," though a humanism of a type. Lovejoy contends that "the whole question [of one's relation to God] was now . . . to be studied quite independently of authority and with the expectation that the answer given to it would more accurately reflect the dignity" of the human race. Still, "Pascal warned against appeal to 'stupid nature' or 'impotent Reason,' (*Pensees*) for we are children of sin" (Lovejoy, pp. 89, 98).

The Course of the Deist Controversy

As we have seen, a complex and interactive set of social and intellectual forces set the stage for the Deist controversy.[13] Toland's arguments in *Christianity Not Mysterious* were not new, but previous statements had not elicited the excitement which his did. Deists were mentioned as early as 1563 by Viret, and Deism had received published replies as early as 1600. Charles Blount had already advanced much of the basic philosophy of Deism in works such as *Anima Mundi* (1678) and *The Oracle of Reason* (1693), and he and other English Deists were answered by writers like Mungo Craig in his *A Satyr Against Atheistical Deism* (1696). The perceived rhetorical character of the Deists is already clearly reflected in the title of Humphrey Prideaux's *The True Nature of Imposture Fully Displayed*, published in 1697. But, then, William Assheton was already warning the Deists against blasphemy in his *An Admonition to a Deist* in 1685. William Stephens, perhaps a Deist himself, thought a history of Deism already in order when he wrote *An Account of the Growth of Deism in England* in 1696. (Another edition appeared in 1710.) Charles Leslie's early response to the Deists, *A Short and Easie Method with the Deists* (1697) was enormously popular both in England and the Colonies.

Nevertheless, Toland's work of 1696 is still conventionally identified as the first important document in the Deist controversy. William Fleetwood's *An Essay Upon Miracles*, published in 1701, represents early efforts to answer an increasingly popular Deism on the issue of miracles.[14] Questions of evidence were very early identified as important to the general debate over religion's supernatural elements, as is revealed in the title of Anthony Collins's first book, *Essay on the Use of Reason and Testimony* (1707).[15] Collins was joined by Shaftesbury, who published his *Letter Concerning Enthusiasm* in 1708 and *Sensus Communis or an Essay on Wit and Humour* in 1709. These works, along with his *Soliloquy or Advice to a Writer*, were issued under the title *Characteristics of Men, Manners, Opinions and Times* in 1711, a foundational work in English Deism. In 1713 Collins published his famous *Discourse of Free Thinking*, prompting Berkeley to enter the dispute. Collins received at least nine other replies within a year. Richard Bentley, Benjamin Hoadley, Samuel Clarke, Francis Hare, and Thomas Sherlock all answered Collins.[16] Swift parodied Collins's work in *Mr. C— — —n's Discourse of Free Thinking Put Into Plain English by Way of Abstract for the Poor*, also published in 1713. That Collins's views were disseminated through coffeehouse societies is suggested by the title of another answer to the *Discourse*: DeFoe's *The Vanity of Free-thinking Expos'd in a Satyr. Dedicated to Mr. C— —ns, proprietor, and the rest of the Thoughtful Members of the Kitt-Katt Club.*

Orthodox writers began to take the attack on revealed religion more seriously after the publication of Collins's *Discourse*. Beginning with John Leng's Boyle Lectures of 1717–18, published in 1719 under the title *Natural Obligations to Believe the Principles of Religion and Divine Revelation*, orthodox apologists were more active in answering Deism. In 1722 the orthodox apologist John Conybeare published two defenses of the Christian miracles, *The Nature, Possibility and Certainty of Miracles* and *The Mysteries of the Christian Religion Credible*, the latter a sermon preached in Oxford on October 21, 1722. The same year, however, William Woolaston strengthened the Deists' philosophical position in his carefully reasoned work *The Religion of Nature Delineated*. Thomas Woolston's assault on the clergy in *Four Free Gifts to the Clergy* appeared between 1722 and 1724. In 1724, Anthony Collins again entered the debate with his provocative *A Discourse of the Grounds and Reasons of the Christian Religion*. Collins attacked the rationality of biblical prophecy and was answered by Edward Chandler, Samuel Chandler, and Benjamin Ibbot.

But the three years from 1727 to 1729 were the most controversial of the decade, largely due to the publication of Thomas Woolston's *Six Discourses on the Miracles of Our Saviour*. Woolston released these scathing works periodically between 1727 and 1729 and in the process elicited dozens of replies, most of them coming before 1730. Woolston, a patristic scholar of repute, though one considered by friends and enemies alike to be mentally unstable, was seen as a dangerous opponent of Christianity. His *Discourses* were the most direct and damaging attack on the Christian miracles yet published. Their caustic satire provided a model for other Deists to emulate. Woolston's rhetorical career is explored in chapter 4.

Collins wrote his *A Discourse Concerning Ridicule and Irony* (1729) in response to Woolston's many opponents. Collins notes that both revered classical authors and respected orthodox divines direct ridicule against their opponents. Also published in 1729 was the most famous orthodox defense of miracles in its day, Sherlock's *Tryal of the Witnesses*. Sherlock's book grew directly out of Woolston's trial, and just as Woolston had set a precedent for later Deists, Sherlock's juridical model was followed by many later orthodox writers. Sherlock's *Tryal* was widely held to be unanswerable and saw numerous editions.[17] Other responses to Woolston included Richard Smalbroke's massive *A Vindication of the Miracles of Our Blessed Saviour.*

The year following Woolston's trial, Tindal's *Christianity as Old as Creation* appeared in print. Tindal, a fellow at Oxford, provided a clear and forceful statement of the basic Deistic position. *Christianity as Old as Creation* appeared at an opportune time. Sentiments over the trial and imprisonment of Woolston were running high. The Deists' case concerning the supernatural elements of Christianity had been persuasive to many. An eloquent and enormously popular statement of Deism come of age, "the Deist's Bible" elicited over one hundred responses, making it the most controversial work of the miracles debate.

By 1730, many arguments on both sides in the Deist controversy had hardened into commonplaces. Thomas Stackhouse reviewed the arguments of ten respondents to Woolston in his *A Fair State of the Controversy Between Mr. Woolston and his Adversaries*, finding remarkable similarities in the basic Orthodox approach. Still, Deism seemed to gain ground—Woolston was widely read at home and in the American colonies; freethinking, Deist, and Masonic clubs met in London and other cities; and several new and provocative radical skeptics such as Annet and Chubb had begun publishing their arguments. A search was on for a new answer to the Deists.

William Law suggested an approach in his *The Case of Reason* (1731). Breaking with Sherlock's juridical model, Law argued vigorously for the limitations of human reason in apprehending the mysteries of God. Berkeley and Conybeare extended Sherlock's method by examining a broad spectrum of evidence in support of Christianity. In *Alciphron*, Berkeley marshaled church history and Near Eastern archeology in the defense of biblical truth. The result was the most thorough case for the miracles yet contrived. Conybeare attempted something similar in his *Defense of Revealed Religion* (1732), a response to Tindal.

Joseph Butler's *Analogy of Religion*, perhaps the greatest literary product of the controversy based on the subtlety and strength of its argument and the elegance of its presentation, was another attempt to find a sure way of defeating Deism. Butler argued that nature, the starting point of the Deists' "natural religion," was full of anomalies, wonders, and even apparent flaws. It thus did not provide a basis for arguing that there can be no mysteries in God. In fact, Butler reasoned that nature's ambiguities and puzzles should lead us to *expect* a divine revelation, and one filled with mysteries at that. Only then could nature and religion be said to be truly analogous.

Law, Berkeley, Conybeare, and Butler made the 1730s a period of orthodox dominance in the controversy. However, the last few years of the decade saw a flurry of controversial activity and the introduction of two powerful new voices for Deism. In 1738 Thomas Morgan published *The Moral Philosopher*, a forceful restatement of the Deists' argument against miracles, as well as a justification of the method of ridicule. Morgan was answered by the able Orthodox writer John Chapman, whose *Eusebius* of 1739 was an important contribution to the Orthodox cause. Morgan wrote an immediate reply to Chapman, *The Moral Philosopher, volume II*. Also published in 1739 was the first important work by Thomas Chubb, *A Vindication of the True Religion of Jesus Christ*. Chubb, a London candle maker, represented a new, more popular brand of Deism.

As the decade of the 1740s opened, activity in the miracles controversy was reaching a crescendo. Morgan published the third volume of his *Moral Philosopher*. In 1741, Chubb published his famous *Discourse on Miracles*, which introduced several important innovations to the basic Deistic case against miracles. Also published in 1741 was the second volume of Chapman's *Eusebius*.

But the most controversial book of 1741 was Henry Dodwell's satirical *Christianity Not Founded on Argument*. Dodwell's work is a parody of Law's fideism in *The Case of Reason*. So subtle was Dodwell's treatment of problems in the Orthodox case that some readers took him to be a sincere Orthodox apologist. More than fifteen Orthodox writers attempted to answer Dodwell, discovering how difficult it can be to refute satire.

Philip Doddridge, however, made it his purpose to see Dodwell thoroughly discredited. Publishing *A Letter to the Author of Christianity Not Founded on Argument* in 1742, *A Second Letter to the Author of Christianity Not Founded on Argument* in 1743, and *A Third Letter* the same year, Doddridge exhibited a characteristic Orthodox zeal to find the right response to Deism's most successful attacks. Thomas Mole, John Mason, and John Leland are among the other Orthodox writers who sought to answer Dodwell's satire.

In the early 1740s, an important new opponent of Orthodoxy appeared on the scene in London. Around 1744, Peter Annet published his *The Resurrection of Jesus Christ Considered by a Moral Philosopher* and *The Miraculous Conception*. The former, a rebuttal of Sherlock's *Tryal* which had stood unanswered for fifteen years, was extremely popular and considered a triumph in freethinking circles. A number of anonymous works published around 1745 are also attributed to Annet. Among the titles are *The Resurrection Reconsidered* (1744), *The Resurrection Defenders Stripped of All Defense* (1745), *The Resurrection Demonstrated to Have No Proof* (1745), and *Deism Fairly Stated* (1746).[18] Annet, the subject of chapter 6, was tried and punished for his writings.

It has been suggested that radical Deism began to wither in the late 1740s. But, in fact, Annet's rhetoric raised the debate to an intense pitch into the opening years of the 1750s. Samuel Chandler's *The Witnesses* is typical of numerous responses to Annet. Though Hume's famous "Of Miracles," chapter 10 of the *Enquiries*, drew the fire of many Christian writers after its appearance in 1748, the radical Deists remained prominent on the English religious stage until about 1770.[19] Hume's argument appeared the same year as the Deist Conyers Middleton's *Free Inquiry*. Though Hume's assault on miracles brought him the controversy he sought, he was bothered that Middleton's argument in *Free Inquiry* was so popular that people were not reading his *Enquiries*. Once the significance of "Of Miracles" was recognized, however, more Orthodox attention was turned to answering it. Thus, Philip Skelton's *Ophiomaches or Deism Revealed* (1749), William Adams's *An Essay on Mr. Hume's Essay on Miracles* (1751), Thomas Rutherforth's *The Credibility of Miracles Defended* (1752), and George Campbell's *Dissertation on Miracles* (1762) were all able responses to Hume.[20] Others replies to the century's greatest philosopher on the question of miracles were written later in the century and throughout the next.

But answering Hume was certainly not the only business of Orthodox apologists after 1748. Dodwell's *Christianity Not Founded on Argument* (1741) was still being answered in 1754 in John Leland's *Remarks on Christianity Not Founded on Argument*, while Leland's *A View of the Principal Deistical Writers*, perhaps the single most important and certainly the most encyclopedic response to Deism, was published in 1752. Even Hugh Farmer's *Dissertation on Miracles* of 1771 is a late reply to Chubb's *Discourse* (1741).

Conclusion

The religious view known as Deism had proponents as early as the mid sixteenth century in Italy and France. Its sources are found in early Christian history, particularly the heresies of the Patristic period, and also in ancient philosophical traditions. Impetus for the Deistic assault on revelation can also be attributed to forces on both sides of the Reformation debate. Tributaries to this powerful intellectual current are thus various and sometimes unexpected: Christian gnosticism, Roman stoicism, Catholic "sceptical" apologetic, and Reformation hermeneutic.

But though this heterodox religious movement was present in various forms for some time before the seventeenth century, it was not until the end of that century that a group of writers in Britain transformed it from an intellectual curiosity into a potent and even dangerous force for radical religious and social critique. This transformation required the particular combination of social stability and relative religious freedom present in England beginning in the mid 1680s. But also necessary to this process of sweeping critique were the rhetorical acumen, textual resources, and iconoclastic motivation of a number of skilled popular religious writers. This study will examine and assess the rhetorical work of these writers, the Deists, as they sought by discursive means to undermine the foundations of England's religious traditions.

Chapter Two

Characteristics of British Deism

But stay: the Deist here will urge anew,
No supernatural worship can be true;
Because a general law is that alone
Which must to all, and everywhere be known;
A style so large as not this book can claim,
Nor aught that bears revealed religion's name.

Dryden, Religio Laici

They stand miserably in awe of fines; they are afraid to speak out their principles, lest they should shock or alarm. It is for these reasons, that they are forced to borrow the name and cloak of Christianity, in order to attack it, and dare seldom or never to rejoin to their answerers, lest they should lose those benefits of their present concealment, from which the greater part of their success is hoped for.

On the other hand, our modern Apologists for Christianity often defend it on Deistical principles.

Deism Revealed

Once treated as a marginal group of rationalist religious writers espousing a natural theology featuring an aloof deity, the Deists are now viewed by some scholars as harbingers of modernism in religion, politics, and social theory. The work of Margaret Jacob, David Berman, Robert Rees Evans, Robert Sullivan, Leonard Levy, and Michael J. Buckley has recently afforded a clearer picture of these enigmatic writers, and they are gradually being awarded a prominent place in the development of modern religious ideas.[1]

One traditional treatment of Deism—as theological rationalism centered on a God who set the universe in motion and then stepped away—though persistent, is no longer tenable.[2] The actual religious convictions of the Deists are so varied and complex as to raise questions about the descriptive usefulness of the term Deist, and controversy surrounds the theological commitments of even individual Deists. Berman has argued recently that Anthony Collins was in fact an atheist and in another place calls him "a strong-minded atheist" (1989, p. 602). Sullivan and Evans, however, affirm that John Toland was a pantheist, and Sullivan denies that Toland was a Deist at all (p. 204). The religious views of Thomas Woolston are equally difficult to identify with certainty, whereas obscure Deists whom historians have chosen to ignore (Jacob Ilive being the most significant example) are best described as gnostic or theosophical in orientation. The picture of Deist theology is further blurred by the Deists' tendency toward misrepresenting their own views in order to avoid prosecution, a point to be developed in the next chapter.

Contributing to the problem of associating Deism with a discrete set of religious ideas is the eighteenth-century tendency to use the words "Deist" and "atheist" almost synonymously. Roger Emerson notes that "early writers did not sharply separate deists from atheists but they did tend to attribute to the former a disbelief in revealed religion" (p. 23). But some twentieth-century writers present the Deists merely as liberal Anglicans or Latitudinarians following Tillotson, while James O'Higgins finds Deism to be the logical extension of Luther's radicalism (p. 50). Other efforts to define Deism avoid religious categories entirely. Jacob has made political liberalism and association with secret societies clearer marks of religious radicalism than any particular theology.[3] Harold Hutcheson finds characteristic of Deism "its profound though empty malcontent, its dissatisfaction with everything that was, with no hope of something else to be" (p. 74). Significant problems, then, attend efforts to define Deism. Nevertheless, the label has been employed since 1562 to describe certain radical tendencies in religious thought, and perhaps practice, with some agreement that a significant number of writers on the Continent and in England between about 1600 and 1800 were Deists and that Deism flourished in Britain between about 1690 and 1740.

The Religion of a Deist?

Uncertainty about a religious definition of Deism should not suggest that Deists did not make theological pronouncements. An early and famous formulation of "Deism" appeared in Herbert of Cherbury's *De Veritate*, published in Paris in 1624. Herbert (1583–1648) suggested that the basic tenets of rational faith were, as summarized by David Edwards, "(1) that God exists, (2) that he ought to be worshipped, (3) that virtue is the chief part of worship, (4) that there should be repentance for vices and crimes, and (5) that there are rewards and punishments after this life" (Edwards, p. 366). More than a century later, Peter Annet provided a representative example of a more developed Deist theology in *Deism Fairly Stated*. "Deism is all, in the Christian Institution," wrote Annet, "that can possibly approve itself, to the true, genuine reason of man." He then identified these six tenets:

I. There is a God . . . a necessarily-existing, self sufficient, and an infinitely perfect being, who is, in and of himself, perfectly happy.

II. Infinite happiness [is] the result of the contemplation of his own essential perfections, and a pure consciousness of an invariable conformity in affection and action, to truth.

III. [Truth] has a necessary existence in nature, independent of and in the order of our conceptions, prior to, the will of any being whatever.

IV. To us, the only conceivable motive the supreme being could have to create us, and every other species of intelligent being, was that of communicating happiness to us, and them.

V. Rational and intelligent creatures are capable of being in their measure happy [as] they are pure as [God] is pure . . . Or, in other words, as they conscientiously conform themselves to the . . . obligations of reason.

VI. [As] we are rendered incapable of perfection, so the kind author of our beings, who could not want us but to be happy, will graciously accept a sincere desire, and endeavour, to know and to do what is right [which is] the nearest approach to perfection, that, in our present state, we are capable of. (*Deism Fairly Stated*, 10–11)

How many Deists would have agreed to Annet's or Herbert's tenets is difficult to know. If Collins, for instance, was an atheist, as Berman argues, then he could not accept any such propositions about God's nature and activities. If Toland was a Pantheist, he would have accepted little of Annet's formula. How much in this credo is for Annet himself mere camouflage or window dressing is also difficult to tell.

Defining Deism Rhetorically

Perhaps the project of defining Deism on theological grounds is best abandoned and another tack taken toward identifying the movement's essential characteristics. A definition more revealing than any particular theology is constructed from Deism's animating controversial impulses as reflected in the recurrent goals and axioms of its public rhetoric. The following seven marks of Deistic discourse, then, are offered as the broad boundaries of the movement's rhetorical definition.

I. The Plea for Rational Liberty

Deism and the call for free rational inquiry are inseparable. In his highly influential volume *A Discourse Of Free Thinking* (1713), Collins affirmed that the essence of Christianity was freethinking, or the free exercise of critical reason in evaluating religious claims. Deists often claimed that the founders of Christianity intended it to be a faith based on free rational inquiry. "The design of the gospel was," writes Collins, "by preaching to set all men upon Free Thinking, that they might think themselves out of those notions of God and religion which were every where established by law. . ." (p. 44).

Jesus himself was, in Collins's estimation, a freethinker. "Our saviour particularly commands us to search the scriptures, that is, to endeavour to find out their true meaning." Thus, "for fear we should surrender our judgments to our fathers, and mothers, he bids us take heed what we hear, and whom we hear, and to beware of doctrine" (p. 45). Later, in his *Discourse of the Grounds and Reasons of the Christian Religion,* Collins wrote that "the grand principle of men considered as having a relation to the Deity and under an obligation to be religious" is that they "ought to consult their *reason* . . ." (p. xiii). Thus, rational criticism of religious claims was the first duty of the Christian and equally the first duty of all people.

It should be noted that Collins's valorizing use of "Christianity," like his use of terms such as "gospel" and "saviour," are strictly disingenuous and diversionary. There is no evidence that he or any other Deist accepted the specific content of the Christian gospel or understood Jesus of Nazareth to be humankind's savior. The problem of the Deists' tactical appropriation of Christian language will be considered in chapter 3.

Free rational inquiry required freedom from religious intolerance and violence. Virtually every writer of the seventeenth or eighteenth centuries who has been called a Deist took a stand against religious persecution and intolerance, an issue to be addressed in chapter 5. So strong was this tendency in Deism that Hutcheson, perhaps overstating the case, makes it the impetus for the entire movement. "The deistic movement must be regarded, in its inception, as a protest against all religious violence and as an attempt to find some practicable formula for bringing that violence to a close" (p. 61). As evidence for his claim, Hutcheson traces the roots of Deism to the Italian Academicians, humanists, and the early European Unitarians such as Laelius and Faustus Socinus, Sebastion Castellio, and Jacobus Acontius, all united principally in their affirmation of religious tolerance.

II. The Preeminence of Reason

Deists affirmed that something they termed the Rule of Reason or Natural Law holds sway in the universe. Not even the divinity is free to interrupt the rational laws governing nature. Deists have thus been viewed as theological dualists by some. "The law of nature is immutable," wrote Tindal in his widely cited *Christianity as Old as the Creation* (1730), "because it is founded on the unalterable reason of things" (p. 61). Nature is always perfectly in accord with reason, and natural law is inviolable. To allow violations of natural law opens the floodgate to innumerable similar violations and brings one at length to an unknowable, irrational cosmos.

Reason is preeminent over other sources of religious truth, which are at best redundant of reason's findings. "God made us reasonable creatures and reason tells us . . . what God requires us to know" (Tindal, p. 30). Reason does not bow to tradition, authority, or revelation. "I build nothing on a thing so uncertain as tradition," writes Tindal, "which differs in most countries; and of which, in all countries, the bulk of mankind are incapable of judging" (p. iii). Similarly, Toland affirmed in 1696 that "since religion is calculated for rational creatures, tis conviction and not authority that should bear weight with them." Nor is revelation above reason. "Nothing revealed," argues Toland, "is more exempted from its disquisitions than are the ordinary phenomena of nature" (pp. xv, 6).

Annet argued that as God "created us with reasoning power" that he will thus "in Justice, require of us a conduct" consistent with reason. God is not so unjust as to require of any human being a standard of conduct or belief not universally attainable. Thus, the refusal of certain religious "obligations" is rational. "If anything else" than what reason teaches "is enjoined as a duty, in any, even the Christian Institution, it cannot be necessary to be observed, in order to eternal salvation." At the point that any religion departs from the religion of reason, it becomes false. Deism is itself the rational core of all religious belief, as it is "all, in the Christian Institution, that can possibly approve itself, to the true, genuine reason of man" (Annet 1746, pp. 9, 10).

But human reason does not, in all cases, arrive at the same or even similar conclusions about religion. Because of their study of other faiths, Deists were more aware of this fact than were most of their contemporaries. They were also aware that such differences posed a problem for their case. If universal human reason has access to religious truth, then why do so few individual minds arrive at the Deists' own conclusions? Why is there such a frustrating variety of religious opinion in the world? The Deists' answer to these questions involved two elements—prejudice and priestcraft.

In his *Letters To Serena*, Toland writes of "the successive Growth and Increase of Prejudices thro every step of our lives" and sets out to prove that there is a "Conspiracy to deprave the Reason of every individual Person." No human being escapes the conspiracy against reason, though some learn gradually to overcome its effects. In fact, we are all implicated as conspirators, for "all the Men in the World are join'd in the same Conspiracy." There exist "Prejudices in all Conditions of Men" which contribute to the conspiracy against reason. The social instruments of the conspiracy include "Schools, Universitys, Churches, [and] Statesmen," but also implicated are the practices of "breeding and nursing up of Children," all of the various "Professions and Trades," and even "ordinary conversation or living in Society." "There is none of these," writes Toland, "without their peculiar Abuses" against reason (preface). The priestcraft hypothesis will be explored in greater detail momentarily.

III. The Rejection of Religious Privilege

Reason is the source of religious truth, and reason has been available to all people in all places and at all times. Thus, religious truth has also been available to all people at all times. Dryden noted that for the Deist:

> God is that spring of good, supreme and best,
> We made to serve, and in that service blest;
> If so, some rules of worship must be given,
> Distributed alike to all by heaven;
> Else God be partial, and to some denied
> The means his justice should for all provide.[4]

Herbert suggested that the true religion of nature is discovered by "internal faculties." We reasonably add to ideas passing this first test "those about which there is the most agreement" among the various religions. In this way the honest searcher arrives at "the worship of the supreme God" (Hutcheson, p. 89).

True religion, it follows, is simple, apparent, ordinary, and universal. It also follows that anything complex, obscure, or mysterious in religion is not true. "All doctrines," writes Toland, "must agree with Natural Reason, and our ordinary ideas" (Toland 1696, p. 6). The simple, universal religious doctrines are "written in the hearts of every one of us." By means of reason alone God communicates truth to *all* people equally. James Andersen was the first historian of the London Masonic Lodge, an institution with links to Deism. In his *The Constitutions of the Freemasons* (1723), Andersen writes that members of the lodge were urged to believe only those elements of religion "in which all Men agree, leaving their particular Opinions to themselves" (quoted in Dewar, p. 33). By this formula, no one person or group of people can lay exclusive claim to salvation. Thus, no community of faith has religious grounds for persecuting any other such community. Hutcheson writes that "the denial of the doctrine of exclusive salvation" was grounded in "scepticism as to the possibility of discovering absolute truth and partly from sheer humanitarian repugnance to the persecutions which that doctrine engendered" (p. 61).

Consistent with their universal view of religious truth, the Deists rejected religious privilege, the notion that one faith has exclusive access to spiritual truth. Deists searched for commonalities among religions in an effort to demonstrate the existence of a common core of universal religious insight. Herbert opens *De Religioni Laici* (1645) with a musing on the varieties of religions in the world. A "Wayfarer" would notice that all faiths make some claim to unique truth and that each rejects such claims made by the others. Herbert wonders how the Wayfarer shall "protect himself if every man's individual dogmas about necessary and excellent truth are so proposed as to damn all the rest?" (quoted in Hutcheson, p. 87). And yet, Herbert noted, each faith also shares many points in common with the others.

Charles Blount (1654–1693) recorded the positions of ancient religions on an afterlife in *Anima Mundi: or, An Historical Narrative of the Opinions of the ancients Concerning Mans Soul after this life* (1678). Toland's *Pantheisticon* (1720) explored similarities in various religious traditions, making it an early work in comparative religions. And the content of that universal faith? The universal "Religion of Law and Nature," ac-

cording to the Mason Andersen, is "to love God above all things, and
our Neighbour as ourself; this is the true, primitive, catholic, and universal Religion, agreed to be so in all Times and Ages" (quoted in Dewar,
p. 34). Nevertheless, individual Deists reserved the right to conceive of
God in any manner commensurate with personal reason, even if that
meant, as it did to at least some of them, as nonexistent. Thus, even in
Deist circles there was no evident consensus on the elements of rational
religion.

IV. The Rejection of Revelation

Any revelation—the Bible being the immediate and principal example for Deists—is necessarily restricted to small groups, often in isolated places. Moreover, varying revelations advance a confusing
multiplicity of specific theological claims. Deists regarded the Bible as
"a tissue of lies and fables," and they sought to propagate this conviction by radical critique (Stromberg, p. 31).[5] Their particular role in developing biblical critical methods will be discussed later in this chapter.
An overview of the Deists' case against revelation is important because
of the centrality of those arguments and assumptions to the general Deist
case against Christianity and all revealed religion.

M. A. H. Melinsky notes that the Deists "saw no place for divine
revelation at all." After all, "God had given all men perfect law by which
to live and sufficient means to know it and do it." As a result, "any special revelation by God is unnecessary," and the particular revelation of
the Bible "is at many points unworthy of Deity" (p. 47). John Yolton
suggests that "by far the most common mark of Deism was the rejection
of revealed religion," the same mark that the eighteenth-century critic
of Deism, John Leland, "singled out in his extended analysis of certain
leading Deists" (1985, p. 172).

Revelation was the foundational cause of much human suffering.
Revealed religion, according to Annet, "is capable of doing any mischief, and of setting up any impositions; of destroying the liberties of
mankind, of demolishing virtue, of dethroning reason, of advancing tyranny, of setting up the most brutal idolatry, and the most unnatural barbarity, for the worship of the Deity." Moreover, "all this it has done."
Special revelation "has been the parent of all sanctified villainy, of all
religious lies and lying wonders, of everything that is scandalous of God,
and pernicious to man." Annet asks, "Can such a foundation as this be
the best to build a religion upon? Reason answers, No" (Annet, *Resur-*

rection of Jesus Christ Considered, pp. 9–10). Crucial to ushering in the new age of reason was removing the great rational impediment of revelation, or, more to the point, of one particular revelation.

At its best, where it repeats the findings of reason, revelation is redundant. At its worst, where it adds doctrine unknown to reason, revelation encourages superstition in the public and abuse of power among priests. "To come to the point," wrote Annet in 1747, revelation is "the grand foundation of the difference betwixt the Deists and the religions of all other persuasions. . . ." If "any doctrine or precept . . . has not its foundation apparently in reason or nature" it cannot be "the essence of religion," nor can it be, for that matter, "a religious doctrine or precept" (p. 14). In other words, any doctrine that rests solely on revelation is, *ipso facto*, false. "Eighteenth century criticism," James Thrower summarizes, "while it included a moral criticism, was for the most part naturalistic and was centered on the idea of revelation" (p. 100).

The specific target of the Deists' fire was not Islam or Hindu but, of course, Christianity. Toland taunts that to say Christianity is supported by a self-endorsing revelation from God is "a noble argument to tell a heathen . . . when all societies will say as much for themselves, if we take their word for it" (Toland 1696, p. 31). And Collins points out that even apparently unique Christian doctrines could be found in other "revealed" sources. After all, *"priests* throughout the world differ about scriptures and the *authority* of *scriptures* . . . the *Talapoins* of *Siam* have a *book of scripture* written by *Sommonocodom*, who, the *Siamese* say, was *born of a virgin*, and was *the God expected by the universe*" (quoted in Berman, p. 602). Annet urged that only the "experience and reason of all mankind" and their "common sense and understanding" were checks against hopeless confusion and false doctrine, the results of revelation (Annet 1747, pp. 74–75). All parties to the controversy "thought that antipathy to the idea of divine inspiration was central to deism" (Sullivan, p. 207).

The Bible was, Deists argued, a confusing and thus divisive document. "How is the gospel the revelation of God," asks Annet, "if men cannot understand it who honestly endeavour to do it?" And of the clergy who sought to defend the scriptures he wondered, "Why should men be so bitter . . . in vindicating what is not of their power to understand, explain, or defend?" (Annet 1745, p. 93). William Stephens also connects a corrupted revelation with a corrupt clerical class. "If those Writings, which they call *Holy Scriptures* are of their side, as [clerics] say they are,

I make no doubt but they were of their own inventing. . . . " But Stephens was willing to extend this argument to include Jesus himself. "If *Jesus Christ* their patron," he writes, "laid the Foundation of those Powers, which both *Popish* and *Protestant Clergy* claim to themselves from under him, I think the old *Romans* did him right in punishing him with the death of a Slave" (p. 7). In response to the Deists' contention regarding the autonomy of reason, Christian apologists argued that reason over-stepped its proper role when it rejected revelation. "In a Word," writes the anonymous author of *Shaftesbury's Ghost Conjur'd,* "I think no Man that professes to be a Christian, should . . . give loose reigns to his blinded understanding to dictate any thing contrary to the Revelation God hath given us" (p. 6). Where reason and revelation conflict, reason is in error. The Orthodox case for revelation, and against reason, is considered in detail in chapter 7.

V. Primitive Religion and the Priestcraft Hypothesis

The original, pristine, and universal religion of reason was gradu-ally lost to humanity. Deist hypotheses explaining this loss were varied and often complex. However, most asserted a massive, ancient, and universal conspiracy by "priests" to dupe a naive populace into accept-ing miracles, rituals, bizarre doctrine, and enslaving superstitions. All of these elements were propagated to ensure the maintenance of priestly power. So common was the priestcraft hypothesis to Deist religious his-tory that Steele remarked: "If one were to take the word 'priestcraft' out of the mouths of these shallow monsters, they would be immediately struck dumb" (quoted in Hutcheson, p. 80).

Blount sought the origins of "superstitions" about the progress of the soul after death in various ancient religions. At the heart of his ori-gins theory were the machinations of opportunistic persons ready to exploit human uncertainty about death. The original proto-priest was "some crafty discerning person, who having observed what is most dear to Mankind, thought by pretending himself able to assist in the preser-vation of that one particular [i.e. life] . . . he might thereby procure an esteem and credit in the world." From this common ancestor the class of priests descended, seizing power by exploiting primal human fears and inhibiting the free workings of human reason. Blount alleges that con-temporary priests employ charges of "Heresies and Schism" as "theo-logical Scare-Crows, with which they . . . fright away such as making an inquiry into it, are ready to relinquish and oppose [religion], if it appear either erroneous or suspicious" (*Anima Mundi,* preface).

The religious confusion brought about by priests is never resolved by them. Priests representing different faiths disagree endlessly about doctrines as basic as the nature of God, the reliability of various prophets, the sinfulness of humankind, and the remedy, if any, to that sinfulness. "It is well known," writes Anthony Collins, "that the priests throughout the universe are endlessly divided in opinion about all these matters; and their variety of opinion is so great, as not possibly to be collected together. . . ." Even Christian priests "differ so much one among another on some of these heads, that it would be an impossible task to give you all their differences" (Collins 1978, p. 47).

The cast of priests had, in fact, *created* religious difference so as to control their various constituencies. Blount identified seven causes "of all the false Doctrine, Idolatry, and Superstition among the Heathens" (Blount 1680, p. 31). All seven, Hutcheson notes, are the work of priests: "forged revelations, forged oracles, ambiguous prophecies, colored interpretations of dreams, pseudo-miracles, traditions, and plain lying" (p. 73). Clerics are thus responsible for much social ill and individual confusion through their self-interested efforts to create religions that require access to God through secrets, mysteries, miracles, and, of course, priests. Of principal importance to the Deist case against revelation, priests were the source of the most damaging religious doctrine of all: inherent human sinfulness (Clark 1994, p. 39).

How could the priestcraft hypothesis be supported, as the origins of revealed religion are lost to view in the mists of early human history? Perhaps the world's primitive people, as yet unaffected by the scourge of priests, might provide a solution to this rhetorical problem. One of the more obscure and yet fascinating documents produced during the Deist controversy is entitled *A Speech Delivered by an Indian Chief in Reply to a Sermon Preached by a Swedish Missionary in Order to Convert the Indians.* This eight-page pamphlet was published in London in 1753 and sold for a penny. The authenticity of the speech cannot be confirmed, though the Chief's religious sentiments are surprisingly similar to those of the Deists. The Chief, when presented with the Christian gospel for his and his tribe's acceptance, asks several probing questions which the missionary is neither willing nor able to answer. The Chief then speaks in favor of "free Enquiry . . . which was never denied our ancestors, who, on the contrary, thought it the sacred, inviolable, natural Right of every Man to examine and Judge for himself" (p. 4). One is left to wonder just how many competing religious systems Native Americans were required to sort through by a process of "free Enquiry" before European

Christian missionaries appeared on the scene. The question also arises as to why these particular people managed to escape the scourge of priests. Was it, perhaps, their isolation from corrupt Middle Eastern and European religious influences?

The Chief, getting the drift of the missionary's message, understands that his own pious forefathers, who had not been Christians, "were all damned" under this irrational system of Christianity. In response to the notion that salvation comes through revelation, preaching, and personal acceptance of a particular religious message, the Chief again takes the Deists' own theological high-road. "It is our opinion," he asserts, "that every Man is possessed with sufficient Knowledge for his own Salvation" (p. 6). Of course, it is greatly in the support of the Deist notion of a "religion of reason and nature" that an untutored person cut off from "modern" civilizations and free to form his own religious notions should come to precisely the Deist position. What better laboratory for testing Deist claims about a pristine, primitive religion of reason than the tribes of the vast American frontier? Clearly priests were responsible, then, for corrupting the pure religion of nature which any unaided and, more to the point, unmolested human intellect could freely and fully apprehend. The Chief even affirms, when told that the Bible is a divine revelation, that "Revelation can't add to natural religion" (p. 6). The plain, untrained reason of the Chief is sufficient not only to discover the means of his salvation but to confute the specious arguments of the religious bigot. Deism and universal religious faith not only enjoy a clear rhetorical victory in this encounter, but Deists can claim anthropological support for their central hypothesis.

VI. Theological Speculation and Secret Societies

Whereas it may not be possible to associate a particular, positive theology with Deism, several of the leading Deists shared a penchant for theological speculation. Toland's interest in theological invention was apparently endless, with Sullivan attributing to him three different theologies.[6] Ilive's theology, set out in his lectures at various guildhalls in London in the 1730s and 1740s, is gnostic. Berman, as was noted, calls Collins a "speculative atheist" (Berman 1988, p. 70). Woolston was not a Deist at all, according to biographer William Trapnell. It is possible to associate Deists with theologies including pantheism, Unitarianism, gnosticism, and atheism. What these writers hold in common is their inability to leave theologies as they find them and their associated incapacity to keep their theological views to themselves. Everywhere Deism is marked by a tendency toward theological generation, experimentation, and advocacy.

Whereas it was once common to allege that Deism was not an organized movement, it is becoming increasingly clear how important secret societies were to its development and dissemination. The allegation that Deists congregated in secret societies or "clubs" was frequent in the eighteenth century. As early as 1800 William H. Reid authored a history of the phenomenon entitled *The Rise and Dissolution of Infidel Societies*. Recently, Margaret Jacob has argued that Toland was a Freemason and had connections to influential lodges in London, Amsterdam, and other cities of Europe (Jacob 1991, p. 91ff.). She has documented the involvement of other Deists in Freemasonry and secret societies such as the Knights of Jubilation between 1710 and 1750 (Jacob 1981, p. 24ff.). Robert Rees Evans has also noted that Toland attended meetings of the Scots Rosicrucians while a student in Glasgow (p. 3). Woolston apparently started a secret society in Cambridge known as the Aenigmatists.[7] Ilive was a leader in the London printers' guilds, which sometimes functioned much like secret lodges. Anthony Collins "is said to have been at the centre of a club which met at the Grecian coffee-house, near Temple-bar" (Berman 1975, p. 92n.).[8] G. Legman's research suggests connections between freethinking groups in Britain and much older secret organizations such as the Knights Templar of the twelfth and thirteenth centuries (pp. 28–38). James Dewar traces the origins of the first Masonic lodges in London to the year 1717 and connects freethinkers with these lodges. The original Grand Lodge of London, organized in 1717, was composed of several smaller groups already meeting in various London taverns, including "the Goose and Gridiron Alehouse in St. Paul's Churchyard, the Crown Alehouse, Parker's Lane, the Apple Tree Tavern, Charles Street, and the Runner and Grapes Tavern, Channel Row, Westminster" (Dewar, p. 34). We have already noted the similarity between Masonry and Deism on the point of universal religion. Bishop Berkeley spoke of infiltrating a "deistical club" under the "pretended character of a learner," whereupon he heard the shocking admission of atheism by a prominent member of the club—Collins (quoted in Berman 1975, p. 89).

The rhetorical efforts of Deists were sometimes directly linked to these societies, where radical religious and political ideas were discussed and refined and where strategies for their propagation were developed. Berman comments that "we have little information about free-thinking clubs." However, he also notes that "one meets the suggestion that some of the free-thinking books, e.g. Toland's *Christianity Not Mysterious* (1696), were written by a number of men in free-thinking clubs." He adds:

There is one instance known to me where this was, to some extent, admitted. In the preface to a later deistic work, *The Moral Philosopher* (1737), the author, Thomas Morgan, says that the book arose from discussions "many years ago by a Society, or Club of Gentlemen in the Country, who met once a Fortnight at a Gentleman's House in a pleasant retired village, with a Design to enter impartially into the Consideration of the Grounds and Principles of Religion in General. . . . " (pp. vii-viii)

Thus, it seems fair to conclude that to be a Deist meant to appreciate the benefits of clandestine associations, including, occasionally, the possibilities for corporate authorship.

Why secret societies? Three reasons suggest themselves. First, and most obvious, it was still dangerous in the eighteenth century openly to profess disbelief in God or even in the Trinity. Blasphemy was a crime under the Act of 1697, punishable by three years in prison and a one-hundred-pound fine. Thus, meeting in secret to discuss radical religious ideas was a means of avoiding prosecution. Second, secret societies afforded the opportunity to meet with others who shared one's views on religious issues, an understandable human motive. Third, the secret meeting held the allure of participation in forbidden religious speculation and even in suspect religious rites. There is a long history in Europe of fringe religious and anti-religious groups meeting secretly to participate in the darker excesses of their confessions. There is some evidence that meetings of Deistical clubs and related groups included heavy drinking, ribald joking, reading of obscene poetry, songs lewdly mocking clergy and other public figures, strange rites of initiation, and forbidden sexual activity.

VII. Rejecting Miracle and Denigrating Testimony

The rejection of miracle is an early and persistent mark of Deism. Suspicion of miracle is expressed in Blount's early *Miracles no Violation of the Law's of Nature* (1683), in which the author draws heavily upon, and even publishes (occasionally without acknowledgment), the works of both Hobbes and Spinoza. Miracles were to the Deist mind "utterly impossible, because contradicting all men's notions of how the universe is constructed" (Annet, *Resurrection Considered*, pp. 74–75). Annet's *Miraculous Conception* expresses well the Deist attitude toward miracle. Concerning the virgin birth of Christ, Annet writes: "In short, a child was begotten in a miraculous, stupendous, astonishing manner; or, in other words, that a child was begotten in an unnatural and irrational way, and consequently repugnant to the established laws of nature" (p. 5). Confirmatory use of miracles by Christians was doubly condemned. For a doctrine to require a miracle in its support proves its falsehood, because miracles are advanced only when a religious teaching is not evident to reason, that is, when it is false.

Even direct sensory experience of a miracle would not convince a rational person, for, as William Woolaston writes, "the reports of sense are not of equal authority with the clear demonstrations of reason, when they happen to differ" (p. 38). And these two always "happen to differ" in the case of miracles. Moreover, St. Paul apparently made acceptance of one miracle—the Resurrection—a *sine qua non* of Christianity's veracity. Writing to the Corinthian Christians, Paul asserts that "if Christ has not been raised, then our preaching is in vain, and your faith is in vain" (1 Cor. 15:14). Thus, John Leland, eighteenth-century Christian chronicler of Deism, noted that "there is scarce anything in which the Deistical writers are more generally agreed than in bending their force against proof from miracles" (quoted in Burns, p. 65).[9]

"By ground of persuasion," Toland writes in the opening of chapter 3 of *Christianity Not Mysterious*, "I understand the rule by which we judge of all truth, and which irresistibly convinces the mind." This standard is derived from "God, the wise creator of all . . . who has enabled us to perceive things, and form judgements of them, [and who] has also endued us with the power of suspending our judgements about whatever is uncertain, and of never assenting but to clear perceptions" (pp. 14, 20). When Toland's standard of proof is applied to miracles, the result is predictable: no event can be considered less certain, and thus less rational, than a miracle.

Deist suspicion of miracle comported with their understanding of natural law. "For the Deists as for their rational predecessors," writes Tennant, "'law' connoted necessity" (p. 8). The notion of inviolable natural law creates obvious difficulties for miracle claims. And the documentary evidence for miracles only underlined the problem of proving such events. The biblical miracles, as all parties to the controversy were aware, rested on a limited set of ancient documents. Christians had traditionally affirmed that the documents were themselves adequate to establish the historical reliability and literal truthfulness of all of the miracle claims contained therein. But this affirmation was widely challenged by the Deists. "Evidence" was not the Christian's bits and pieces of mythical narratives and historical hearsay, but "the idea's [sic] of the operations of the mind." We ought to "strictly require this evidence in all the agreements and disagreements of our idea's in things merely speculative," writes Toland (Toland 1696, p. 19). That is, disputable or contingent claims—which all miracle claims must be—are tested against the criterion of propositional indubitability, the very foundation of rational thought.

In his *Discourse on Miracles* (1741), Thomas Chubb hammered away at the logical possibility of proving miracles, as well as at their potential *as* reasonable proof. Chubb questions the authenticity of miracle accounts, the agency for miracles, and their significance. The deduction from "the *raising* a dead person to life [being] a work above the natural ability or inherent power of any created being" to the conclusion that "therefore, it must be performed by the *immediate* operation or *agency* of God" constitutes a mistake in logic. "[H]ere is a point *presumed* without *sufficient* ground, and on *consequences* drawn from that presumption, which in *argument*, is not allowed" (p. 15).[10]

As the biblical documents amounted to testimony supporting a set of disputed events, the status of testimony as evidence was of critical importance to the Christian case. Thus, Deists denigrated testimony. For Annet, to accept testimony as evidence for miracles is to take "things said, for granted" and to prove "the truth of a fact, by other facts which equally want proof" (*Resurrection Considered*, p. 10). Believing any report by another is an act of faith, and "what we call faith . . . is mere credulity." He adds, "we take reports upon faith without examining the truth of them; or knowing that what is reported of them whose name they bear, is their report; or that their judgment and veracity were equal if it be" (Annet 1742, p. 10). *A fortiori*, testimony for *miracles* can be rejected out of hand, because "that testimony cannot be credible which relates incredible things" (*Resurrection Considered*, p. 71).[11]

Reason evaluates testimony by the criterion of experience. "The use of reason in matters of whose evidence depends upon testimony, is to perceive the credibility of the witness or witnesses, and the credibility of the thing testified . . ." (Collins, *Use of Reason*, p. 16). Testimony does not have the evidential status of sense perception or of the indubitable ideas of the mind. The only credible testimony, then, is redundant of other and better sources of evidence. And, of course, miracles are never confirmed by these higher evidential sources. Deists dismissed all of the primary documentary evidence for Christian miracles by this argument against the credibility of testimony.

The Deists and Biblical Criticism

In *Discourse of Freethinking,* Collins defines "freethinking" as a commitment to rational criticism. "By Free-Thinking," he writes, "I mean, The Use of the Understanding in endeavouring to find out the Meaning of any Proposition what soever, in considering the nature of the Evidence for or against it, and in judging of it according to the seeming Force or Weakness of the Evidence" (p. 5). Nowhere was this habit of criticism more evident than in the Deists' approach to the Bible.

Some histories of biblical criticism treat English Deists as a minor contributing source to the major stream of European criticism in the seventeenth and eighteenth centuries. Edgar Krentz, for instance, pays little attention to critical developments among English religious radicals in his history of biblical interpretation. Though Nigel M. de S. Cameron acknowledges that scriptural "problems" had been identified long before Spinoza, and "in English Deism they had their most widespread and popular discussion" (p. 8), he does not make any effort to link Spinoza's critical approach to that of the Deists, nor does he make the Deists a link in the critical chain from Spinoza to the nineteenth-century British and German biblical critics.[12] A similar failure to acknowledge early English contributions is true of other histories of biblical criticism as well.[13] On the other hand, Emanuel Hirsch has written of Annet, one of the most notorious Deist critics, that "he is the originator of scientific criticism of the Easter stories and thereby gave impetus to the field of New Testament studies" (quoted in C. Brown 1985, p. 4). Who, then, invented modern biblical criticism?

Many scholars take for granted that biblical criticism evolved out of the German Enlightenment of the late eighteenth century and that its sources are found in the Renaissance return to texts and Spinoza's attack on revelation in the *Tractatus.* On this view, modern biblical criticism came late to Britain, not being practiced there until the nineteenth century.[14] Some recent histories of biblical scholarship challenge this conventional view, however, forging strong and direct links between the critical work of Deists in the late seventeenth and early eighteenth centuries and significantly later German developments. Henning Graf Reventlow, for instance, finds English Deism to provide the intellectual and methodological foundations of German biblical criticism. He writes that "the direct and indirect influences of English Deism on the German Enlightenment . . . are great." Reventlow notes "the numerous translations of English Deistic literature which appeared on the German market after the publication of Johann Lorenz Schmidt's popular translation of Tindal's *Christianity as Old as Creation*" in 1741. "We cannot overestimate," he concludes, "the influence exercised by Deistic thought, and by the principles of the Humanist world-view which the Deists made the criterion of their biblical criticism, on the historical-critical exegesis of the nineteenth-century; the consequences extend right down to the present" (p. 412).

Reventlow, however, presents the Deists as similar in purpose and presupposition to the Orthodox apologists with whom they fought so vigorously. He transforms the Deists into rationalist defenders of Christianity, referring to some of them as "apologists." On this view, Deist critics sought to strengthen the rational foundations of Christianity, not to destroy them. But this understanding of radical English Deism is untenable, unless "Christianity" be understood as a meager moral teaching, lacking a Messiah and making no particular reference to a revelation for its legitimation. All Deists rejected revelation, and, as Colin Brown insists, they "shared a common rejection of the Christian theistic view of a personal God whose interaction with the world culminated in the incarnation." Moreover, it was precisely the Deists' intellectual and moral rejection of Christianity which "provided a theoretical basis for their critique of orthodox Christian beliefs" (C. Brown 1985, p. 51).

Like Reventlow, however, Brown does find that the influence of English Deism on German thinking increased dramatically after the publication of Schmidt's translation of Tindal in 1741. Deist influence on German approaches to biblical criticism was well established "for half a century before the publication of the *Fragments*" of Lessing, often viewed as the watershed event in the development of German higher criticism (C. Brown 1985, p. 51).

Lessing's Fragments and the Origins of German Criticism

It may be helpful to take a closer look at the early history of German criticism and some specific Deistic influences on that history noted by Reventlow, Brown, and others. Modern biblical criticism is conventionally traced back to Herman Samuel Reimarus (1694–1768). Reimarus taught for a time at Wittenberg and travelled in England, where "he came under the influence of English Deists," before taking a position teaching oriental languages at Hamburg, a post he held for forty years.[15] Reimarus held "doubts he had long nursed about revealed religion, the historical worth of the Bible and the origins of Christianity" (C. Brown 1985, p. 2). He recorded these doubts privately and revealed them only to a small group of friends. Publicly he maintained an outward adherence to Christianity throughout his life, even though his *Fragments* questioned the divinity of Christ and denied the historicity of the Resurrection (Gay, p. 381).

Not long after his death, Reimarus's *Fragments* were published through the offices of his friend Gotthold Ephraim Lessing (1729–1781), who "kept the deist cause alive in Germany" (Gay, p. 381). Lessing's publication of Reimarus's critical literature sparked the famous *Fragments* controversy and immersed Lessing in a long debate with Orthodoxy.[16] A dramatist and literary critic and not himself a theologian, he was fascinated by Reimarus's learned questioning of the origins of Christianity. Lessing had also been "deeply impressed" with the journalist Christolb Mylius, who praised both "the learned Toland" and the "searching Woolston" (Gay, p. 380). Thus, the connection to English Deism was established for Lessing both through and independently of his association with Reimarus.

Lessing, fearing the controversy that the *Fragments* would generate, falsely attributed them to Tindal's translator, the well-known skeptic and heretic Schmidt. Lessing was fully aware of the true authorship of the *Fragments*. Like Reimarus and the English Deists, Lessing questioned the authenticity of the scriptural records, miracles, prophecy, and claims about Christ's divinity and miracles. Like the Deists, he proclaimed a "religion of humanity" (Gay, p. 332). Lessing was, moreover, like some Deists, interested and involved in secret societies. He was a Freemason and a friend of the grand master of the German Lodges. He may also have been, like Toland, a pantheist (C. Brown 1985, pp. 17, 22). Like Woolston, he held that "Christian mysteries are symbols and allegories, aids to understanding" (Gay, p. 333). Brown concludes of Lessing's public polemic that "it was Deism . . . which inspired the *Fragments* controversy" (p. 31).

Other German writers associated with the origins of biblical criticism have English Deistic connections. Johann David Michaelis, "one of the first scholars to attempt a thoroughly historical approach to Scripture," was influenced by English Deism during a visit to England in 1741–1742. He subsequently rejected pietism. Brown connects the Deists directly to such theologians of the German Enlightenment as C. M. Pfaff, C. Lemker, C. C. Woog, C. Kortholt, Christian Gottlieb Jocher, G. W. Alberti, Heinrich Gottlob Schmid, Johann Heinrich Meyenberg, Urban Gottlob Thorschmid, J. A. Trinius, and S. J. Baumgarten. The only real novelty introduced by the German critics, he concludes, was "the open espousal of the criticism" (C. Brown 1985, pp. 51–52). But this is a curious claim, as Brown is familiar with the work of Woolston and Collins, who both openly espoused such critical practices fifty years earlier in England. Thus, there were no German innovations in the field of biblical criticism, which originated and was developed in England between 1680 and 1745.

Even early experiments in German biblical criticism occurred after the publication of the major works of Deist criticism had been widely circulated in Britain, France, and Germany. Perhaps inspired by the comparative linguistic work of Blount and Toland, the early Church history of Woolston and Middleton, and the philosophical explorations of Collins and Tindal, German theological scholars began to work in disciplines such as philosophy, history, and philology. This work led directly to the first German excursions into higher biblical criticism. Johann Lorenz von Mosheim (1693–1755) began to use primary sources in his study of early Christianity, *Commentary on Christian Matters before Constantine,* and thus to "examine the textual tradition of Scripture in a critical way." Other German writers of the middle and late eighteenth century also examined biblical accounts critically. The work of Johann August Ernesti (1707–1781) in Leipzig focused on the New Testament documents, while Michaelis in Gottingen examined the Old Testament. Such writers found "traditional dogmatics . . . less important" as a result of their critical ventures (H. Brown, p. 404).

Virtually all of the early German advocates of a scientific criticism were directly or indirectly influenced by the English Deists of the late seventeenth and early eighteenth centuries. These early English biblical critics influenced subsequent generations of scholars, and that influence is felt, in Reventlow's phrase, "right down to the present." Thus, the history of higher criticism is firmly rooted in the Deists' iconoclastic invention—a method for dismantling and discrediting biblical narratives. Biblical criticism was developed by the English Deists to serve their destructive polemical goals of overturning revelation and thus the church. Moreover, the method of biblical criticism was grounded on the Deists' *a priori* rejection of the supernatural, the mysterious, the miraculous, the monotheistic.

The biblical critical method often associated with the German enlightenment was not a scholarly invention but rather a strategic one and not a German discovery but an English one. Peter Gay rightly calls the English Deists "ruthless controversialists in an age of ruthless controversy" (p. 375). Biblical criticism was an engine of rhetorical war, employed with abandon for half a century in English coffeehouses and Deistical clubs prior to its transportation to German Masonic lodges and universities. And the motives of the English Deists and those of the early German critics were not dissimilar, though the academic training of the latter was in several important instances greater.

The Deists' Search for a Critical Method

We return now to the Deists' own rhetorical problem of discovering a particular kind of critical method unavailable to them in sixteenth- and seventeenth-century philosophy or rhetoric. To be precise, English Deists sought a means of dismantling the New Testament narratives in order to demonstrate their fallibility and to do so in a way that would attract the attention of a literate though not well-educated audience of the English general reading public. The ultimate goal was to discredit the Bible and the clergy and so to inaugurate a new era of religious, social, and political reform. Methodological developments prior to 1680, though substantial, did not supply Deists with the specific tools appropriate to their rhetorical work.

The classical rhetorical tradition was largely inventional rather than critical in its method. Cicero's canons of invention, arrangement, style, memory, and delivery, for example, had a constructive goal: to guide orators in discovering and arranging the material for, and to assist them in the effective presentation of, public speeches. Method in later rhetorical writing often meant a short or economical route to a goal and thus later the most direct approach to solving a problem, a systematic way of preparing a speech, an organizing principle for the curriculum in a school, a systematic approach to a practice (an art), or a way of teaching an art (Ong, p. 220ff.).[17]

However, literary criticism was practiced by a number of ancient rhetoricians and grammarians such as Dionysius of Halicarnassus in the effort to differentiate genuine from forged or altered classical works such as the speeches of Lysias or the plays of Sophocles. Criteria such as consistency of style and content were developed for separating "genuine" from "spurious" works of such masters as Homer. Possibilities such as forgery, editing, multiple authorship, deletion, and pseudonomy were all discussed in connection with disputed works. Robert Grant notes that in resolving "questions about authenticity, critics generally relied on methods of refutation and confirmation taught in the rhetorical schools," and in rhetoric treatises such as the *Progymnasmata* of Theon (Grant, pp. 15–16, 16ff., 30). Hermogenes set out refutational criteria that were freely applied in textual criticism: "You will refute from the obscure, the unconvincing, the impossible, the inconsequent and contradictory, the unsuitable, the inconsistent" (quoted in Grant, p. 31).

Early opponents of Christianity such as Porphyry and Celsus, and heretics like Marcion and Simon Magus, criticized biblical texts and advanced alleged biblical documents of their own. Marcion set out contradictions between Old and New Testaments in the second century in *Antithesis* and advanced his criticism of the New Testament in other works such as *Gospel* and *Apostle*. These works include historical criticism, social history, word studies, and close comparison of documents. Tertullian accused Marcion of "try[ing] to destroy the status of the Gospels . . ." (Grant, p. 43). The late-second-century heretic Appeles sought logical contradictions in the Genesis accounts of creation, the temptation of Adam and Eve, and the flood. Christian writers such as Gaius, Irenaeus, and Origen developed aspects of textual criticism in their own efforts to answer the arguments of the skeptics and heretics.

Discussions of method in medieval and renaissance rhetorics were closely related to the topical logics of writers such as Agricola—ways of discovering a direct path to an argument or ways of teaching argument. By the seventeenth century, method as a rhetorical concept was understood in two or perhaps three ways, each of which was largely constructive. Following Peter Ramus (1515–1572), method was a means of communicating that which was already known. Ramus thus offered a method suited to perpetuating received truth. Embedded in the tradition of method following Ramus, however, was the notion of *iudicium*, or judgment, which involved, according to the early-sixteenth-century dialectician Johann Sturm, "the art of examining, judging, and discoursing about what something is and of what sort it is when it is proposed as a matter for investigation and teaching" (quoted in Ong, p. 235). Bacon may be said to have added to these two a third rhetorical approach. Method was "a technique for the rediscovery of something previously known but temporarily forgotten" (Howell, p. 367).

Two other writers in the rhetorical tradition advanced a method which held potential application to religious issues. In the *Port-Royal Logic* (1662), Antoine Arnauld (1612–1694) and Pierre Nicole (1625–1695) argue that "ideas and . . . judgments . . . arise in the soul, [that] are false and unreasonable." As such "obscure and confused ideas" are also "common to all men who have not corrected them," these writers sought a means of purging the soul of them. "The only way of remedying this inconvenience," they maintain, "is, to throw aside the prejudices of our youth, and to believe nothing which is within the province of reason through that which we have judged of it before, but only through that which we judge of it now." By this means "we shall arrive at natural ideas . . ." (pp. 68, 71).

The Port-Royal logicians also express a suspicion of unexamined language, an issue central to Deist method. "The necessity which we have for employing outward signs in order to make ourselves understood," they write, "causes us to attach our ideas to words, [and] we often consider the words more than the things. Now this is one of the most common causes of the confusion of our thoughts and discourse" (p. 76). Logic, understood as "the art of managing one's reason aright in the knowledge of things" takes on methodological significance as a means of alleviating the confusions inherent to language use. The influence of Arnauld and Nicole's *Port-Royal Logic* was considerable, and "the general conception of logic which they expounded . . . dominated the treatment of logic by most philosophers for the next 200 years" (Kneale and Kneale, pp. 315, 320).

Descartes (1596–1650) sought a method of scientific inquiry, not one for communicating received knowledge like he found in Ramus and the scholastics (Howell, p. 348). In the *Discourse de la Methode* (1637) he resolved

> never to accept anything for true which I did not clearly know to be such; that is to say, carefully to avoid precipitancy and prejudice, and to comprise nothing more in my judgment than what was presented to my mind so clearly and distinctly as to exclude all ground of doubt. (quoted in Howell, p. 345)

Descartes's goal was the discovery of indubitable knowledge. Thus, even his method of doubt was fundamentally constructive in orientation (Krentz, p. 13).

Benedict de Spinoza (1632–1677) laid the groundwork for much of

Deist philosophy and religious theory in his *Tractatus Theologico-Politicus* (1670). He affirmed the principle of the supremacy of reason to revelation. The only religious truths were ones taught universally, a doctrine closely related to Herbert's doctrine of *notitiae communes*. Spinoza determined to "examine the Bible afresh in a careful, impartial, and unfettered spirit, making no assumptions concerning it, and attributing to it no doctrines, which I do not find clearly set down therein," a theme often repeated by the Deists (p. 8; quoted in Cameron, p. 16). Moreover, he suggested that certain implausible passages were "foisted onto the sacred writings by irreligious hands," and the corresponding claim that "whatsoever is contrary to nature is also contrary to reason, and whatsoever is contrary to reason is absurd, and *ipso facto*, to be rejected" (p. 92; quoted in Cameron, p. 14). Spinoza questioned the dating and authorship of many biblical books, particularly in the Old Testament. He also advanced philosophical arguments against the possibility of miracles.

Spinoza advanced a rudimentary method for "interpreting" scripture grounded in natural history. "[T]he method of interpreting Scripture does not widely differ from the method of interpreting nature—in fact, it is almost the same." He explains that

> as the interpretation of nature consists in the examination of the history of nature, and therefrom deducing definitions of natural phenomena on certain fixed axioms, so Scriptural interpretation proceeds by the examination of Scripture and inferring the intention of its authors as a legitimate conclusion from its fundamental principles. (quoted in Cameron, p. 11)

Thus, the principles of scriptural interpretation are discovered in the "history" of scripture, by which Spinoza meant (as Cameron summarizes):

> first, its full linguistic or grammatical description; secondly, its full context; and, thirdly, "the environment"—that is, the life, the conduct, and the studies of the author of each book, who he was, what was the occasion, and the epoch of his writing, whom he wrote for, and in what language. (pp. 11–12)

Spinoza's method was not benign in its intent, but corrosive, providing a means of discrediting the notion of traditional authorship and doctrinal inspiration. Spinoza wished to turn biblical criticism in a "negative and destructive" direction, and, Krentz notes, with the publication of the *Tractatus*, "the tools of destruction were at hand." Spinoza began with the assumption that "revelation as such does not happen" and had in mind to "discuss biblical interpretation [in order] to discredit the appearance of supernatural authority" (Krentz, p. 14). In his assumptions and goals he was of the same house as the Deists.

Herbert of Cherbury speculated about method in *De Veritate*. He made "common notions," truths innate to all normal rationality, the judge of other claims to truth (Popkin, p. 152). Herbert's proposed method was relatively simple and probably overly hopeful. It involved ensuring, as Richard Popkin explains, "that the proper conditions of perception and concept formation have been met, and then employ[ing] the proper Common Notion or Notions, thereby gaining knowledge which conforms to the thing itself" (p. 152). Herbert applied his method to two types of truths: the truths of things as they are (*veritas rei*) and the truths of things as they appear to us (*veritas apparentiae*). Thus, he did not envision his method as a test of received knowledge or of documentary evidence. However, later Deists criticized scriptural claims according to the doctrine of common notions.

Locke also encouraged critical approaches to biblical texts in his *The Reasonableness of Christianity* (1695). Appearing the year before Toland's *Christianity Not Mysterious*, Locke's book suggested that "scripture [is] a series of documents written at different times, the authenticity of which must often be called into question" (Colie, p. 40). Though he sought to appear friendly to revealed religion, and though he may have thought many Deists had gone too far with their criticism of the Bible, Locke had a significant influence on Deist writers. J. C. D. Clark writes that "Locke's significance for the eighteenth century was not chiefly in introducing contractarianism into political theory, but heterodox theology into religious speculations" (Clark 1985, p. 280). Collins, Toland and Bolingbroke all were professed disciples of Locke.[18]

Several seventeenth-century religious writers assisted the project of biblical criticism by contrasting biblical history to scientific and historical knowledge. In 1655 Isaac de La Peyrere's *Prae-Adamitten* was published, in which the "new knowledge" of an infant science was driven next to scriptural accounts. He concluded, for instance, that geographical and chronological evidence suggested that Adam was not the first man. The benedictine monk Jean Mabillon's *Acta Sanctorum* (1668) "worked out the means for determining the date and authenticity of ancient documents, a cornerstone in historical method" (Krentz, pp. 12, 13).

French Oratorian Richard Simon (1638–1712) is often credited with having been "the direct founder of the historical-critical method," though other founders are alleged (Krentz, p. 15). *Histoire Critique du Vieux Testament* (1678) aroused tremendous controversy within the Catholic church, and Simon was expelled from the Oratorians (C. Brown 1985, 281n.58). Undaunted, he proceeded to author a series of books intending to show that the Protestant standard of *sola scriptura* was untenable as a criterion of biblical scholarship and ended only in confusion.[19] His own suggested standards were "the evident and the rational," though he also argued that biblical interpretation must be guided by tradition (Krentz, p. 15).

La Peyrere, Mabillon, and Simon suggested directions Deists would explore in their critical work on the biblical texts. Works by Astruc (1684–1766), credited with laying the foundation for critical studies of the Pentateuch, came later in the century and were not available to the early Deists. As Krentz writes, during the seventeenth century "the scriptures were more and more treated like ordinary historical documents. The process of objectification had begun" (p. 16).

Though they borrowed freely from the methodological contributions of earlier critics, the English Deists sought a method not specifically available in the rhetorical, philosophical, or theological traditions of the sixteenth and seventeenth centuries. That method's first objective was to demonstrate the implausibility of biblical narratives, specifically miracle accounts. The method must also be adapted to arguing against established authority before a popular audience. That Deists borrowed ideas from many earlier methodologists seems clear, though usually they modified what they found to suit their particular rhetorical needs. For instance, their rejection of authority and revelation is in keeping with Descartes's method of doubt. But Descartes erected a barrier between sacred and profane knowledge in an effort, perhaps, to protect the former from his method. Moreover, Descartes's concerns were scientific and apologetic, the Deists' were neither. Thus, they kept the method of systematic doubt while ignoring Descartes's protective barrier. But the particular destructive and, importantly, popular method required for an outright assault on revelation was not available in any previous writer, not even in Spinoza.

G. Legman, in his remarkable study *The Guilt of the Knights Templar,* writes of the initiation rituals of the "House of Sciences or Abode of Wisdom," active during the Fatimite dynasty in medieval Egypt. The

House of Science instructed the neophyte in "the contradictions between religion and reason" as well as the "extravagences" of religious revelation. The society also practiced rituals of a sinister brand of gnosticism. This unexpected combination of elevation of reason, rejection of revelation, and communal occult spiritual practices leads Legman to comment:

> We are here clearly in the presence of one of the original sources of that atheistic or anti-Christian spirit hidden in Europe for centuries, though always very close to the surface, in both secret rites and secret thoughts; finally breaking into open expression in 1537 in *Cymbalum Mundi* of Banaventure Des Pieres. . . . (Legman, p. 82)

Deism is in many ways the first genuinely public and popular expression of this spirit in Europe, and the alarm felt by many in Britain at this development is correspondingly genuine, profound, and warranted. The next chapter explores the specific ways in which the sharply anti-Christian spirit of Deist rhetoric was exhibited in their public documents and their opponents' efforts to marginalize the Deists based on the style, strategies, and overall manner of their argument against revelation.

Chapter Three

The Rhetoric of Subterfuge and Characterization

But to curse the Figtree . . . was as foolishly and passionately done, as for another Man to throw the Chairs and Stools about the House; because his Dinner is not ready at a critical Time, or before it could be got ready for him.

Thomas Woolston, *Discourses*

The *Free-Thinker,* who scarcely believes there is a God, and certainly disbelieves Revelation, is a very terrible animal.

Joseph Addison, *Evidences*

A solemn judicial Death is too great an honour for an Atheist. . . .

Spectator, n. 389, May 27, 1712

In addition to their arguments against revelation and the clergy, Deists developed a discourse of subterfuge characterized by strategic lying, linguistic camouflage, scandalous allegation, and scathing ridicule. In response, the Deists were characterized by Christian opponents as vermin unfit for membership in a civilized society. To support this *ad hominem* assault, Christian writers drew evidence from the tactics and style of Deist rhetoric, as much as from the specific theological claims of Deism. The controversy's social and political nuances are revealed by exploring rhetorical tactics having little connection to the specific theological issues which ought to have occupied the center of a theological debate. We will focus attention first and longest on the Deists' use of ridicule, the most common, defining, and controversial strategy in their assault on Christian revelation. Other important strategies of subterfuge and characterization will also be considered.

Deist Ridicule

Deism's assault on Christian revelation began with attacks on mystery, prophecy, and miracle, but by the 1720s the force of the attack was directed at miracles.[1] Miracles, Christians maintained, supported essential doctrines such as Christ's divinity and the effectiveness of his atoning death. Moreover, the Crown's right to rule and the state's authority to require religious observance were rooted in the dictates of scripture. The Bible's authority resided in its unique status as the one authentic divine revelation. This status was, in turn, validated by a limited set of New Testament miracles—the virgin birth of Christ, his various wonderful works, and perhaps especially his resurrection. Attacking the foundational miracles, then, endangered not only the faith of individual Christians but Christianity generally and thus the stability of the state.[2]

As self-professed rationalists who opposed all "mystery" in religion, the Deists might be expected to pursue rigorous and serious argumentation guided by a recognized critical method. Instead, they built much of their case against miracles on ridicule. The practice of ridicule was theoretically defended in books by Deist authors and generated great public controversy in popular periodicals, books, and essays for much of the eighteenth century.[3]

The Deists' persistent use of ridicule reflects the power relationships that marked their long controversy with the Church. Though the theory of ridicule was developed by aristocratic writers like Shaftesbury and Collins, the actual practice of ridicule was perfected by writers of lower social rank who wrote for an audience of their peers. By ridiculing revelation, a socially marginal group of rhetorical tacticians could mock the ideology of an established clerical/aristocratic class. Gary Allen Fine writes that "through humor one can express ideas which are inappropriate for serious communication, given the legitimate boundaries of talk." By ridiculing Christian miracles, Deists articulated the inexpressible idea that the sacred is, in fact, laughable. Fine adds that "since Plato and Hobbes many theorists have argued that humor permits the teller and listener to feel superior to the butt of the joke" (Fine, pp. 85, 89). In Deist hands, ridicule created a social inversion wherein those of a lower social station were momentarily superior to their betters. George Orwell noted that "whatever is funny is subversive" (Orwell, p. 176; quoted in Palmer, p. 11), and Deists exploited this fact with expert grace and virtuous persistence.

Shaftesbury and the Theory of Ridicule

The principal methodological theorist among early-eighteenth-century skeptics was Anthony Ashley Cooper, the First Earl of Shaftesbury. In 1708 Shaftesbury published *Letter Concerning Enthusiasm* and in 1709, *Sensus Communis, or an Essay on Wit and Humour*. Both works explored the notion of free critical examination of all ideas. Shaftesbury was especially interested in the critical potential of humor. His suggested critical method of ridicule was instantly the topic of a popular debate.

Shaftesbury asserted that "any thinking Christian must be sceptical about the biblical tradition" (Reventlow, p. 314). In the opinion of Henning Graf Reventlow, Shaftesbury argues that "historical truth handed down in writing" must, prior to its acceptance by a rational reader, "undergo a thorough testing of the character and genius of its author and the capacity of the historian who handed it down to make an unbiased judgment. . . ." Under the principle of "critical truth," Shaftesbury called attention to possible corruptions in ancient texts due to copyists' blunders, editors' mistakes, and translators' errors (p. 316). But Shaftesbury's most important and controversial suggestion was that ridicule could be employed to test a text's truthfulness. One must test the "real temper of things," and this can *only* be done "by applying the ridicule. . ." (Cooper 1711, p. 12).

Shaftesbury affirmed a natural sense of the ridiculous, an inherent human capacity to detect falsehood. Falsehood is often obscured by gravity, tradition, ritual, and the appeal to "mystery." But, ridicule reveals falsehood whether it has been cleverly concealed or unintentionally obscured. In fact, ridicule is the only means of achieving this critical goal. The critic's goal is to discover which things are truly serious and which ridiculous. "And how can this be done," asks Shaftesbury, "but by applying the ridicule to see whether it will bear?" (p. 12). Thus, ridicule is one of the textual critic's principal tools. Later Deist writers rehearsed and modified Shaftesbury's theory. For instance, Collins wrote that "ridicule is both a proper and necessary method" for determining the truth of a proposition (Collins 1729, p. 22).

The Light of Ridicule

"That which can be shown only in a certain light," Shaftesbury writes, "is questionable." "Truth," on the other hand, "may bear all lights," and "one of those principal lights or natural mediums, by which things are to be viewed, in order to a thorough recognition, is ridicule itself . . ." (Cooper, 1711, p. 61). Shaftesbury here describes ridicule as a kind of light, and exploring this image assists our understanding of his critical theory.

Bacon had earlier employed the metaphor of light in much the way Shaftesbury did, but to describe rhetoric rather than ridicule. Wilbur Howell clarifies the metaphor's connection to the rhetorical tradition. "When Bacon calls rhetoric the illustration of tradition," he writes, "the image behind his words is that of shedding light so as to make anything visible to the eyes." Thus "illustration within the context of the theory of communication would mean the shedding of light so as to make knowledge visible and hence deliverable to an audience." Howell quotes the late-sixteenth-century rhetorical theorist John Marbecke to amplify the rhetorical device called "illustration": In illustration, "the forme of things is so set forth in words, that it seemeth rather to be seene with the eies, then heard with the eares." This, according to Howell, "is what illustration meant to Bacon, [and] his theory of communication assigned to rhetoric the task of presenting the form of things so that they could be seen as if in a great light" (Howell, p. 371).

Shaftesbury likely was influenced by Bacon's notion of rhetoric as illustration in developing his theory of ridicule. Shaftesbury clearly intends ridicule as a persuasive tool and particularly as a means of testing and exposing the false claims of Orthodox Christianity. Shaftesbury taunted clerics by asking why they "appear such cowards in reasoning, and are so afraid to stand the test of ridicule?" While "gravity is the very essence of imposture," ridicule provides a method for examining revelation and miracles which no honest person could object to (p. 11).

Shaftesbury's views on ridicule caught on quickly in skeptical circles, the method eventually becoming the principal weapon employed to discredit Christian miracles. Shaftesbury's recommendation of ridicule in biblical criticism reflected a willingness to examine the Bible not influenced by any feeling for it as a sacred text. This critical turn "produced a new relationship to the Bible in the Enlightenment both in England and outside it" (Reventlow, p. 318). Moreover, Shaftesbury's appropriation of an element in earlier rhetorical theory to forge his critical method suggests that rhetoric is at the very center of the history of biblical criticism, a fact which historians Grean, Reventlow, Cameron, Krentz, and Brown neglect to mention.[4]

Other Theorists of Ridicule

Though Shaftesbury suggested some of the tools of a critical method, he did not develop them, nor did he explore extensively their application to biblical texts. Anthony Collins's *A Discourse Concerning Ridicule and Irony* (1729), Thomas Morgan's *Moral Philosopher* (1739), and the anonymous *An Essay on Ridicule* (1753) extended Shaftesbury's basic argument in elaborate theoretical justifications of ridicule.

Ridicule is for Collins "the true method to bring things to a standard" for "decency and propriety will stand the test of ridicule, and triumph over all false pretenses to wit." Collins found biblical precedent for ridicule in the tale of Elijah's ridiculing the prophets of Baal (Collins 1729, pp. 21, 22). Collins adds that "ridicule of certain kinds, and under reasonable directions and rules, and used in proper time, place, and manner" is both a "proper and necessary method of discourse in many cases, and especially in the case of gravity, when that is attended with hypocrisy or imposture, or with ignorance, or with soreness of temper and persecution" (p. 21).

Morgan finds ridicule an important critical method as well. Moreover, it is a virtually foolproof, for ridicule is self-refuting when misused. "If some things are ridiculous in themselves," he writes, "I cannot see why they should not be considered and treated as they are." And "when a man places the ridicule wrong, it must certainly recoil upon himself; but whenever it sticks where it is laid, it must always be just." This is because "nothing can be odd or absurd but what is unreasonable" (Morgan, pp. 19, 20).

The anonymous author of *An Essay on Ridicule* continues in the tradition of Shaftesbury, Collins, and Morgan. Advocating ridicule as a critical method, he writes that it is "one of the methods best founded, easiest comprehended, and the least subject to fallacy." In theology as in other matters, "an argument that will not bear ridicule, is certainly false logic" (pp. 17, 31).

The Paradox of Ridicule

The Deists' choice of ridicule as a critical method poses what John Redwood calls "the paradox of ridicule." Why would writers committed to rational criticism of the biblical texts focus so much of their energies on the theory and use of ridicule? Ridicule was so characteristic of

Deist rhetoric in the eighteenth century that Redwood asserts that "the age of reason could perhaps more eloquently and adequately be called the age of ridicule, for it was ridicule, not reason, that endangered the Church" (p. 196).

Most scholars take one of two tacks to resolve the paradox. The first approach subsumes ridicule under the literary genre of satire, emphasizing the continuity of Deist ridicule with satirical literary works in the eighteenth century. Several historians and critics have sought to explain Deist ridicule in this way.[5] However, these scholars fail to account for ridicule as either a critical method or as a rhetorical tactic in the long-lasting public debate between the Deists and the Church. Ridicule as it appears in Deist pamphlets and tracts can hardly be fully explained as a species of literary satire.

The second kind of resolution does attribute a limited rhetorical significance to the approach. However, these efforts do not assign to ridicule sufficient rhetorical force to account for its longevity and popularity or its selection by such a wide range of writers. Redwood, for instance, proposes that ridicule was simply faster and easier than serious argument (p. 14).[6] William Lane Craig affirms that in some cases the "strategy was to make the biblical miracles look so silly that no amount of scholarly reasoning could generate belief in them" (pp. 130–31). Stanley Grean writes that ridicule had "a kind of *proving* power" for the Deists (p. 124). John M. Bullitt makes some effort to set Shaftesbury's theory of ridicule in a rhetorical context, but his principal concern is with Swift, not the Deists, and with satire, not ridicule.[7]

Though these two approaches—making ridicule a species of satire or a minor rhetorical tactic—provide some insights into the Deists' choice of method, each leaves the paradox of ridicule largely unresolved. In fact, the paradox is only finally resolved when ridicule is viewed as a carefully selected critical apparatus and as a sharply honed rhetorical weapon. This understanding of ridicule takes in the Deists' social context and rhetorical agenda, as well as ridicule's rhetorical benefits.

The most infamous and dangerous practitioner of ridicule was Thomas Woolston, whose *Six Discourses on the Miracles of our Saviour* appeared between 1727 and 1729. Woolston's rhetorical career is examined in detail in chapter 4, but some excerpts from his writings will serve here to exemplify Deist use of ridicule. In the following passage, Woolston ridicules Jesus' cursing the fig tree:

> *Jesus* was hungry, it seems, and being disappointed of Figs, to the Satisfaction of his Appetite, cursed the Figtree. Why so peevish and

impatient? Our *Divines,* when they please, make *Jesus* the most patient, resign'd and easy under Sufferings, Troubles, and Disappoint-
ments, of any Man. If he really was so, he could hardly have been so
much out of Humour, for want of a few figs, to the Allay of his Hun-
ger. But to curse the Figtree upon it, was as foolishly and passionately done, as for another Man to throw the Chairs and Stools about
the House; because his Dinner is not ready at a critical Time, or before it could be got ready for him. . . . Where was *Judas* his Steward
and Caterer with his Bag of Victuals as well as Money? Poor Forecast,
and Management amongst them, or *Jesus* had never trusted to the
uncertain fruits of a Figtree, which he espy'd at a Distance, for his
Breakfast. (Third Discourse, pp. 5–6)

Woolston also ridiculed Jesus' healing of a woman with a "flow of
blood" on the basis of an ambiguity in the account. As "neither one of
the evangelists signify of what degree her hemorrhage was, nor from
what part of her body it proceeded, nor how often or seldom she was
addicted to it," there can be no basis for discerning a great miracle in the
account. "It might be, for ought we know, only a little bleeding of the
nose, that now and then she was subject to." Woolston does not find
that "any of our divines have determined what sort [of bleeding] it was.
But a great miracle was wrought, they think, in her cure, without knowing the disease" (Second Discourse, pp. 10–11).

Woolston's ridicule, as other instances of the Deist tactic, is enhanced
by hyperbole. That the precise nature of the woman's problem is not
stated in a general historical narrative is not surprising, particularly considering the level of medical sophistication current in Palestine in the
first century A.D. That the illness might have been as trivial as "a little
bleeding of the nose" is unlikely, but Woolston insists that the account's
ambiguity allows such a reading.

Anthony Collins ridiculed, in addition to the biblical miracles, ecclesiastical practice and history. The elements of the Eucharist are said to
become the body and blood of Christ, despite what sense perceptions
indicate. This, writes Collins, "is a piece of Impudence equal to that of a
Man's Wife, who, when her Husband caught her in bed with a priest,
told him, *It was nothing but a Deception of the Devil to abuse a Man of God,*
and that she *hoped he would believe his own dear Wife befor his Eyes*" (Collins
1978, p. 25). Collins hopes that his *reductio* by analogy will be found
persuasive as well as amusing.

Collins ridiculed medieval Catholic miracles as well. His use of jux-
taposition is enhanced by his timing and sense of comedic crescendo.

Collins asks his readers to recall miracles "such as that of St. Dominick, who when the devil came to him in the shape of a monkey, made him hold a candle between his toes, till it burnt them." Readers should also consider miracles

> such as St. Patrick's heating an oven with snow and turning a pound of honey into a pound of butter: Such as Christ's marrying nuns and playing at cards with them; and nuns living on the milk of the blessed virgin Mary; and that of diverse orders, and especially the benedictines, being so dear to the blessed virgin, that in heaven she lodges them under her petticoats; such as making broken eggs whole, and of people who had their heads cut off, walking with their hands, which were sometimes set on again: Such as fasting a hundred years . . . and turning butter into a bell; and making a bull give milk. (Collins 1729, 8–9)

These, "the clearest miracles God ever wrought," are in fact "the most extravagant, whimsical, absurd, and ridiculous legends and stories imaginable" (p. 8). *A fortiori*, the less well-attested biblical miracles are condemned, while Collins protects himself from the still-present possibility of prosecution for blasphemy by focusing attention on "Roman" miracles.

Ridicule was not used exclusively to attack miracle accounts. Morgan ridiculed "spiritual" interpretations of the scriptures which sought to reconcile contradictory notions such as law and grace:

> Literal *Judaism* then, it seems, was figurative Christianity, and literal Christianity is mystical *Judaism;* the Letter of the Law was the Type of the Gospel, and the Letter of the Gospel is the Spirit of the Law; the Law was the Gospel under a Cloud; and the Gospel is the Law unveil'd and farther illuminated; *Moses* was the shadow of Christ, and Christ is the Substance of *Moses:* But tho' this Sort of Connexion and Harmony between the Law and the Gospel, or between the *Old Testament* and the *New,* may give intire Satisfaction and appear perfectly just and beautiful to Men of deep Discernment and Penetration; yet it must, as I imagine, be a little puzzling to vulgar Understandings. (Morgan, p. 19)

Morgan's clever linguistic turns both point up the contradictions and inconsistencies in the doctrines he attacks while they also "raise a laugh."

Ridicule's Goals

What were the Deists' intentions in ridiculing miracles? Several strategic goals influenced their selection of this method. First, Deists advocated "freethinking," reasoning liberated from the traditional constraints of authority and revelation. In this way "writers such as Toland and Collins regarded themselves as soldiers in the cause of Enlightenment," according to Maximillian Novak (pp. 96–97). Ridicule expressed the freedom to inquire into religious questions unrestrained; it was reason flaunting authority and as such appealed to a reader's sense of adventure and, perhaps, latent rebelliousness.

Second, ridicule undermined the revelation-based clerical hierarchy. Miracles endorsed biblical revelation and thus were crucial to clerical power. Annet recognized the direct connection between miracles and clerical power when he argued that "the No-Resurrection being proved as satisfactorily, as a negative can be proved, to all, that will make the least use of their reason, it is hoped, we shall hiss parsons off the stage . . ." (Annet 1742, p. 9). Clerical power, Collins argued at length, was employed to kill innocent people, ruin reputations, lie, and encourage superstition (Collins 1978, 46–99). Ridicule afforded the opportunity to embarrass members of the clergy by changing public attitudes about the foundation of their power.

Third, the clergy increasingly used miracles as proof of revelation in the opening decades of the eighteenth century (Burns, p. 12). A new, miracle-centered approach to Christian defenses invited skeptical attention. Miracles themselves suggested ridicule, particularly as Christian writers persistently claimed that miracles should be treated as historical events. Historical examination yielded quickly to ridicule as Deists sought to show that miracle accounts were either incapable of historical proof or rested on the flimsiest of historical evidence.

Ridicule's Strategic Advantages

Ridicule expressed a new intellectual freedom and was a weapon for attacking guardians of the old order. Clerics could be wounded by ridicule, mysteries exposed as beneath reason, and miracles unmasked as historical impostors. For minority advocates attacking an established religious view, ridicule held several strategic benefits. Most generally, it allowed Deists to forge a case against miracles that was both damaging and difficult to answer. "The risible faculty, when suitably directed, hath often proved a very potent engine," writes Orthodox apologist and rhetorical theorist George Campbell (p. 20). Several particular advantages associated with ridicule in a public debate on religious issues are worth considering.

Deists often noted the distracting and soporific effects religious language had on the public. They also affirmed with pleasure ridicule's ability to cut this verbal fog protecting miracles. Shrouded in religious language, miracles inhabited a realm beyond criticism. But, as Lord Kames argued, "any subject" may, "by the influence of fashion or custom," acquire "a degree of veneration to which by nature it is not entitled." When this occurs, "the proper means of wiping off the artificial colouring, and displaying the subject in its true light" is to "apply the test of ridicule, which separates it from its artificial connections, and exposes it naked with all its native improprieties" (p. 205). Once ridicule entered the repertoire of talk about miracles, their rejection was possible. Ridicule reclassified sacred events. By means of ridicule miracles are moved from the category "religious wonder" or "sacred mystery" to new categories such as "forgeries," "pretended wonders," and "tricks." Collins writes, for instance, of the "*Trick* of *casting out devils*" (*Free-Thinking*, p. 23). Ridicule introduced a range of new discursive possibilities in religious debate. As Richard Hughes writes, "once a subject has been defined as ridiculous, it can be treated with greater freedom than would ordinarily be allowed" (p. 22).

Moreover, as many Orthodox writers discovered by excruciating experience, ridicule is difficult to answer by traditional argument. It does not appear in discourse *as* argument; its premises and conclusions are obscure. Respondents are forced to maneuver on the opponent's ground, trying to answer the claim that one's own position was not worthy of serious consideration. A "contemptuous silence" would have been better than to "argue at length" with Deist ridicule, suggested Leslie Stephen in the nineteenth century. By arguing with ridicule, apologists fell victim to "the danger of a purely defensive line of argument" (volume 2, p. 5). Deists boasted of leaving their opponents "beating the air," an apt description of efforts to refute ridicule by argument (Berkeley, p. 284). John Brown writes, "ill qualified, indeed, is the saturnine complexion of the dry reasoner, to cope with this mercurial spirit of modern wit: The formalist is under a double difficulty; not only to conquer his enemy, but to find him" (J. Brown, p. 9).

Ridicule also focused attention on individual miracles to the exclusion of considerations such as general consistency among accounts, the degree of "fit" with the narrative context, or support from potentially corroborating evidences. Isolating a miracle distracts attention away from narrative and contextual considerations so important to its defense, focusing it instead on the particular event under scrutiny (Fisher, pp. 47–49). By this means, ridicule attacked miracles in their weakest form—as decontextualized wonder-stories. Stories such as Jesus' cursing a fig tree and causing it to wither—a favorite target of ridicule—are more vulnerable to attack as isolated accounts than as integrated elements in a narrative incorporating the life and teachings of the miracle worker, set against the narrative backdrop of, for instance, Jewish messianic prophecy.

In addition, ridicule magnifies minor problems such as ambiguities within accounts or insignificant inconsistencies among various miracle narratives. Thus, Annet searched the Resurrection accounts microscopically for inconsistencies. On a broader or more charitable view, such problems might be construed as strengths, proofs that there was no collaboration by the authors of the four gospel accounts.[8] Moreover, a respondent is bound either to explain every flaw in the narrative—a nearly impossible task—or to shift the grounds of debate altogether, leaving open the question of why problems in the text are not addressed by its defenders.

Ridicule and the Popular Audience

Deists were also aware of ridicule's strategic advantages before a popular audience. Ridicule provided a rational shortcut, a pleasant alternative to long and tedious deliberations. William Whitehead writes that ridicule as a "method" was among "the easiest comprehended." Nevertheless, ridicule is "as much serious as any method of reasoning" and "one of the most forceful and expeditious of all the methods of reasoning." It is precisely suited to detecting "that sort of falsehood, which we call the ridiculous" (pp. 17, 22).

Before an audience unaccustomed to religious disputation, but who nevertheless enjoyed the give and take of verbal battle, ridicule held obvious attractions. John Brown noted that ridicule was universally understood, as compared to traditional modes of argument:

> *Daedalian* arguments few can trace,
> But all can read the language of grimace.

> Hence mighty Ridicule's all conquering hand
> Shall work *Herculean* wonders thr'o the Land.
>   (quoted in Templeman, p. 27)[9]

Collins also noted that "there is a universal love and practice of drollery and ridicule in all" (Collins 1729, p. 47). Ridicule enjoyed a widespread appeal that academic argument and serious exegesis simply could not. This observation held special significance for Deists, for whom universality signified the natural and the rational.

Simply put, ridicule entertained, placing matters in "a pleasant and gay light." Ridicule's pleasantness was an incentive to free rational inquiry. "Men can never be better invited to the habit" of reasoning, wrote Shaftesbury, "than when they find pleasure in it." In fact, "a freedom of raillery, a liberty in decent language to question everything, and of unravelling and refuting any argument . . . are the only terms which can render such speculative conversations agreeable" (p. 69). As for himself, the earl would "hardly care so much as to think on this subject, much less to write on it, without endeavouring to put myself in as good humor as possible" (1711, p. 21). Whitehead also identified ridicule's capacity to "please by the novelty and contrast of its application" (Morgan, p. 81). Charles Bulkley noted that "the test of ridicule is no other than the test of free and chearful inquiry" (Bullitt, 76n.).

Ridicule's direct appeal to the common reader rendered it an attractive strategy for Deist writers, most of whom lacked actual political power, and some of whom were not well educated. Ridicule circumvented the institutional and formal constraints which inevitably worked to the advantage of the powerful. It appealed immediately to the larger audience whose members shared, as the Deists knew, a suspicion of power and intellectualism and a love of laughter.

But ridicule also carried risks. Cicero warned in Book II of *De Oratore* that in employing ridicule "[you must be] especially tender of popular esteem, so that you do not inconsiderately speak ill of the well-beloved" (p. 375). The Deists sometimes ignored this warning to the detriment of their case. Though skepticism may not have been uncommon in early-eighteenth-century Britain, much of the British public was not ready to hear the Virgin Birth and Resurrection ridiculed. Their careless and caustic treatment of sacred matters won the Deists some adherents but probably violated the religious sensibilities of many more readers. Christian writers frequently alleged that ridicule was inappropriate to the treatment of serious subjects such as religious faith. Robertson comments, "arguments that might have been made convincing were made to pass as banter, and serious spirits were repelled" (pp. 727–728).

Style, Status, and Common Sense

Language has often been identified as providing reliable signs of class. Less frequently has the same claim been made about methods of argument. Nevertheless, in the Deist controversy, one's manner of argument was taken as a sign of one's character, class, and worth. Hester Lynch Piozzi argued that ridicule is appropriate only in limited contexts. Addison, she notes, "detests all drollery on serious subjects," even though she recognizes that "a quotation out of Hudibras shall make some blockheads treat with levity an obligation wherein their welfare is concerned in this world and the next" (pp. 226–27). A willingness to ridicule religious subjects reveals defects in character, a loathsome nature, and low social standing.

Ridicule's ubiquity "in fashionable circles" is Shaftesbury's fault, which author has "shown us how happily and airily we might laugh at Heaven and its judgments" (Piozzi, p. 227). Interestingly, though Piozzi finds Mandeville's ridicule of Shaftesbury's *Characteristics* to be "admirable," Shaftesbury's introduction of ridicule into literary circles has had a generally disastrous effect:

[S]ince that book appeared, which taught mankind how RIDICULE alone was to be considered a test of truth, every character, however venerable by virtue of conduct or dignity of situation—every transaction, however trifling in itself, has been torn out and hung before the public eye to excite DERISION of authority, and promote BANTER where 'tis difficult to imitate merit.

Ridicule in the wrong hands is dangerous even to virtue, for "a man may lose his eye from the stroke of a boy's pop-gun, if not aware of its sudden approach." Moreover, "the present are beyond all preceding times fruitful in sarcastic merriment, so I recollect no age less fertile of elegant humours and harmless gaiety than the present." (Piozzi, p. 228)

There is a distinct class consciousness to Piozzi's criticism of ridicule.[10] Even "high people" have been corrupted by "broad mirth and coarse representation of mean manners, and the rough scenes of life," which draw them to "the tricks of Miss Hoyden and Miss Tomboy" on the stage. Moreover, people of quality show "the same disgraceful eagerness" for such low humor "that detains a lower set with liquorish hope of seeing somewhat at a printshop window capable to inflame the appetite in unintellectual and empty youth, or to restore it in debauched though half inert old age." Ridicule reveals "the retrograde progress of false refinement . . ." (p. 229).

Piozzi's lament in 1794 may be the last gasp of a dying order that depended in part on sharp distinctions in language to maintain its social identity. Carey McIntosh writes that while "upper-class social status" belonged to the "peerage and gentry," "upper-class linguistic status accrues to any locutions that are unambiguously associated with this elite group." Refined language and traditional modes of argument were linguistic emblems of the social privilege of a relatively small upper-class that faced the brute reality of a burgeoning lower class by century's end. "There were never more than 170 peers at any one time before the middle of the eighteenth century, and probably not more than 18,000–23,000 gentry, in a population that was growing from roughly five million to ten million between 1700 and 1800" (p. 7).

Language just as clearly marked the lower classes. MacIntosh notes that "in the very lowest social classes, among nonliterate working people and unemployed, English was entirely colloquial and entirely unregulated." She adds that "whatever got the message across was acceptable, including slang, profanity, dialect, theives' cant, grunts, signs, gestures, jargon, and quotations from the Bible" (pp. 7–8). Thus, the concern of Piozzi and others that the Deists were conduits for lower-class language into cultural arenas such as the theater and intellectual arenas such as theological debate was well founded. The social implications of this invasion were profound. Moreover, the relative fluidity of English society in the eighteenth century was a factor in the rise to considerable social status of Deist writers with their roots in the yeomanry. Thomas Chubb, a chandler's son with little formal education, associated with influential members of the clergy and aristocracy on the basis of his many published writings.[11]

Piozzi's anxiety about language, and especially about ridicule, reflects a strenuous social struggle that marked the eighteenth century in Britain. As the landed gentry sought to protect themselves from the encroachments of a rapidly growing and often rebellious lower class, laws such as the Black Act of 1723 were enacted that prescribed horrific penalties for relatively minor infractions involving property. The act "extended the death penalty to cover crimes against property as trivial as cutting down young trees or deerstalking in disguise" (Richetti, pp. 86–87). E. P. Thompson has drawn attention to the "class struggle without class" that characterized English social history in this period.[12]

Ridicule appealed directly to the common sense and social sensibilities of this broad new public. Ridicule, like humor generally, "requires an immediate audience response" (Fine, p. 84). Thus, in successful ridicule, speaker and audience must share a conception of common sense, that taken-for-granted store of values, beliefs, and experience that distinguishes a community (Perelman and Olbrechts-Tyteca, p. 99). Deist ridicule contrasted the common sense of the broader public to the narrowly conventional sense of the Church hierarchy. The strained and artificial reasoning of the clergy, reflected in their acceptance of the most preposterous stories, was shown to oppose the "natural" sense of "the people." Thus, Deist ridicule again emphasized and benefitted from the social tensions energizing the miracles controversy. Michael Billig has argued that "minorities can challenge the previously unchallenged assumptions of common-sense, and this challenge can substantively affect the nature of common-sense." Billig adds that such a challenge "may force the majority to justify assumptions which were previously unjustified, and, thereby, the status of the assumption is altered" (p. 219). This was precisely the situation facing the Church during the Deist controversy. Christian assumptions which had once enjoyed the status of common sense now required rational justification.

This fact does not imply that the Deist case was more widely accepted or clearly stronger than the Christian, for even "the probings of a minority [may] have the effect of disrupting the epistemological status of the majority's assumptions." In fact, "the mere questioning of a statement is," according to rhetorical theorists Chaim Perelman and Madame L. Olbrechts-Tyteca "sufficient to destroy its privileged status" (p. 68). By simply calling a matter in question before the public, "the unquestioned elements of common sense can be relegated to matters of controversy, on which attitudes are expected to be held" (Billig, p. 220). Thus, clergy were forced to justify Christian tenets which had previously been accepted more or less uncritically.

Lies and Disguise

David Berman has noted the tendency of Deists to espouse religious views which they apparently did not hold (Berman 1987). Berman argues that major Deists engaged in "the art of theological lying." This subversive rhetorical form was used to advance socially unacceptable and dangerous views by insinuation, while avoiding prosecution for blasphemy by hiding behind the mask of the lie. Lying was a rhetorical adaptation to the pressures under which the Deists wrote. "Given the oppressive forces of the time, the basic choice for a free-thinker was between silence or lying. . . ." Berman adds that "the free-thinker was in a moral dilemma: if he was silent, the truth (as he saw it) would suffer by omission; if he told the truth, he would suffer." Deists resolved the dilemma by a paradoxical moral compromise: "lying for the truth, lying so that the intelligent would know or could unravel the truth, while the authorities could not punish or victimize the writer" (Berman 1992, p. 256).

Previous scholarship on the Deists has failed to recognize the public dishonesty of these writers. Berman writes regarding assessments of Collins, for instance, "those scholars who see Collins as a Deist must also accept that he was a liar—that is, he did not mean what he said" (Berman 1987, p. 61). Berman holds that Collins—as well as Blount, Toland, and Tindal—four of the most important early Deist writers, lied in their public rhetoric about their belief in immortality, God, and biblical authority. For instance, John Toland wrote in his *Vindicus Liberius:* "I have no doubts concerning the Excellence, Perfection, and Divinity of the *Christian Religion* in general as it is delivered in the holy *Scriptures,* and I willingly and heartily conform to the Doctrine and Worship of the *Church of England* in particular" (pp. 105–6; quoted in Berman 1992, p. 257). But Berman correctly points out that anyone familiar with Toland's work would immediately recognize that this cannot be an honest claim. Toland was far from being an Anglican, or a Christian of any sort.

Berman finds a rationale, though no excuse, for theological lying in "a fear or unwillingness to write truthfully about religion" (1987, p. 62). The Deists feared prosecution for their anti-Christian tracts. Lying about their belief in biblical authority and immortality allowed Deists to maintain a facade of Orthodoxy before a gullible public while disseminating their decidedly unorthodox views. Berman calls the approach a "technique," that is, lying was a rhetorical maneuver, an adaptation of discourse to an audience and to the constraints of controversy (1992, p. 258).

Lying allowed writers like Toland to accomplish three goals, each requiring adaptation of their discourse to a different audience. First, the Deists sought to avoid prosecution. Their audience in this regard was "the civil and legal authorities." Second, Deists sought to communicate their true religious opinions to discerning readers. Their audience is now "free-thinking friends." Finally, the Deists recognized the persuasive power of insinuation, hiding their real message under layers of what Blount termed "bouncing compliments"—disingenuous affirmations and outright lies regarding cherished Christian doctrines. Here their audience is "unwary and/or open-minded believers" (1992, p. 259). Toland writes to his correspondent in the second of his *Letters to Serena* (1704) that "You have no doubts, I'm Certain, about the Soul's Immortality, and Christianity affords the best, the clearest Demonstration for it, even the revelation of God himself" (quoted in Berman 1987, p. 66). Having made his "bouncing compliment," the force of the remainder of Toland's argument in this piece is, as Berman notes, "*against* belief in immortality" (p. 66).[13]

The tactic of the lie was not simple irony. Deists recognized that their clerical opponents knew they did not mean what they said about the nature and existence of God, the truthfulness of revelation, and the reality of an afterlife. But they also suspected that the average reader would believe them sincere and would thus be more willing to accept the covert message that such beliefs rest on the flimsiest of foundations. "We are apt to underestimate the gullibility and uncertainty of the average eighteenth-century reader," writes Berman (1987, p. 69). Berman also argues that the Deists sought by insinuation to "influence at an unconscious level. They were trying to bring about a belief without the unwary reader being aware of it." Thus he concludes that "free-thinkers like Blount should be seen as vehicles of a subversive, threatening social unconscious" (1992, p. 264).

John Leland Exposes the Deists

Berman's thesis about the Deists' tactical lying finds support in Christian polemic, which clearly reveals that the Deists' dishonesty was recognized by their clerical opponents. John Leland, the most important eighteenth-century historian of the controversy and a major respondent to the Deists, exposed their extensive use of deception in *A View of the Principal Deistical Writers* (1752). "Never in any country where Christianity is professed, were there such repeated attempts to subvert its divine authority, carried on sometimes under various disguises . . ." (p. i). Leland seeks to elucidate "the different disguises and appearances

[Deists] have put on, and the several schemes they have formed," which are "all directed to one main end, *viz.* to set aside revelation, and substitute mere natural religion, or, which seems to have been the intention of some of them, no religion at all, in its room" (p. ii).

Leland, like other Orthodox writers, finds covert and subversive rhetoric a sign of an unprincipled adversary.[14] "[T]he enemies of Christianity have not generally behaved as became fair adversaries, but have rather acted, as if they judged any arts lawful, by which they thought they might gain their cause" (pp. ii–iii). Deception, he notes, was an aspect of Deism from its inception. The earliest continental Deists, mentioned by Viret in 1563, were men who maintained an "outward appearance" of religion, though they regarded the religion of Jesus and the apostles as "fables and dreams." They "laughed at all religion." The efforts of these early Deists to propagate their religious views is condemned by Leland, paraphrasing Viret: "[N]ot content to perish alone in their error, they took pains to spread the poison, and to infect and corrupt others, by their impious discourses, and bad examples" (p. 2). Ultimately, the Deists' rejection of Christianity and their corresponding tendency toward deception is rooted in "corrupt lusts and passions" (p. 404). The argument against heterodox theology again is linked with an *ad hominem* argument regarding the adversaries' moral character. Lying propagated the "poison" of unbelief. Even "the name of Deists, as applied to those who are no friends to revealed religion" was affected to cover their unbelief. The label "is said to have been first assumed about the middle of the sixteenth century, by some Gentlemen in *France* and *Italy*, who were willing to cover their opposition to Christian revelation by a more honourable name than that of Atheists," writes Leland (p. 2).

Leland unmasks present-day Deists, exposing them as liars and deceivers. Collins, for instance, "lays the greatest stress upon a passage from *Victor* of *Tmuis*, in which it is said that at the command of the emperor *Anastasius*, the holy gospels were corrected and amended." Certainly if true, such a charge would damage claims of scriptural historicity and authority. However, Leland continues:

This our author calls *an account of a general alteration of the four gospels in the sixth century.* And he says, it was discovered by Dr. *Mills*, and was very little known before. But then he should have taken notice of what Dr. *Mills* has added, *viz.* that it is certain as any thing can be, that no such altered gospels were ever published; and that if the fact had been thus, it would have been mentioned with detestation by all the historians, and not be found only in one blind passage of a puny chronicle. (p. 86)

Much of Leland's two long volumes is taken up with similar efforts to expose what he alleges are intentional Deistic deceptions. It is an educated Christian's duty to answer the Deists' subversive rhetoric, "and it should be the matter of our earnest prayers to God, that all those who value themselves upon the honourable name and privileges of Christianity, may join in united efforts to support so glorious a cause," on which depends "the preservation and advancement of true religion and virtue, the peace and good order of society, and the present and eternal happiness of individuals" (p. vii).

Identifying and repudiating the rhetorical tactic of lying became important components in the Orthodox case against Deism. Lying was a deceptive strategy of cowardly lower-class writers afraid of open and direct discursive confrontation with qualified opponents. Lying reflected moral cowardice, mental laziness, and political unscrupulousness, all rooted in atheism. On the other hand, open and honest statement of one's views signaled fairness, reasonableness, high social status, and Christian piety. In short, atheists and infidels deceive and pretend in argument, Christian gentlemen reason fairly and openly. Thus did rhetoric reveal character. In constructing his own arguments against the Deists, "great care has been taken to make a fair representation of them" (p. iv). Leland will not be found guilty of the subversive tactics which characterize his unbelieving opponents.

Though Berman's thesis that leading Deists were liars runs counter to the widespread view that they were sincere theists, their theological dishonesty was widely alleged in the eighteenth century. For this reason as much as for their heterodoxy and hatred of the clergy, Deists enjoyed the profound disrespect of the powerful clerical-academic hierarchy. Moreover, their rhetorical tactics were taken as marks of the Deists' low social estate, indeed of their low rank in the great chain of being. Their efforts to overturn the existing social order by whatever means necessary were not, then, surprising. Such moral and social tensions account in large measure for the harsh treatment many leading Deists received in the period of relative religious freedom following passage of the Toleration Act.

Mental Pests and Hydras of the Soul

The literature of the Deist controversy reveals a bitter social struggle joined by advocates who loathed not simply one another's theology but one another. Deists viewed clerics as despotic spiritual slaveholders and political tyrants. The clergy saw their opponents as agents of demonic bondage and harbingers of moral degeneracy.[15] "Atheistical" writers were not simply political opponents of the established elite but social vermin and pariahs worthy of the severest punishments. "In my opinion," wrote E. Budge in the *Spectator* on May 27, 1712, "a solemn judicial Death is too great an honour for an Atheist . . ." (quoted in Berman 1975, 90n.). The Reverend Robert South wrote colorfully of his non-trinitarian opponents as "impious blasphemers, whose infamous pedigree runs back (from wretch to wretch) in a direct line to the devil himself; and who are fitter to be crushed by the civil magistrate, as destructive to government and society, than to be confuted as merely heretics in religion" (quoted in Clark 1985, p. 283). As South's statement suggests, the battle between the forces of heterodoxy and of orthodoxy was more than a religious fight; it was cultural warfare.

From Britain's social fringes, Deists attacked a privileged elite by means of a scandalous and profane rhetorical appeal to an emerging literate and urban audience of tradesmen and mechanics. This audience, drawn from "an increasing reading public," was particularly prepared to resist the "practice and mentality of 'dependence'" and to respond to a rhetoric that challenged the long-established notion that citizens "were expected dutifully to obey their betters . . ." (Rack, pp. 6, 22). The Deists' principal audience was one prone to riot, both physical and mental. London in the early eighteenth century, particularly those parts of London inhabited by mechanics, guild members, and the "hack" writers of Grub Street and its surrounding burroughs, was the scene of frequent and often brutal rioting.[16] Moreover, the "rioting mob had its own notions of what was just" (Rack, p. 7). Similarly, London was the refuge of Deist writers like Woolston and Annet, sons of the mechanic class, who sought and found an audience among this same public for a violent assault on holy writ, sacred notions, and powerful churchmen.

Defoe on the Deists

The social or class animosity Deists and social conservatives harbored for one another is seldom far from the center of this debate. Deists would cut society free from its moral moorings grounded in divine dictate. Thus, they were the enemies of civil society. "Freethinkers," wrote Defoe in 1721, "are profane" and erase "the Awe of God in their hearts. ..." They publicly advocate "Freedom in all Manner of Vice,—using the Pretence of Liberty for a Justification of Crime, as if the Liberty God gave to man of being a free Agent, disengaged him entirely from all the restraint of Laws, whether Human or Divine" (quoted in Novak, p. 96). Silencing the Deists was important to maintaining social order.

Deists were lawless renegades bent on the destruction of manners, freedom, and Christian society. Defoe was "an active advocate for the Societies for Reformation of Manner from their inception," who viewed "the civilizing of English behavior during the transition from the Restoration to the eighteenth century as the product of a moral code enforced by religious sanctions" (Novak, pp. 96–97). Thus, for him and other social conservatives, the Deists' "religion of reason and nature" was literally the work of the Devil, with the goal of undoing British-Christian society. Deism, as the invention of evil men, was "of an Original deeper than Hell, and out of the Reach of the *Devil*" (quoted in Novak, p. 104).

Novak takes Defoe's several books on the occult as rhetorical adaptations of his attack on Deism and atheism to a popular audience which would not sit still for a serious discussion of false ideologies. Not that Defoe thought such a tactic was the best one, only that it was necessary given the level to which religious debate had descended in response to Deism. "Unhappy Times! where to be serious, is to be dull and grave, and consequently to write without Spirit" (quoted in Novak, p. 105). Defoe laments the rhetorical climate engendered by Deist ridicule.

Addison on the Deists

Joseph Addison (1672–1719) also wrote with great venom against the Deists, especially Shaftesbury and Collins. Though his *The Evidences of Christianity* advances a series of sophisticated rebuttals of Deist arguments, Addison's book is also characterized by harsh *ad hominem* attacks intended to support a call for prosecution of the Deists. Deists were subhuman creatures, judging from their manner of life and the intent of their writings. "It is my opinion," he affirmed, "the *Free-Thinkers* should be treated as a set of poor ignorant creatures" who "have no sense to discover the excellency of religion" and who "proclaim aloud to the world, that they have less motives of honesty than the rest of their fellow-subjects. . ." (Addison, p. 189).[17] On the other hand, Addison's own work (according to his editor) reflects "the politeness and beauty" which appeals to "persons of a superior Character and more liberal Education" (p. iv).

Addison addressed the Deists' charge that Jesus' miracles were worked by magic, emphasizing the moral direction of Jesus' own works and teachings in contrast to those of the socially iconoclastic Deists. Employing a commonplace of the time, he responds that magic does not assist the development of piety and virtue. "Was it the business of magic," he asks "to humanize our natures with compassion, forgiveness, and all the instances of the most extensive charity. Would evil spirits contribute to make men sober, chaste, and temperate?" (p. 16). Addison also argues from the surprising early progress of Christianity and from the record of the numerous early converts to the faith, including many learned people. Some of the early converts had opportunity to debunk the faith were it not true. The fulfillment of Christian prophecies, such as Jesus' claim that his followers would be brought before magistrates and kings, is further evidence of the faith's truth.

Addison also attacked the deceptive tendencies of "sober *Free-Thinkers*" who assert that "virtue indeed is beautiful, and vice deformed" on one page, while on another such doctrines as "the immortality of the Soul, or eternal punishments and rewards . . . are openly ridiculed, or rendered suspicious by the most sly and laboured artifice." Based on this kind of rhetorical evidence, Addison develops a pointed *ad hominem* argument against the Deists. They are "treacherous," "joyless," and "dull" writers who "think to surmount their own natural meanness" by "laying offense in the way of such as make it their endeavour to excell" by pursuing the "honest arts of life" (pp. 188, 245).

Addison translates such *ad hominem* into a potent strategy of reclassification. Deists are transformed from un-Christian nuisances into sub-human creatures lacking the emotional capacity to understand religion. The "Free-Thinker is a creature unacquainted with the emotions which possess great minds when they are turned for religion, and it is apparent that he is untouched with any such sensation as the rapture of devotion." Moreover, the Deist "wants capacity to relish what true piety is." Deists as a group are "scroners" and "low and narrow in their opinion of things." The typical Deist is a "blockhead" who is "vain" and by whom "mischief is done for mischief's sake." It is a testimony against the age that such men have been listened to. "When such writers as this [Collins], who has no spirit but that of malice, pretend to inform the age, *Mohocks* and Cut Throats may well set up for wits and men of pleasure" (pp. 246–47, 248, 257).

The exclusion of the Deists from civil society, and their eventual transformation into "creatures" who lack basic human emotions, is in Addison as other Christian writers preparatory of the argument for prosecution. With Collins especially in view, Addison argues that as "the peace and tranquility of the nation, and regards even above these, are so much concerned in this matter . . . it is difficult to express sufficient sorrow for the offender, or indignation against him." With effort, however, the latter is possible: "But if ever a man deserved to be denied the common benefits of air and water, it is the Author of *a Discourse of Free-Thinking,*" that is, Collins (p. 250).

Pursuing the strategy of reclassification, the Deist is likened to a fly on the ceiling of St. Paul's Cathedral. The fly would, from its limited vantage point, claim that there was no pattern to the ceiling. From a broader point of view, however, the pattern is seen to be exquisitely beautiful. The Deists focus their flylike capacities on small questions and in so doing fail to comprehend the wonders of God. Moreover, such insects dare to criticize Christians for their narrowness. Addison's anger at this criticism is unvarnished. "There is not," he writes, "any instance of weakness in the *Free-Thinkers* that raises my indignation more, than their pretending to ridicule Christians, as men of narrow understandings, and to pass themselves upon the world for persons of superior sense, and more enlarged views." Finally, Addison asserts that the despised Pharisees of Jesus' day were religious pretenders who rejected the Messiah and who "believed neither Resurrection, nor Angel, nor Spirit." They were, "in plain *English,* . . . *Deists* at least, if not Atheists" (pp. 256, 259).

Other Characterizations of the Deists:
Berkeley and Whitehead

The Deists' mental laziness was consistently alleged by their Christian opponents. Berkeley, whose dialogue *Alciphron* (1731) is perhaps the best of the anti-Deist books, took the Deists' use of ridicule as evidence of their rational sloth in matters demanding careful critical inquiry. A Deist in *Alciphron* rejects the notion that all of the evidences for Christianity should be examined. "Such an inquiry," he argues, "would cost too much pain and time." Deists like himself "have thought of another method—the bringing religion to the test of wit and humour: this we find a shorter, easier, and more effectual way" (p. 284). Thus, the undisciplined Deists are careless reasoners more interested in having fun with one another at the expense of religious faith, than with ascertaining the truth regarding the questions they pretended to be investigating.

William Whitehead's *Essay on Ridicule* was published in 1743, near the height of Annet's popularity. Whitehead takes ridicule like Annet's as evidence of laziness in intellectual matters, for "if too harsh each boistr'ous Labour proves," the Deist "conducts us to more happy groves" (p. 11). Serious intellectual inquiry is too taxing for these advocates who find ridicule easier and more enjoyable. But, ridicule also indicates intellectual narrowness. Ignoring studies about which they know or care little, Deists judge that "all's ridiculous, but what they know" (p. 10).

The Deists are philosophical dabblers who know too little to engage in the kind of textual criticism they claim to be doing. It is precisely because of this ignorance that ridicule appeals to them and to their audience. Ridicule wins assent only from "th' unthinking crowd," who mistakenly equate laughter with refutation (p. 13). Deists are shiftless cheaters in debate, willing to stoop as low as need be to make their case appeal to the most unreliable of audiences.

The Deists' portrait is given even more sinister tones when Christian writers cast them as vermin, criminals, and agents of the Devil who must be opposed, if need be, by violence. Whitehead suggests the proper treatment of these "mental pests":

> Here then we fix, and lash without controul
> These mental pests, and *Hydra's* of the Soul;
> Acquir'd ill-nature, ever prompt debate,
> A zeal for slander, and delib'rate Hate:
> These court Contempt, proclaim the public Foe,
> and each, *Ulysses like,* should aim the blow.

Deists are animals to be controlled with the whip, miscreants who deserve punishment and respond only to force:

> Hope we to mend him? Hope, alas, how vain!
> He feels the lash, not listens to the Rein.
> And if to quell, not pierce, the *Sword* we draw,
> The Hardy Felon quite contemns the law.
>
> (p. 13)

Animal metaphors were also common in portrayals of the Deists, one more strategy in an ongoing rhetorical effort to redefine Deists as subhuman. Monkey-like, skeptics raise laughter by imitating rational human beings:

> O fruitful Source of everlasting Mirth!
> For fools, like Apes, are Mimes from their Birth.
>
> (p. 17)

E. P. Thompson has written, in fact, that members of the upper (gentry) and lower classes in England at this time "seem scarce to regard each other as of the same species" (Thompson 1974, p. 395; quoted in Speck, p. 44). And then we have Defoe hinting darkly in *A System of Magick* that the "Atheists, and Deists," are the Devil's agents and thus deserving of "Fire and Faggot" (quoted in Novak, p. 103).

The Deists' portrait in the rhetoric of prominent opponents such as Defoe, Addison, Berkeley, and Whitehead was intended to suggest the great social gulf fixed between the righteous and those sitting in the seat of mockers. Moreover, their persistent subhuman portrayal in Orthodox rhetoric legitimated the harsh treatment of important Deists such as Woolston and Annet, treatment that included harassment, trials, fines, imprisonment, and the public stocks.

But clearly both Deists and their opponents in the Church developed and employed rhetorical strategies questionable when judged by the standards of conventional *topoi* of argument. Deists lied about their theology, assumed religious "disguises" so as to avoid prosecution, and made ridicule the centerpiece of their case against miracles so as to gain readers while escaping the restraints of theological language and argument. Christian writers, in turn, seized on deception and ridicule in building a powerful *ad hominem* case against the Deists' moral character. As might be expected of blasphemers and heretics, clerics argued, Deists employed rhetorical strategies unworthy of serious writers deliberating sober religious questions. Such tactics provided clear evidence of moral degeneracy, which was itself the only explanation for the Deists' ruthless assault on "the faith once delivered to the saints." Christian polemicists appropriated the Deists' more questionable rhetorical tendencies as an opening for a potent countertactic aimed at social marginalization. Clerics employed discursive evidence of moral corruption—lying, disguise, ridicule—to warrant their strategic definition of the Deists as not merely beyond the pale of polite society but literally beneath the human species. Deists were insects, animals, monsters, and demons. Once so defined, these miscreants could be treated in a manner in keeping with their true nature.

Chapter Four

The Rhetorical Career
of Thomas Woolston

To Woolston recommend our youth
For learning, probity and truth,
That noble genius, who unbinds
The chains which fetter free-born minds,
Redeems us from the slavish fears
Which lasted near two thousand years,
He can alone the priesthood humble,
Make gilded spires and altars tumble.

Jonathan Swift, *A Dialogue*

On March 4, 1729, Thomas Woolston was tried at the Guild Hall before the King's Bench in London for blasphemy. Woolston's scandalous attacks on Christian revelation in his *Six Discourses on the Miracles of our Saviour* and other works had sped "the rapid torrent of spiritual Deceit" which was flooding all of England in the early eighteenth century (*A dialogue Between Mr. Grounds and Schemes*, p. 1). In many respects Woolston was an unlikely candidate for criminal prosecution under England's Blasphemy Act of 1697. Born into a working-class family in Northampton in 1670, he rose to become an ordained cleric, fellow of Cambridge's Sidney-Sussex College, a leading expert on the early Church fathers, and the author of scholarly and popular books and tracts. "He bore the repute," writes one biographer, "of a sound scholar, a good preacher, a charitable and estimable man."[1]

But between 1720 and 1729, Woolston was the single most troublesome enemy of the Church of England and one of the most important rhetorical voices of the decade. His early polemical works angered Cambridge administrators sufficiently to bring about his dismissal from the University in 1721. Edmund Gibson, Bishop of London, twice brought blasphemy charges against Woolston and published a widely read pastoral letter condemning him in 1728. Other prominent church leaders

also wrote against him, and Woolston even attracted the personal attention of both the Archbishop of Canterbury and Queen Caroline. His scandalous *Six Discourses* (1727–1729) elicited more than sixty published
replies. By 1729, he had generated serious and consequential religious
debate in England, on the Continent, and in the American colonies. His
highly controversial trial, which was followed with great interest in
England and abroad, set important precedents for blasphemy cases (Levy
1981, pp. 317–30). Woolston's life, works, and trial constitute an important and largely ignored chapter in the history of eighteenth-century
British rhetoric.

Woolston was a paradoxical figure who has elicited strikingly
equivocal responses from historians. More than a century ago, Sir Leslie
Stephen branded him "a mere buffoon jingling his cap and bells in a
sacred shrine" (p. 231); his evaluation has probably influenced many
subsequent assessments of Woolston. Harold Hutcheson muses, regarding the controversy that Woolston touched off, that "rarely has so unim-
pressive a charge produced so momentous an explosion" (p. 77). Peter
Gay writes of Woolston's "clinical insanity" (p. 375) while Henning Graf
Reventlow has recently referred to him as "eccentric" and as "psycho-
pathic" (p. 149). John Redwood calls Woolston's attack on miracles the
work of an "evil genius" (p. 149). But Robert M. Grant and David Tracy
find Woolston to have been "the most influential" of all English skeptical writers (p. 109). Similarly, Herbert Morais maintains that Woolston
subjected the New Testament miracles to "a searching analysis" (p. 39).
Colin Brown also finds Woolston's analysis of the biblical miracles to
prefigure later critical developments (C. Brown 1984, p. 50).

Judgments about his character and sanity obscure Woolston's specific rhetorical accomplishments. But Woolston's clash with the Church
is important to understanding the serious problems facing Orthodox
Christianity in early-eighteenth-century England, as well as the radical
changes taking place in public attitudes toward religion. Woolston was
a catalyst in the debate over miracles and biblical interpretation, and he
personified the skeptical threat to traditional beliefs. This chapter as-
sesses the rhetorical career of Thomas Woolston, particularly the impact
of his last and most important work, the *Six Discourses on the Miracles of
our Saviour*. It considers Woolston's rhetorical context, motives, strategies, and accomplishments, as well as the discursive and legal efforts
mounted by opponents to silence him.

Woolston is an important figure in the history of religious rhetoric
for several reasons. First, his madness, whether real or feigned, was

methodical enough to force a popular discussion of vital religious issues such as the authenticity of Christ's miracles. He thus helped to move these issues from the domain of a clerical elite to the arena of public rhetoric. Second, Woolston introduced both a critical method and an interpretive approach which seriously challenged literal understandings of scripture. In this way Woolston made an important and largely unrecognized contribution to the development of modern approaches to biblical interpretation. Finally, though this chapter's primary concerns are to locate and to assess Woolston's rhetorical career in its historical context, Woolston's life also illustrates how the rules of a discourse community can be challenged and altered. Woolston developed both an extravagant rhetorical style and a flamboyant public persona which made his views impossible to ignore. The controversy and trial touched off by his blasphemous claims permanently altered the boundaries of religious rhetoric in the English-speaking world. His trial for blasphemy also revealed the lengths to which the Church would go to silence Deist rhetoric and perhaps the frustration engendered by efforts to silence Woolston and others by strictly rhetorical means.

Woolston's Rhetorical Career

In 1705, Woolston, a Cambridge tutor and student of the Church fathers, published his *An Old Apology for the Truth of the Christian Religion*, in which he argued that biblical miracles were largely allegorical rather than historical in nature. Woolston based his argument on the Alexandrian school of biblical interpretation that developed in the second and third centuries under the direction of Origen.[2] Although the *Old Apology* received little response, it was held by some to express a heretical nonliteral interpretation of Christ's miracles. In the face of growing skepticism, a literal and historical understanding of the New Testament miracles was becoming increasingly important to Christian defenses (Burns, pp. 9–18). Recognizing that further efforts on his part to discover a more rational basis for Christianity could be dangerous, Woolston did not publish again for fifteen years. William Trapnell suggests that Woolston may have been confined during this period as his writings were taken by friends and opponents alike to be evidence of insanity.

In 1720–1721, however, Woolston resumed his attack on literal readings of biblical miracles by publishing tracts defending strictly allegorical interpretations of scripture. He maintained that the Apostles were allegorizers and that the New Testament miracles were never intended to be taken as literal accounts of historical events. Following Spinoza, Woolston drew attention to "absurdities" in Christian miracle accounts. A consistent reading of the New Testament was possible without recourse to supernaturalism. Early respondents like William Bowman were troubled by what they called Woolston's "method of arguing from Absurdities," an approach that failed to respect the authority of scripture (pp. iii–iv). The full implications of Woolston's non-literal hermeneutic were, however, only beginning to become clear.

Woolston could not be dismissed by the Church as unqualified to speak on matters of interpretation, nor as a rabid atheist. He was both a recognized expert on early church history and an ordained minister. Woolston presented the hierarchy with a daunting problem—a damaging assault by an Anglican cleric and Cambridge scholar on the foundation of Christian orthodoxy, biblical literalism. Early efforts to silence him tended to be punitive rather than rhetorical. For his tracts of 1720–21 Woolston was relieved of his fellowship at Cambridge, with allegations of mental instability being reasserted. Woolston was shunned by former colleagues, and few friends stood by him. The pain of expulsion, exclusion, and denigration was, by his own account, almost more than he could bear. The "Reproaches and Defamations" from the clergy for his books, and "the Shame of them" nearly drove Woolston to suicide (Woolston 1728, p. iv). His credibility as a writer and scholar suffered predictable and calculated damage. "I need not tell the World, Sirs," he wrote to the clergy in 1724, "what a mean and contemptible Person you have made me, beyond Measure, to the Prejudice of any thing I can publish . . ." (p. 4).

In order to draw attention to his works, Woolston developed a strategy of answering his own tracts in satirical imitation of his critics. An example of the technique occurs in *An Answer to Aristobuls's two Letters to Dr. Bennett. By a Country Curate* (1721). Woolston further angered clerics by identifying them by name. Well-known figures such as Whitby, Waterland, Clarke, Sacheverel, Ibbot, and Sherlock were also referred to as *"Dunces," "ignorant Blockheads," "Black Guards of Hell,"* and *"Pluto's Liverymen"* (pp. 25, 37).

Woolston moved to London around 1722, where he occupied himself with writing popular works intended to embarrass his clerical enemies and undermine scriptural literalism. In order to attract the general reading public to his books, Woolston joined his hermeneutical arguments to a sensational style and venomous satire. The combination of volatile theological themes, caustic prose, and penetrating wit proved explosive.

Woolston filled his first genuinely popular series, *Four Free Gifts to the Clergy* (1722–1724), with extravagant insults directed at his former colleagues, who were "the cause of infidelity" and "as ignorant of the Gospel of Christ, as the most illiterate of their Congregations that they preach to." Christian ministers are "the real *Scribes* and *Pharisees*, against whom our Saviour muttered so many Invectives," as well as "*Caterpillars, Makebates, Necromancers, Dark Lanthorns*, and the like." In sum, the Anglican clergy were "the greatest *Hereticks* and *Apostates* of all ages" (pp. 7, 19, 28, 43). Woolston admitted that his insults were intended to "invite [clerics] into Combat with me" (p. 33). And he could not have failed to recognize that they attracted readers and created controversy.

Woolston was an ejected cleric and a madman undeserving of dignified response. But this lunatic clergyman was now making a public mockery of the Church's leadership and in the process winning a wide hearing for a dangerous view of scripture. Refutations of his works ran the dual risk of lending credibility to his views while making respondents look foolish for choosing to answer a lunatic.

Woolston's madness, real or feigned, evoked contradictory associations. The mad were considered by some to have yielded their souls to the Devil, who now tormented their minds and caused them to utter blasphemies.[3] By another ancient tradition, however, "only madmen and angels can speak the truth" in opposition to the wise and powerful (Rosen, 154ff.).[4] Perhaps recognizing the dilemma he posed the hierarchy, Woolston reveled in the role of madman. In the *Four Free Gifts*, for instance, he boldly proclaims that "*Origen*, who lived Fifteen Hundred Years since, is pleased to say of me . . . that I am best skilled of any Man in the Spirit of Prophecy" (p. 32). He had also claimed to have spoken with "*Elias* on the *Sublime Mountain* of *Vision*" (A. B., p. 4).

Like his insults, madness had the desired effect of provoking angry responses from the clergy. And when responses were not forthcoming in sufficient number, Woolston would write them himself, parodying his powerful enemies after the fashion of a court jester.[5] Thus, one frustrated respondent noted, "you have got a scurvy trick of answering yourself" (A. B., p. 10). By such tactics, Woolston became the most damaging and infamous opponent of Christianity in England in the 1720s.

As frustrating as was Woolston's ludicrous assault on the clergy in

Four Free Gifts, his sustained critical examination of miracles posed a more serious threat. In *A Moderator between an Infidel and an Atheist* and two *Supplements to a Moderator* (1725), Woolston questioned the historicity of biblical miracles. The *Moderator* series provoked Gibson to bring blasphemy charges against Woolston in early November 1725, but the prosecution was dropped because such a course might win sympathy for Woolston and make the Church appear both to fear a challenge and to favor persecution. The archbishop himself visited Woolston, stating that he "was against all such prosecutions" (Woolston 1733, p. 12). Despite warnings and a brief period in prison, in the spring of 1727 Woolston published the first two issues of his most important and controversial works, *Six Discourses on the Miracles of Our Saviour.*

The Six Discourses

By 1726, Woolston had succeeded in pressing two crucial issues on the Church, making each the subject of a broadly public and highly embarrassing controversy. First, Woolston called in question the competence and necessity of the clergy. Second, he challenged the authenticity of biblical miracles. Although the former provided his opponents with ample personal motive for going after him, the latter was the more serious challenge for it threatened Christianity's historical foundations. As John Redwood explains, a literal view of the miracles was vital to both Christian apologetic and faith:

> Miracles were needed as proof of Christ's divinity; without them the unitarians had a chance of swaying opinion. Miracles were needed to attest essential doctrines; without their proof the whole fabric of New Testament Christianity seemed unstable . . . ; miracles were necessary as proof of God's powers, as proof of God's concern, as evidence of revelation. (p. 149)

Thus, the threat posed by Woolston's *Discourses* was complex. He challenged clerical privilege, questioned the historicity of miracles, and introduced a radical new vocabulary of biblical criticism.

The *Six Discourses,* published separately between May 1727 and March 1729, were instantly popular and controversial.[6] They received dozens of replies, and Voltaire noted on a visit to England that 30,000 copies were sold there in a short time, while many copies were sent to the American colonies (Burns, p. 10). One respondent wrote in 1729 that the *Discourses* were "too well known to need to be particularly named" (*Miracles of Jesus Vindicated*, volume 1, p. 4). Swift acknowledged the *Discourses* fame in satiric verse:

> Here's Woolston's Tracts, the twelfth Edition;
> 'Tis read by ev'ry Politician:
> The Country Members, when in Town,
> To all their Boroughs send them down:
> You never met a Thing so smart;
> The Courtiers have them all by Heart.
>
> (Swift 1958, p. 564)[7]

All six *Discourses* were satirically dedicated to prominent bishops who had opposed Woolston.[8] In shocking language Woolston argued that "the literal History of many of the Miracles of Jesus, as recorded by the Evangelists, does imply Absurdities, Improbabilities, and Incredibilities, consequently they, either in whole or in part, were never wrought. . . ." Deliberately severing the traditional link between miracles and Christian defenses, Woolston asserted that the miracles of Christ are not "a good Proof of his Divine Authority to found a Religion." Woolston justified his critical agenda as an effort to provide Christianity with a rational foundation not dependent upon supernaturalism and superstition. He opens the *Discourses* with the taunting assertion that it is "to the Honour of our *Messiah,* and the Defence of Christianity, I write this Treatise on Jesus's Miracles . . ." (*First Discourse,* p. 4).[9]

In the *Discourses* Woolston's rhetoric of insult and ridicule reached Jesus himself. Jesus was a "magician" and a "sorcerer" whose miracles were "nauseating" displays filled with "absurdities" and "tricks" for which he would have been "made to swing" had he performed them in modern England (*First Discourse,* p. 34).[10] The insults and sensational claims that punctuated the *Discourses* drew popular attention to Woolston's general argument: the New Testament miracles are ridiculous as historical events and carry only symbolic content.

Woolston organized the *Discourses* around two related tasks, one critical and the other interpretive. Following Shaftesbury's suggestion that ridicule was a natural method for testing the truthfulness of ideas, Woolston employed the technique extensively with the miracles to "clear the way" for allegory, that is, to eliminate the possibility of a literal reading. Woolston pursued this two-stage approach with each of Jesus' miracles, which made the *Discourses* the most comprehensive critical examination of the New Testament wonders ever advanced in English. In the scope of his investigations and in his refusal to allow any historical merit to Christ's miracles, Woolston stands as the first major figure in modern biblical criticism. A closer look at his hermeneutic is warranted.

Woolston's criticism of the miracle of Jesus' healing a blind man with clay made from spittle and dust, discussed in the *Fourth Discourse,* is typical. Discrediting the story as a literal account involves several procedures, all of which he groups under the heading "ridicule." First, Woolston asserts that the miracle is not proved on the basis of the interested testimony of Jesus' followers. For a healing miracle to be established, convincing medical evidence would be necessary, such as the testimony of a trained physician. "When it is spoke of the Cure of a Disease, as of Blindness or Lameness, it ought to be so represented, as that skillful *Surgeons* and *Physicians,* who can do strange and surprizing Cures by Art, may give it upon their Judgment, that no skill of Man could reach that Operation" (p. 7).

Woolston next suggests alternative explanations of the miracle, such as the use of a medicine. Jesus' "miracle" is compared with the healings attributed to "Mr. Moore, the Apothecary," and "the notable cures he performs, by the means of medicines" (p. 7). Perhaps Jesus was "a *juggling Impostor,* who would pass for a miraculous Healer of Disease, tho he used underhand, proper Medicines" (p. 6). Asking such questions of the miracle is only to test it "by Reason and Sense" which, he notes, "*Bishop [Richard] Smalbroke* does not disapprove of." He adds, "If [miracles] will not abide the test of Reason and Sense they are to be rejected, and *Jesus's* Authority along with them" (p. 16).

Having undermined a literal reading of the passage, Woolston notes the "absurdities" that this story is "clog'd with" (p. 15). He ridicules in particular the use of the mud, writing that "*Jesus's Eye-Salve,* for absurdity, whim, and incongruity, was never equall'd, either in jest or in earnest, by any *Quack-Doctor*" (p. 11). Woolston's final conclusion about the literal reading of the miracle is that "The miracle, which consisted literally in the Cure of a blind Man by the use of an Ointment made of *Dirt* and *Spittle,* is absurd, senseless and unaccountable . . ." (p. 22).

Having dispensed with the literal sense of the miracle, Woolston urges that "our *Divines* must of necessity go along with me to the Fathers for a mystical and allegorical Interpretation of the story of this

Eye-Salve; or the miracle will fall to the Ground, and *Jesus's* divine Power be in great danger with it" (p. 17). Citing passages from Eusebius, St. Cyril, Origen, St. Augustine, St. Jerome, and St. Theophilus, Woolston catalogues a variety of mystical understandings of the blind man, his blindness, the mud, and the healing itself. The blindness is, for instance, "Ignorance, Error and Infidelity, or the want of intellectual Sight and Knowledge of God and his Providence" (p. 20).

Strikingly, even Jesus is to be understood mystically, for "right Reason and Truth . . . are his mystical Names." Jesus is thus merely a stand-in for rationality in the narrative. Woolston is selective in the Church fathers he follows in discovering the correct allegorical interpretation of the miracle. Rejecting St. Theophilus of Antioch's interpretation as "too hard to apprehend" and that of Origen as mistaken, Woolston opts for St. John of Jerusalem's interpretation that the mud of spittle and dirt was *"perfect Doctrine,* which is Truth may open the Eyes of Mens Understanding." Such perfect doctrine emerges when "the *Water* of the Spirit is instill'd into the *Earth* of the Letter of the Scriptures" (p. 21), that is to say, when one follows the allegorical method of interpretation.

Ridicule was a key component in Woolston's new critical approach. Ridicule separated Jesus and his miracles from the veneration that attended them and shocked readers out of the stupor of education and prejudice. Before examining the miracle of Jesus' turning water into wine at the wedding feast in Cana, Woolston reflected in the *Fourth Discourse* on ridicule's role in his interpretive method:

How shall I force Nature and Faith to ridicule this Story? How shall I lay aside the profound Veneration for the Holy Jesus, which Conversation with the Fathers more than the Prejudice of Education has begotten in me, and ludicrously here treat him and his miracle too, as is incumbent upon me, to make way for this mystery? (p. 28)

In spite of his "Veneration for the Holy Jesus," Woolston brings himself to ridicule the story for several pages, attributing his own scathing commentary to a "Jewish *Rabbi"* who makes several appearance in the *Discourses.* This device provided Woolston with a transparent means of attributing his harshest textual criticism, and some of his coarsest language, to a suspect commentator.[11] The Rabbi's style and critical approach are, of course, Woolston's own. Nevertheless, introducing this new voice into the narrative breaks the monotony of Woolston's predictable, often forced questioning of the miracle accounts, while at the same time increasing the scandal and thus the appeal of the *Discourses.*

The Rabbi condemns Jesus and Mary in shocking terms. They are invited to the wedding because of their reputation as "boon Companions" of drunken revelers at celebrations. Jesus' harsh reaction to Mary when she requested that he do something to ameliorate the problem of the wine's depletion—*Woman, what have you to do with me?*—"was certainly the effect of Drinking." Mary knew that her son was "initiated in the Mysterys of *Bacchus*" when she asked his help with supplying more wine (p. 33). The Rabbi's pursuit of ridicule and insult for fifteen pages makes his criticism of the miracle the lengthiest component in Woolston's discussion of the story.

Although Woolston surveys treatments of the miracle by Justin Martyr and Origen, he spends the most time on the interpretation of St. Augustine, who believed that "by *Water* is meant the Letter of Scriptures; and by the best *Wine* is to be understood spiritual interpretations" (p. 48). Thus, this story, like others, becomes a justification of Woolston's hermeneutic of allegory. Woolston follows a similar critical pattern with each of Christ's miracles: ridicule, then rejection of the literal and historical sense of the miracle, and finally an allegorical interpretation of the miracle.

Woolston's treatment of Christ's miracles was accessible to virtually anyone who could read, and, undoubtedly, his *Discourses* were also read aloud for the benefit of the illiterate. All six are written in a plain and forceful style, with an abundance of Woolston's characteristic rhetorical tactics—ridicule, insult, folly, named opponents, assumed identities—to capture and hold the reader's attention and generally to enhance the ribald effect. That several prominent bishops had opposed his tactics only added to the appeal of Woolston's prose.

But a more visceral issue than the attack on miracles attended the *Discourses.* Woolston offended many readers by his defamation of Christ's character. As part of his criticism of miracles, Woolston claimed, among other things, that Christ was a "Quack-doctor," a drunkard, a sorcerer, and a felon deserving of death. This character assassination, in the view of Church leaders, shifted the *Discourses* from the status of the marginal rhetoric of an offensive, impious, and imbalanced nuisance into the realm of blasphemy.[12] In his public assault on the very person of Christ, Woolston violated one of the last boundaries of religious rhetoric. Religious faith, public morality, clerical authority, civic life, and government power were all threatened if Christ could be described in such terms, if authors were free to write such blasphemy, if presses were free to print and sell such profanity, and if even the lowliest literate members of British society could purchase and read such sacrilege.

Woolston's *Discourses* constituted an extensive and damaging public attack on Christ and his miracles. In rejecting all of Christ's miracles as absurd and unnecessary and in suggesting that historical literalness was unimportant to the moral sense of scripture, Woolston had impugned the very foundations of orthodox, historical Christianity. He added to this injury a series of low insults directed toward bishops and Christ himself. Augmenting the Church's frustration with the whole Woolston affair, the *Discourses* were in some measure persuasive. Simon Browne, an Orthodox apologist, was "surprised to see so many reasonable people moved to doubts by Woolston and others" (Browne, p. i).

Both the magnitude and the nature of Woolston's threat to their foundational documents and teachings forced Church leaders to respond to his "mad ravings." But how to respond? Certainly Woolston's critical method of ridicule had to be addressed, the allegorizing interpretive scheme challenged, and the actual historicity of the miracles reaffirmed. Woolston's rhetoric, however, offended by more than its argument; his irreverent and blasphemous language—particularly when directed toward Christ—was also a serious concern. Never before had a skeptical writer with broad appeal as well as scholarly and ecclesiastical credentials engaged in such a sustained sacrilegious assault on the person and works of Christ. The precedent could not be allowed to stand.

Bishop Gibson's Pastoral Letter

One of the most important answers to Woolston was the *Pastoral Letter* authored by the influential Bishop Edmund Gibson of London in 1728. The fifty-four-page *Letter*, "occasioned by some late Writings in favour of Infidelity," went through six editions in less than two years and was nearly as popular as the *Discourses*. The *Letter* rebutted Woolston's arguments, while at the same time preparing the ground for a second blasphemy charge.

In Gibson's *Letter*, Woolston is guilty of "pretending to raise the Actions and Miracles of our Saviour to a more exalted and spiritual Meaning" while in fact he has "labour'd to take away the Reality of Them, and by that, to destroy one of the principal Evidences of Christianity." In addition, Woolston has exhibited a "*Licentiousness*, in treating the serious and important Concerns of Religion in a *ludicrous* and reproachful manner" (p. 3). The specific danger is that Woolston will "corrupt and poison" the faithful "both in their Principles and Morals" (p. 4).

First, the Bishop attacks Woolston's pervasive use of ridicule as specious; it proves nothing about the content of miracle accounts and is a trick intended to fool careless readers. That Woolston aims his rhetoric at a popular audience is a clearly implied concern of the Bishop's. "There is no subject how grave and serious in itself, but may be turn'd into jest and ridicule; and by being so turn'd, may be made to appear mean and dispicable." Woolston knows that ridicule can "take off the Reverence that belongs to Religion" with the result that "the Minds of the people are easily carried into a disregard of it and an indifference about it" (p. 8). Gibson sternly warns his readers to

> be sure therefore to avoid this Snare; and do not only lay aside, but abhor all such Books as turn Religion into jest and mirth: For, next to writing and publishing them, there is not a more certain sign of a deprav'd and irreligious Mind, than the finding of any degree of *satisfaction* and *complacency* in them. (p. 8)

Gibson was aware that ridicule might shift the discursive frame in which religion was discussed. As Richard Hughes has pointed out, "once a subject has been defined as ridiculous, it can be treated with greater freedom than would ordinarily be allowed" (p. 22).

Having dealt with the critical method of ridicule, Gibson attacks the allegorical argument, vehemently upholding the historical authenticity and apologetic function of miracles. The testimony of miracles is "a most sure, plain and easy Proof; which the meanest Capacities are capable of apprehending and entering into; and which therefore was evidently intended to be the principal means of convincing all Mankind of the Truth of Christianity" (p. 24). Just as ridicule was defended as a universally accessible critical approach, miracles were affirmed as possessing a kind of convincing power available to anyone. Thus, against the Deists' natural method of ridicule, Gibson pitted the natural proof of miracles.

Gibson drives the case hard for the literal sense of miracles. To reject the literalness of miracles is "to deny what the bitterest Enemies of Christianity of old had not the Hardiness to deny" (p. 24). Insisting on the connection between a literal reading of the miracles and their status as proof, Gibson affirms that "miracles could be no Testimony at all, if they were not *true* and *real*. . . ." The stories themselves are so clearly an authentic history that they by themselves "shew the Vanity and Wildness of a late Attempt to prove that" they were "merely *Allegorical*" (p. 27). Allegory commits Woolston to the absurd position "that when the People were amazed to see the Miracles [Jesus] did, they were amazed at *nothing*" (p. 33).

Gibson attacked Woolston's Patristic justification of allegory, arguing that by this technique the Church fathers sought to highlight the moral sense of the scriptures but not to deny the historical. Borrowing the "method of arguing from absurdities" to attack allegory, Gibson finds in Woolston's allegorical hermeneutic evidence of stupidity, insanity, or bigotry:

> The truth is, the Supposition of an Allegorical and Mystical Meaning, exclusive of the literal carries in it so many strange Absurdities, that nothing could lead any one into it, but either great Weakness of Understanding, or great Disorder of Mind, or very strong Prejudice against the Christian Religion. (p. 32)

Gibson angrily denounces the "*Blasphemous Manner* in which [Woolston] has taken liberty to treat our Saviour's Miracles and the Author of Them." Like other Christian apologists, he maintains the legitimacy of "clear, decent and serious" religious rhetoric. Nevertheless, "*ludicrous*, or . . . *reproachful*" language is disallowed in such discussions (p. 35).

Gibson changes his focus from Woolston's style and manner of argument to the legal implications of ridiculing scripture. Hinting at the impending blasphemy charge, he writes that it is "the duty of the Civil Magistrates at all times, to take care" that "Books and Writings" that pursue such a course be strongly discouraged. Not only are "Religion . . . Truth, Virtue, Seriousness, and Good Manners" at risk from such discursive exploits, but so is "the Foundation of Civil Society" (p. 35). Gibson thus treats Woolston's angry and insulting language as what Michel Foucault terms "excluded discourse" in the religious arena, discourse that is controlled by being prohibited. And since blasphemy was a civil crime—a form of seditious libel or speaking against the authority of the Crown—Gibson's linking of Woolston's discourse to the corruption of social order is more than a patriotic flourish. The power of the Church and that of the State were inseparably linked as the Crown's right to govern was taken to be derived from divine revelation. Thus, crimes against the Church, or, to be more precise, against the Bible, could be prosecuted as crimes against the Crown.

Just as he had argued against Woolston's impious rhetoric, the bishop also argued *from* it, drawing evidence of insanity and rhetorical malice from Woolston's discursive excesses. The opposition of reason to folly is an important means of excluding discourse, and Gibson pursues the strategy with an intensity born of moral indignation and the sting of personal insult (Foucault, pp. 216–17). "When you meet with any Book upon the Subject of Religion, that is written in a *ludicrous* and *unserious* manner," he warns his readers, "take it for granted that it proceeds from a *deprav'd* mind" (p. 8). Gibson adds that "there is not a more evident Testimony of a corrupt and deprav'd Disposition, than an irreverent Treatment of things Sacred. . . ." Woolston's goal, evidenced in his rhetoric, is to "bring [religion] into Disuse and Contempt, to banish Christianity out of the Nation" (p. 43). Woolston is an aberration in the human race, and his mad discourse proves that "there are Monsters of Mind, as well as in Body . . ." (p. 12).

The argument regarding Woolston's insanity and vulgarity was seldom advanced without an attending contrast to reason and civility in religion. To Woolston's "deprav'd" and "irreligious" thinking, Gibson opposes a respectful and reverent frame of mind when contemplating the sacred. The "rule" he supplies his readers

> is this, that you be careful to preserve upon your Minds a serious Regard and Reverence to Things Sacred; that is, to every thing that bears a Relation to God and his Religion, particularly his *Word*, *his Name*, *his Day*, *his House*, and *Ordinances*, and his *Ministers*. (p. 42)

One page later the bishop again pleads for "a constant and serious Regard to every Thing that bears a Relation to God, and to consider it as *Sacred* on that account" (p. 42).

Toward the end of his *Letter*, Gibson returns to those most troubling questions of Woolston's "prophane" language and his use of ridicule. These linguistic issues exercised Gibson much more than did the allegory argument. Pious persons should express "abhorrence of making [religion] the subject of Wit and Jesting, and of raising Mirth from un-serious Allusions to the Language or Matter of it. . . ." Although such language may be "usual in loose Company and among unthinking people,: it clearly reveals "a very great degree of Impiety and

Prophaneness" (p. 43). The danger was the introduction of irreverent and mocking discourse into the public religious arena. The allegorical argument was troublesome in its tendency to undermine historical literalness, but it did not in itself pose an immediate threat to public faith and morals. Ridicule, insult, and vulgarity, however, did. Arguments could answer allegorical interpretations; folly, profanity, and banter resisted reasoned response and invited repudiation on grounds that must have appeared to many readers matters of mere preference.

Woolston's allegorical argument had been refuted. But allegory was not the principal issue in Gibson's response to Woolston; language and style were. Woolston had not disproved the historicity of scripture, simply challenged it, and a persuasive counterargument, albeit one colored by harsh *ad hominem*, could be advanced. In fact, a new evidentialist apologetic was emerging which gained credibility by candidly facing historical questions. Bishop Sherlock showed the way in his classic response to Woolston, *The Tryal of the Witnesses to the Resurrection.*[13] Sherlock's case was impressive: a powerful, self-assured, historically based argument for the Resurrection. But Woolston's angry disrespect, blasphemous language, and utter disdain for Christ and his works could not be tacitly endorsed by the Church by being allowed into religious debate.

Other Responses to the *Discourses*

Gibson's *Letter* was one of more than sixty published replies to the *Six Discourses*, and the themes Gibson developed marked other responses as well. In a sermon preached at Magdalene College, Oxford, on Christmas day of 1728, Thomas Bowles simply affirmed that "the History of the Life of Christ contain'd in the New Testament, is a true revelation of Matters of Fact," and is not allegorical (p. 22).[14] Bishop Smalbroke also found Woolston's *Discourses* to express "a flagrant sort of profaneness." Like Gibson, he is "ready to Consider any Objections against [Christianity]," but he also insists that there is a "real Difference between Arguments and Buffoonery, or that licentious invective against the Founder of our Religion, and the professed Ridicule of those Miracles that Confirm the Truth of it. . . ." As the co-sponsor with Gibson of the second blasphemy charge, Smalbroke also affirms that such discourse is not protected by "the *Liberties* of a *Christian Nation*. . ." (preface, pp. A2, A4).

Thomas Stackhouse is less concerned about Woolston's antiliteral interpretations than he is by the practice of "exposing the *Mysteries* of our most holy Faith to contempt and Ridicule" (Stackhouse 1733, preface). The anonymous author of *A Defense of Scripture History . . . in answer to Mr. Woolston's Fifth Discourse* also notes of Woolston's discourse that he "could not pursue [his case] with more spite and ridicule" (p. iii). William Tilly found Woolston's discourse to be "light, empty, frothy, foul, insolent, impious, and infamous," while Woolston himself was a writer "most inclined to do mischief in the world . . ." (Tilly 1729, p. vi). Despite such strenuous objections, however, the damage had been done. Once Woolston's impious discourse had been introduced into the arena of religious rhetoric, it could not be expunged.

Gibson's allegation of insanity, based on the evidence of Woolston's rhetoric, also became an important strategy for other respondents to the *Discourses*. An anonymous opponent asked who could believe "such Rapsodies of Madness as these Discourses are filled with?" (*An Answer to the Jewish Rabbi*, p. 15). A writer identified only as A. B. remarked that "the only further Amendment that can be made in the *Toleration* Act to do you service, is a provisional Clause, for proper Accommodations for such as fall into your way of thinking in *Moor-fields*," a lunatic asylum in London. By charging Woolston with blasphemy, "my *Lord* [Gibson] has *kick'd* the *clown* on the Shin" (pp. 13, 26). The *Discourses* were sometimes attributed to the Devil, popularly held to be the cause of madness. Thus, John Entwick was "destroying only the Works of the Devil" in answering Woolston (p. x). One anti-Woolston tract of 1728 casts the following dilemma in its title: *For God or the Devil, or Just Chastisement no Persecution . . . for . . . that Wretched Woolston.*[15] Woolston mocked allegations of his madness in a clever anonymous satire of 1728 entitled *Tom of Bedlam's Short Letter to his Cozin Tom W—lst—n*. A resident of Bedlam is surprised to find that "the *Late Fellows of Sidney*," the Cambridge college from which Woolston was expelled seven years earlier, "would soon be fellows of *our College*" (p. 4). The bishops had other plans for their own and Woolston's futures.

In *An Answer to the Jewish Rabbi's Two Letters Against Christ's Resurrection*, the anonymous author addresses Woolston's treatment of the Resurrection with a straightforward evidentialist argument reminiscent of Sherlock. How many guards were placed at the tomb? How many men would it have taken to overpower them? If the guards had been asleep, wouldn't the disciples have made enough noise moving the stone to arouse them? Another sort of difficulty was dealt with as well, for a certain Dr. Rymes had recently pretended to have been raised from the dead and was gathering a following. The evidence for this modern-day resurrection was dispensed with, and the good doctor's followers dismissed as weak-minded people or deceivers. This author also appeals to the disciples' character in building his case against "the Jewish Rabbi's" arguments:

> Let us again consider our Rabbi's Disingenuity, in supposing, *That the Disciples*, who were educated by *Jesus* to a life of Piety, and in all the precepts of Virtue and Morality, as he confesses our Saviour's Doctrines were, that such Men could (contrary to their reasonably grounded Expectation of their Master's Rising, with which they were undoubtedly possessed, with a fix'd Faith) take such a mistaken Course, as to risque their expectation, and so foolishly traverse all, by so faithless and imprudent a Step, as to think of stealing away his Body, before the Time of his promised rising was expired. (*An Answer*, p. 18)

Wade's Response to Woolston

George Wade was Woolston's most thorough and effective respondent. In his *Two Discourses*, Wade sets a high standard for miracles employed as evidence of Christ's divinity. John the Baptist's disciples, sent to inquire about Jesus' identity and mission, had received a decidedly evidentialist response from Jesus himself. "Go, says Jesus, and shew John again those things which ye hear and see: The Blind receive their sight, and the lame walk, the lepers are cleansed, the deaf hear, and the dead are raised up." Wade comments that Jesus made "*Appeal* to his *Miracles*" as his "*Credentials*" and "*Evidences*" on the basis of which John should "judge whether I am He, *who was to come*, or *another* is still to be look'd for." On the evidence of miracles, Jesus "not only tacitly owns himself to be the *Messiah*, but supports his Right and Title to that Character by the clearest and strongest Evidence, that God himself can give, or Man require; I mean doing such *Miracles* as *no man could do, except God was with him*" (pp. 8–9).

Jesus' miracles are physical proofs of his claims about himself, his relation to the Father, and his messianic mission. They appeal to the rational and affective capacities of any who cared to know who he was or, for that matter, any who did *not* care to know who he was. Seeking a clarifying metaphor to explicate the significance of Jesus' miracles, Wade argues that "*miracles* are to a Person, who pretends, as *Jesus* did, to come from Heaven, and to be God's Messenger to Man, what the King's *Letters of Credence* are to an *Ambassador* sent to a foreign state" (p. 9).

Wade recognized that his evidentialist reasoning was open to a number of challenges. For example, miracles may be forged, as even the Bible makes clear in the book of Acts. There, sorcerers and magicians such as Simon are capable of working wonders in order to deceive the gullible. Even Moses encountered this problem in his confrontation with the Pharaoh's magicians, an episode which was the source of endless debate between Deists and Christian apologists. Wade takes the standard, and highly hopeful, line of defense: false miracles will always be discovered as such. If miracles are forged, "the *Fraud* soon must be discovered, and laid open to the World" (p. 9). But, of course, Woolston, Annet, Morgan, and other Deists were arguing that the Resurrection itself was just such a fraud which they *were* laying open to the world. Who was the final judge of such matters? Was it not individual reason? And if reason judges that Jesus' resurrection is insufficiently supported, who can disprove this judgment? It is a contest of one person's reason against another's. The evidentialists, by making their own appeal to individual reason, had opened the way to just such a rationalist response.

Wade acknowledged that "God may suffer *evil Men*, assisted by *evil Spirits*, to shew surprising Prodigies, and do *Signs and lying Wonders*, which from the known laws of nature we cannot account for." His only answer to this observation is to affirm that "God will not let his own miracles be imitated" (p. 10). But how is the objective observer to know the difference between a genuine work of God and a "lying wonder"? Wade answers that one particular quality of genuine miracles, inexplicable power, speaks irrefutably to the unbiased observer. Jesus' miracles, "in the manner that they were done, by a *Touch*, or by a *Word*, were far above the reach of *Art*, and such as Devils neither could nor would perform" (p. 11).

Nevertheless, the observer must apply various critical criteria when assessing a miracle's authenticity. First, the miracle must be "above art," that is, is not magic or illusion. Thus, the "manner" in which the miracle is performed—e.g. by merely speaking a word—must be noted. Second, the miracle must not be of a type likely to be performed by a devil. For instance, miracles tending toward good consequences or confirming sound doctrine are not diabolical. Jesus' own miracles were plainly good in this regard and thus not of the magical or diabolical sort. Wade's opponents responded that such judgments were nothing but autobiographical reports of a writer's theological commitments. A Muslim, a Jew, or a skeptic might regard the miracles of Jesus in an entirely different light. Perhaps to underline this point Woolston put his criticism of many of Jesus' miracles in the mouth of a critically minded rabbi.

Woolston devoted considerable time in his own *Discourses* to examining what was usually considered to be the central Christian miracle—the Resurrection. Thus, Wade's *Second Discourse* is devoted entirely to an evidentialist defense of the Resurrection. Christianity itself, Wade insists, rests on the authenticity of the Resurrection:

> And this indeed is a Point of that extraordinary Weight and Moment, that if this main Pillar of our Religion stood not on so firm a Basis, as to defy all the Batteries that can be rais'd against it, the Whole Fabric of *Christianity* must soon drop into Ruin. (p. 26)

St. Paul had argued in his first letter to the Corinthians that "*if* Christ *is not risen*, or, (which is the same thing) if there is not sufficient Evidence of his *Resurrection; then is our preaching, and your faith in vain also*" (Wade, p. 26). Wade's equating of Paul's existential claim with an evidential claim is revealing—the claim that a miracle occurred is now no different from the claim that there is evidence for that miracle. But *is* the historical claim that Christ rose from death the *same* claim as that there is convincing evidence of that fact? Moreover, *is* the Resurrection itself intended by Paul as evidence of the kind that Wade and his colleagues employ it as? By conflating two different kinds of claims—historical and evidential—Wade contributes to the increasing tendency on the part of Christian writers to see the miracles almost solely as evidences of the type brought in court. Correspondingly, the miracles are less often viewed as wonderful or mysterious events. The judicial metaphor dominates from this point on in Christian apologetic, and the resurrection achieves the status of the central miracle in the evidentialist case. This tradition's most powerful and influential treatment appeared in Sherlock's *Tryal of the Witnesses*.

Much as the Deists cast Christ as a rationalist, Wade makes Jesus himself an evidentialist. The Messiah advances his own resurrection as proof of his mission. Jesus "promised in Proof of his divine mission to Rise the Third Day from the Dead; and if after such a Promise he rose not accordingly; he himself was a Deceiver, his Disciples false Witnesses, and his religion a lie" (p. 27). Wade moves through the evidences like an attorney pleading a case. Witnesses to the Resurrection such as the Roman soldiers are brought forth, accounts are carefully compared, alternative hypotheses are tested and rejected, and a verdict is rendered: Jesus Christ rose again to life after his execution and burial.

Woolston's Trial

Trials for blasphemy were not common in the first quarter of the eighteenth century. Thomas Emlyn was tried and convicted in 1703 for his *An Humble Inquiry into the Scripture Account of Jesus Christ*. He served two years in prison. Edward Elwell was prosecuted in 1724 for publishing *A True Testimony for God and His Sacred Law* (Clark 1985, p. 286). But these cases did not generate anything like the public interest and outcry that Woolston's trial generated in the opening months of 1729.

By 1728, Woolston and his *Discourses* were infamous. His work had garnered a level of public awareness and interest unprecedented for a skeptical writer. In the late spring of 1728 Bishops Gibson and Smalbroke again brought blasphemy charges against Woolston, this time for the first four *Discourses*. He was taken into custody by Lord Townshend on May 23, 1728, charged with "being the author of several printed Discourses about our Saviour's Miracles" (*Monthly Chronicle*, May 1728, p. 119). Woolston was brought to trial before judge Sir Robert Raymond at the Guild Hall in London on March 4, 1729 (*Monthly Chronicle*, March 1729, p. 50).

The prosecution's case, like Gibson's *Letter*, emphasized Woolston's "prophane" and "ludicrous" language in the *Discourses*. The allegorical argument was not specifically at issue in the trial, though Woolston used it in his own defense. The charge read as the trial opened was that Woolston had alleged the miracles of Christ were performed "by the Power of Magick Art, to the scandal of Our Holy Religion, and bringing in Contempt, the Life and Doctrine of Our Lord and Saviour *Jesus Christ*" (*An Account of the Trial of Thomas Woolston, B.D., Sometime Fellow of Sidney College in Cambridge*, p. 3). One prosecutor accused Woolston of "prophanely making as familiar with the Great Name of *Jesus*, as if he was a Ticket Porter" (*Woolston's Works*, volume 1, p. 14). He was also charged with "stating Our Saviour's Miracles as Romances, idle tales and Rodomantadoes, and not an Evidence to his Divinity, but vile Absurdities, Incoherencies, and Contradictions." Woolston's *Discourses* were "the most Blasphemous Book that ever was Published in any Age whatsoever, in which Our Saviour is compared to a Conjurer, Magician, and Imposture, and the Holy Gospel, as wrote by the Blessed Evangelists, turn'd into ridicule and ludicrous banter. . ." (*Account*, p. 3).

The prosecution's evidence consisted of reading passages from the *Discourses* aloud in court; almost any page could have been selected. Had not Woolston repeatedly held Jesus himself up to scorn? Had he not written of Christ and his miracles, "But they are such, if literally true, as our divines do believe, as are enough to turn our stomachs against such a prophet; and enough to make us take him for a conjuror, sorcerer, and a wizard, rather than the Messiah and the prophet of the most high God"? (*First Discourse*, p. 19). Christ's character had been impugned, and he had been ridiculed and insulted. Moreover, each of his miraculous works, important evidences of his divinity, had been publicly mocked, not once, but many times over a period of years.

Woolston was defended by a Mr. Birch, who took the case without a fee. Woolston also made several brief speeches in his own defense. The defense's case rested on rendering the allegorical argument a means of apologetic. Birch emphasized that allegory had long been used as an exegetical approach, particularly by the early Church fathers. Woolston had used this defense of his approach since *An Old Apology* was published twenty-four years earlier in 1705. Woolston's strange and angry language, the mocking denunciations of Christ and his miracles on which the prosecution built its case, were not, in fact could not be, denied. Instead, Birch claimed that Woolston sought by allegory "to put Our Religion upon a better footing, and shew, that the Miracles of Our Saviour were to be understood in a Metaphorical Sense, and not as they were Literally Written" (*Woolston's Works*, volume 1, p. 14). Church history and tradition endorsed allegory as a legitimate medium for discussing the miracles of Christ and even Christ himself.

The prosecution answered the claim by deriving Woolston's intent from his style and method, as had Gibson in his *Letter*, and by again contrasting these to the appropriate discourse of traditional argument:

If Mr. Woolston's intent was to [strengthen Christianity], he would not have turned the Miracles of Our Saviour into Ridicule, and proceed in so Ludicrous a Manner, as he has done, but to have endeavour'd to prove, They were not to be taken as they are Literally Wrote, by a Serious Discourse, and Sound Argument. (*Account*, p. 4)

Attacking the literalness of Christ's miracles was allowable within proper rhetorical limits. Arguments advanced by the prosecution did not focus on Woolston's nonliteral hermeneutic. Rather, the prosecution's case emphasized the language Woolston had employed to attack Christ and his miracles. Challenging Christianity was not in itself a crime, as both Gibson and Smalbroke had already affirmed. Ridicule, insult, prophanity, and defamation were, however, legal violations when employed against Christianity's founder and its foundational wonders. The trial of Thomas Woolston turned on the issue of the rhetorical means—the language, manner, and even style—that might be employed to criticize Christianity. Woolston's "profane" rhetoric was contrasted with, was tried by, the legitimate rhetoric of "Serious Discourse and Sound Argument." The former, if allowed into religious debate, could not be effectively controlled by either debate or prosecution. The latter could be met with traditional rhetorical weapons wielded by scholars and debaters within the Church who were at least the equals of even the most talented critics.

More passages from the *Discourses* were read, and the trial closed. The prosecuting attorney concluded that "these, and such like Indignities" had been directed by Woolston "to the *Holy Jesus*, Our Blessed Saviour, the Author and Foundation of Our Hope." Emphasizing the fact that blasphemy was, in point of law, an offense against the Crown as well as the Church, the prosecutor affirmed that any person who would turn the religious foundations of British society "into Burlesque and Ridicule, cannot escape with Impunity" (*Account*, p. 6).[16]

And Woolston did not. The jury was polled four times, once for each of the four counts of blasphemy deriving from the first four *Discourses.* Each time it reached a decision quickly without leaving the chambers: Woolston was guilty of four counts of blasphemy. He was sentenced to a year's imprisonment and a fine of one hundred pounds. He was held in the King's Bench prison "where he continued after the Expiration of the Year, through Inability of paying the Fine" (*Woolston's Works*, volume 1, p. 6). After paying expenses with what remained of his royalties from past books, Woolston gave his small remaining savings to the tradesman who had boarded him in London.

Woolston was a figure of great public interest after his trial, a monster or a hero who was the subject of much discussion and writing. He was mocked as a homosexual and criminal in a very popular account of the life and trial of Britain's most notorious sex criminal entitled *Some Authentick Memoirs of the Life of Colonel Ch[artre]s, Rape Master of Great Britain* (pp. 44–45). Woolston published two defenses of his *Discourses* while in prison. The *Discourses* themselves were translated into French and published with a brief biography and an account of Woolston's trial, and the controversy he generated "provoked lively involvement on the continent" (quoted in Reventlow, p. 611n.159). Antoine Louis Seguier (1726–1792) reprinted d'Holbach's translation of Woolston's *Discourses* along with other Deist works in 1770. On August 18 of that same year the *Discourses* were ordered burned in France.

Thomas Woolston died of stomach cancer on the evening of Saturday, January 27, 1732/3. "I am sincerely grieved," wrote one commentator on the occasion of Woolston's death, "when I think that in the Annals of this excellent Reign it will be told that a Person dyed under a Persecution for Religion" (*Woolston's Works*, volume 1, p. 31).

That Thomas Woolston was a madman whose marginalized rhetoric can largely be ignored is, it seems, wide of the mark. His ten-year battle with religious orthodoxy constitutes an important episode in English rhetorical history and in the history of religious discourse generally. Woolston's critical method, his nonliteral hermeneutic, his strange tactics, and especially his provocative language placed increasing pressure on the Anglican hierarchy between 1720 and 1729. The Church mounted both punitive and rhetorical efforts to silence Woolston with limited success; his rhetorical influence is felt to this day. Examination of Woolston's rhetoric and responses to it suggests several conclusions.

First, Woolston's hard-edged and irreverent brand of textual criticism seriously threatened the integrity of the biblical texts as historically authentic and doctrinally authoritative. Woolston called in question the evidence for miracles, provided naturalistic explanations for miraculous events, and advanced standards of proof for such events. Where he found the evidence for the New Testament miracles wanting, which was in every case, he was willing to brand the stories absurd. He thus undercut the use of miracles as supernatural endorsements of Christianity. Moreover, "Woolston was arguing a position," Redwood notes, "that would become more and more popular as particular parts of the Bible were brought into doubt by advances in natural science and in historical understanding" (p. 149).

This hermeneutical approach represents Woolston's most lasting effect on religious discourse, an effect that has too seldom been recognized or acknowledged. Historians may be reluctant to locate one important source of modern biblical criticism in an intentionally destructive project: Woolston's effort to demolish biblical literalism. Nevertheless, Woolston influenced the development of several critical schools; his insistence that biblical texts be read without a predisposition to find them historically accurate became the hallmark of the approaches that still dominate biblical criticism and distinguishes Woolston as one of the first modern biblical critics.[17] Cambridge scholar Conyers Middleton pursued Woolston's method of providing naturalistic explanations for miracles, as did later German biblical critics who are often credited with having developed the approach.[18] Woolston's allegorical interpretations provide an early example of a thoroughly nonliteral reading of the Bible's supernatural accounts. Allegory complemented ridicule, leaving the biblical texts historically dubious and "demythologized." Woolston's allegorical readings "anticipate the mythical theory of Strauss."[19]

Second, Woolston's accessible and scandalous style and his corresponding appeal to a popular audience popularized important religious issues including the historical authenticity of miracles, the necessity to religion of the supernatural, and the primacy in religion of moral over historical issues. His education and credentialing by the Church meant that he could speak with authority about scripture and interpretive approaches, while his provocative rhetoric of insult, mockery, folly, and "profanity" drew numerous curious readers and prominent respondents. Thus, Woolston helped to move debates concerning foundational religious issues out of the domain of academic dialectic and into the arena of a broader public discourse.

Third, in spite of the best efforts of his opponents, Woolston demolished many of the boundaries of religious discourse. He introduced an expanded language of religious criticism employed by later skeptical writers such as Peter Annet, the most important Deist author of the 1740s. Annet's most damaging work, *The Resurrection of Jesus Examined by a Moral Philosopher* (1744) is a direct response to Woolston's detractors and imitates Woolston's style as well as his language. Woolston challenged every discursive barrier to religious criticism. The Church found this his most dangerous rhetorical tactic and vigorously opposed him on the point. Bishops Gibson and Smalbroke objected strenuously to this new critical language. The reverence for sacred persons and events which traditional religious language protected was now widely challenged by a new and radical brand of discourse. The hierarchy saw the serious threat this linguistic shift posed and anticipated the problems for public faith engendered by Woolston's sacrilegious rhetoric of religion.

Finally, the extensive efforts to silence Woolston are probably instructive on the issues of both the influence and the control of radical rhetoric. Woolston's initial attacks on biblical literalism and clerical power raised the important strategic question of whether he should be answered at all. Answering his inflammatory rhetoric meant lending a measure of legitimacy to his views and posed the additional risk of making respondents look foolish by arguing with a lunatic. Failing to respond, however, opened the way for further such attacks by making the Church appear weak and indecisive. Woolston's persistence and his provocative tactics necessitated response, resulting in a public debate on the most delicate religious issues and in a measure of popular status and polemical success for Woolston. The punitive measures attempted in order to control his rhetoric—his dismissal from Cambridge and threats of prosecution—increased his insistence to be heard. The legal actions against him catalyzed Woolston's peculiar genius for both popular rhetoric and damaging textual analysis.

Woolston's astute rhetorical maneuvering drew the fire of powerful figures in the Church, thus further popularizing his views. Insanity was alleged in the effort to poison the well of Woolston's angry pen, but the scandal and attending popularity of the debate were only enhanced. The blasphemy trial carried some liabilities for the Church as well. Woolston appeared as a celebrity from society's fringes being persecuted by a powerful elite. Public opinion was polarized and Woolston's sympathizers emboldened by the trial. Even after his death Woolston's strange discourse continued to exert considerable influence in England and abroad. Echoes of his criticism can be heard in the rhetoric of Paine, Voltaire, and Lessing. German intellectuals of a later generation embraced him as a prophet.[20]

Impoverished, a convicted blasphemer, branded insane and a servant of the devil, expelled from his occupation as well as his home, refuted by numerous respected opponents, libelled, abandoned by friends, Woolston was as thoroughly discredited in his time as any intellectual figure can be. Moreover, his reputation for mental imbalance and rhetorical recklessness has persisted and has colored assessments of his contributions. But Thomas Woolston's significance to the history of religious rhetoric, biblical interpretation, and the development of skeptical attitudes in the West is likely greater than has heretofore been either understood or, for reasons discovered in his rhetoric, allowed.

Chapter Five

Tolerance, Expression, and Prosecution

Let but the Search go freely on, and the right Measure of every thing
will soon be found.
            Shaftesbury, *Letter Concerning Enthusiasm*

The British Deists were ardent proponents of freedom of expression, particularly on religious issues. Their influence in this regard has
not been fully appreciated, but it is impossible to separate the debate
over Christian revelation from the attending debate regarding freedom
of expression and the Church's right to prosecute blasphemers. This
chapter overviews the controversy over freedom of expression, religious
tolerance, and prosecution for religious crimes that attended the miracles
controversy.

Persecution for unorthodox religious views has a long history in
England. A statute of 1400 decreed death by burning for heretics and
remained in effect, though seldom used after 1533, until 1676. The Arian
Bartholomew Legat was "burnt . . . at Smithfield, at London, *March 18,
1611*" (*Blasphema Detestanda*, p. 3). The last two heretics to be burned in
England were tied to the stake in 1612 (Hutcheson, p. 68). As late as 1648
the Puritans provided impetus for an ordinance which "made anyone
liable to the death penalty 'who denied the Trinity, Christ's divinity, the
inspiration of the scriptures, or a future state,' and set prison penalties
for other heresies" (Hefelbower, p. 4).[1] Dissenting pastors as well as
Quakers were still being tried and imprisoned in the 1680s. Only late in
the seventeenth century did freedom of religious expression become a
real possibility in England, and even then tolerance was not extended to
all religious opinion.

Though Locke's *Letter Concerning Toleration*, written during his own
exile in the Netherlands, argued forcefully for religious liberty, Locke
"expressly denied full liberty to atheists and papists," a strange restric-

tion considering that his close friend Anthony Collins was an atheist (Hefelbower, p. 8). Nevertheless, after 1689 an "atmosphere of tolerance" encouraged "free debate about the hallowed doctrine of the ancient faith." This debate, importantly, was popular as well as scholarly. It transpired "both in conversation among those who frequented taverns and coffee-shops, and in print as the intellectuals or the ambitious hastened to persuade or insult each other in pamphlets and books" (Edwards, volume 2, p. 395).

At the beginning of the eighteenth century, "four formal routes were open for the reproof or punishment of religious radicalism" beyond dismissal from clerical and university posts. J. C. D. Clark enumerates the four: "a motion in Parliament; a prosecution in the civil courts; a prosecution in the Church courts; or a motion in Convocation." Increasingly, though reluctantly, magistrates turned to criminal prosecutions for blasphemous libel in their efforts to silence Deists and other religious radicals. Blasphemy trials were noisy and controversial affairs that garnered great public interest. Local authorities could also mark works as "public nuisances." Most effective was early intervention by civil authorities to prevent the publication of suspicious materials (Clark 1985, pp. 285, 286, 287).

The Deists and Free Expression

Deists are seldom mentioned in histories of free expression. Though Thomas Spragens discusses the contributions of philosophers like Hobbes, Hume, and Kant to thinking about the relationship between reason and free expression, he does not mention any of the Deists in this regard. Roscoe Pound tracks this history in legal theorists such as Coke and Jefferson, but finds no place for the Deists as advocates of free speech. Craig Smith traces free expression's seventeenth- and eighteenth-century roots back to English and Colonial Puritan theologians, but not to the Deists. Paul Murphy writes that American colonists were "convinced by Enlightenment thought that diversity of opinion was a guarantee that eternal truths would not be obfuscated by the false authority or custom or by transient prejudice" (p. 11), but does not mention the writers who challenged authority and custom for a century in England prior to the writing of the Constitution. Samuel Eliot Morrison's account of personal liberties pits "Englishmen" against "regimes" in the seventeenth century and emphasizes documents such as the "Magna Carta, the Petition of Right, the Habeas Corpus Act of 1679 and the Bill of Rights of

1689" (p. 14). The Deists, however, are not mentioned in his history of freedoms. What is perhaps most surprising about the Deists' general absence from the history of freedom of expression is that such well-known proponents of this right as Thomas Paine and Thomas Jefferson had clear ideological links to early-eighteenth-century English Deism.

The Case of William Whiston

William Whiston (1667–1752), a friend of Thomas Woolston, was "Newton's successor at Cambridge in the Lucasian chair of mathematics . . ." (Clark 1985, p. 285). He was dismissed from Cambridge in 1710 and threatened with legal proceedings for advocating the Arian heresy in published works. The arguments advanced regarding the action against Whiston are an early salvo in a long battle over religious expression and its limits. The general controversy over free expression reached its crescendo following the trial of Woolston in 1729.

Whiston was widely considered an Arian, as he seemed to deny Christ divine status equal to that of the Father. His views were condemned in works such as the anonymous *The New Arian Reprov'd, or, a Vindication of some Reflections on the Conduct of Mr. Whiston in his revival of the Arian Heresy* (1711). The deep concern in the Church over the spread of anti-trinitarianism brought pressure to bear on Cambridge authorities to censure or dismiss Whiston.

In *Reasons for not Proceeding against Mr. Whiston By the Court of Delegates*, a letter to Reverend Dr. Pelling, rector of St. Anne's Westminster, becomes a vehicle for explaining why Whiston should not be tried. The anonymous author of this letter is "a lover of truth and true religion" who argues "against going on any further with Mr. *Whiston*." Prosecuting Whiston "seems plainly to be *Unfair*, and contrary to the common Rules of Justice and Equity," the reason being "that Mr. *Whiston* has been guilty of no real crime in this matter." In other words, heterodoxy was no crime. Moreover, Whiston had not resisted the actions against him for professing Arianism and had even "largely and movingly" acknowledged the "Fairness of his Proceedings, in one of his Papers." Thus, "'tis almost impossible to suppose Mr. Whiston guilty of any crime" (pp. 5, 6).

Charges against Whiston were adjudicated privately, which raised another important issue. The author of the letter objects to the fact that Whiston's views were not "openly and freely debated with Mr. *Whiston*, before the Convocation, or any Committee thereof; or indeed in the face of any free and publick Conference whatsoever. . . ." It is not Christian to conduct a private trial of an individual who has earnestly reached heterodox conclusions following a free inquiry into the content of the Bible. "This method of yours, in prosecuting him before the Delegates, seems to be not only Unfair and Absurd, but utterly *Unchristian* also" because "it is to punish him for exactly obeying the Laws of Christianity." Our writer adds that "those Laws oblige him, and every Clergyman especially, to *search the Scripture*," a favorite Deistic allusion to a verse in the Acts of the Apostles (p. 6).

The author also argues that most suspected heretics were not brought to trial in 1713, so Whiston should not be singled out for prosecution. But the fundamental concern is that trials for heresy simply are wrong because they violate the right of free religious inquiry and thus inhibit religious progress. Deists such as Collins frequently argued this last point in forging their case for freedom of expression, as will be shown momentarily. Whereas Catholics might be expected to suppress religious inquiry, Protestants should know better. "This Method of prosecuting Men at Law for honestly Speaking or Writing what is the result of their Enquiries, is the known way of *preventing all Reformation* of what is amiss; and so is in all Protestant and Reformed Churches utterly unreasonable and unjustifiable." Even Christ himself was a religious reformer who advocated and practiced criticism of the received tradition. "Where had the Protestant Reformation been at this day! Nay, let us suppose the same of the Gospel it self, and its doctrines were the right to free religious inquiry and expression denied?" (p. 15).

Finally, this writer argues that Whiston's conscience is a sufficient punisher of his errors. "This Method of Prosecution can be to no purpose as to his real *Degradation* and *Silence*, any farther than his own Conscience has made him" (p. 19). Prosecution would only cause Whiston to separate from the Church and to spread his ideas further. Trying heretics makes them "considerable in the World, and will gain them greater reputation than they either desire or deserve" (p. 23).

The case advanced by the letter's author was difficult for the Church to answer because Whiston had expressed his views with decorum and conducted himself with respect for the authorities. Moreover, was the Church arguing that Whiston had not a Protestant's right to read and interpret the scriptures for himself? Had he not the additional right of a Christian and a British subject to express his theological views openly, as long as he did so reverently? Was not the proper, Christian, and gentlemanly manner for dealing with such offenses a public debate? The

Church would also be forced to face the issue of whether blasphemy consists in the matter or the manner of religious rhetoric. Whiston left Cambridge and moved to London, where he was perpetually engaged in controversial writing and where he translated the works of Josephus.

Collins's Case for Free Expression

Following the action against Whiston, discussions of the rights of religious investigation and expression became a feature of Deist rhetoric. Anthony Collins, among the ablest of Deist advocates, made free expression a social obligation in the service of correct opinion. His argument is set out in the second part of his 1724 publication *Discourse of the Grounds and Reasons of the Christian Religion*. Collins begins by affirming that "in matters of opinion, it is every man's mutual right and duty to think for himself, and to judge upon such evidence as he can procure to himself, as he has done his best endeavours to get information" (p. v).

Just as such freethinking is a "natural right and duty," so free expression is as well. Every individual "should be allowed *freely* to *profess* his opinions, and to endeavor when he judges proper, to convince others also of their truth, provided those opinions do not tend to the disturbance of society." Freedom of expression is, in fact, a social responsibility by virtue of discourse's role in building societies. "A man by himself, can make no great progress in knowledge," writes Collins, and "a single man is unable, by his own strength, to take in the compass of things necessary to understand his own opinions fully" (pp. vi, vii). Thus, knowledge, even personal knowledge, is corporately constructed. This corporate process of building knowledge depends on free expression, which inevitably has a critical quality. Communication itself is a social and critical endeavor, and "free profession or communication" is the fundamental social enterprise.

The connection between free expression and freedom of religious belief is very close indeed for Collins and the Deists. Religious ideas are foundational to societies and must for that reason be tested more rigorously than other ideas. Freedom of thought and expression are religious duties, almost acts of worship: "The grand principle of men considered as having a relation to the Deity and under an obligation to be religious" is that they "ought to consult their *reason*." But then, prudentially, Collins hastens to add, "and of Christians, and Protestants, that they ought to consult the scriptures as the rule of their faith and practice" (p. xiii).

All sociocritical uses of reason depend upon liberty. For example, "would Transubstantiation pass in France without an attack made upon it, if men could freely write against it?" (p. xviii). Religions generally, and Christianity in particular, have been harmed by repression of the liberty to express doubt. The result is confusion and a serious departure from the original pristine teachings of the "primitive institution" of Christianity (p. xx). Collins thus links the priestcraft hypothesis with the argument against religious repression. Priests as agents of repression, and thus of doctrinal corruption by preventing inquiry, have ruined religion.

Trials and punishments are the greatest blunder possible in the social conduct of religious debate. When writers "are chiefly conducted by *authority* and compelled by force" to refrain from expressing their opinions, the inevitable result is "monstrous absurdities" and "excessive ignorance." And in most of the world "this state of things has endured among men." Thus, Collins argues that "*authority* and *force*" are clearly not the means to "put an end to error, or make men wiser," but rather have always "contributed to encrease the errors and follies of men." Thus, Collins vigorously advocates "*free inquiry, profession,* and *debate,*" which cannot make men more erroneous and foolish than they are." These discursive practices are "the only way to make men less erroneous and more wise than they are" (pp. xx–xxi).

Thomas Chubb on Tolerance and Free Expression

Thomas Chubb was born into a poor family in the hamlet of East Harbham on September 29, 1679. His father died when he was young, and Chubb was apprenticed to a glove maker. He eventually abandoned this profession to become a candle-maker. Like many other Deists, Chubb joined a debating society—this one in Salisbury—and studied rhetoric and religion on his own. Whiston's *Primitive Christianity*, the work that led to the mathematician's dismissal from Cambridge, influenced Chubb profoundly. Chubb wrote toward the end of his life that Whiston's Arianism interested him for the first time in religion (Chubb 1748, volume 2, p. 5).

Chubb and some acquaintances with Deist leanings wrote pieces back and forth on the question of Christ's divinity. Whiston himself first spotted Chubb's talent for popular theological writing when Chubb read publicly a statement defending Arianism. Whiston urged him to publish the piece, entitled *The Supremacy of the Father Asserted.* Whiston introduced Chubb to Sir Jospeh Jekyll, who was drawn to Chubb's plain manners and quick wit. Jekyll became Chubb's patron for life.

The meeting with Jekyll proved fateful for Chubb, who now found himself in the company of minor aristocracy, fringe intellectuals, and rationalist clerics in London who shared a common interest in theological speculation. The group included Thomas Emlyn, the first Unitarian minister in England; Samuel Clarke; Arthur Onslow, later speaker of the House of Commons; and Baptist scholar John Gates. Chubb's many published works between 1730 and 1747 reveal a tenacity and patience with important theological issues that some of his fellow Deists lacked.

Chubb advocated freedom of speech and the press and religious tolerance. He published on the subject as early as 1727, the same year Woolston's *Discourses* began appearing in London. Chubb, like Collins, grounds religious freedom in the enterprise of building and maintaining society. "It is full time for Christians to think," he writes, that religious persecution is "but a blemish to their profession and that their obligation to love and do good to each other arises from their being *men* who are, by nature, entered into one great society" (Chubb 1730, p. 298).

Chubb argued that the Bible was subject to a multitude of interpretations, and thus any definitive view of "orthodoxy" was out of the question. It is *"human understanding"* that discovers "Meanings in Scripture." Thus, "man must exercise his reasoning capacity, by a careful reflection" in doing any work of interpreting scripture. Chubb's logic is disarmingly simple: the Bible may be "the rule of faith, yet it cannot, in the nature of the thing, be an absolute security against error" (Chubb 1730, pp. 286, 287). Thus, differences in understandings are merely matters of error in understanding, and who can know who erred? As a result "one man is not answerable to another . . . for his sense of Scripture" (quoted in Bushell, p. 69). Moreover, "if another man should give a different sense" to a biblical text "to what I may put upon it, it would be unmanly and cruel for me to disrespect him, and treat him ill upon that account" (Chubb 1730, p. 287).

In this argument Chubb challenges the very concept of "orthodoxy." But in so doing he also was tacitly attacking the source of authority for both the Church and the state—if no one knew *what* scripture said on any particular question, and if one interpretation was literally as good as any other, then there was no basis for a God-ordained clergy or king. Because it challenged government authority, Chubb's argument was a matter of seditious libel under the blasphemy laws as they were being interpreted by the Court of the King's Bench.

Chubb's case for religious tolerance was subtle and persuasive. The Bible is subject to different interpretations, and human minds draw varied conclusions from the same evidence. Moreover, though one's reasoning may be in error, one cannot *will* to make an error in reasoning. Thus, no one can be held criminally liable for arriving at unorthodox conclusions from the evidence of the Bible (Bushell, p. 72). To this reasoning Chubb added a minimalist view of government's role, a position which was rapidly gaining adherents in the American colonies, where the Deists had a wide following. Governments exist only "to guard and secure the common good . . . by making such laws as are proper to secure men's persons, properties, and reputations, and to execute those laws by punishing transgressors" (quoted in Bushell, p. 74).

It is not the role of government to establish one religion over another, nor to punish those who do not adhere to the established religion. And to hold speakers and writers in prison on the claim that their views were potentially harmful is absurd. T. L. Bushell writes, "to restrain on the strength of an hypothetical injury to society is to do so upon the absurd presumption that at some future time a man will be guilty of a crime" (p. 74). To this argument, Chubb added the contention that it was not the government's place to regulate forms and types of worship (Chubb 1730, p. 296). Restriction of religious liberty causes great harm and is a result not of differences of opinion but of priestly power and, interestingly, greed. "It would be endless to enumerate all the *evils* which attend the *restraint* of liberty in this case," he writes. Moreover, "the disorders and injuries done to *society*. . . . did not, strictly speaking, spring from men's *different* religious opinions, or modes of worship, but from that *worldly wealth*, and *authority* to direct understanding and consciences of men" (pp. 296–97). Were money not involved in religion, there would be little religious persecution. Chubb concludes that "as persecution is an evil thing, and bitter, and which can by no means be justified," so it is "high time that it were *banished* out of the *Christian world*" (p. 298).

Freedom from religious persecution opened the door to free religious inquiry, the foundational liberty of conscience and culture. Such freedom underlined the point that religion is a matter of personal preference and not of legislative fiat. Chubb's position marks a distinctly modernist turn in western religious discourse: One's religious views cannot be criticized by another, for conclusions regarding God and worship are matters strictly of private reflection and personal conviction. Everyone ought to be allowed to believe whatever he or she wishes; to hold otherwise is to act tyrannically toward the citizen's private conscience. "We of this *age* and *nation* enjoy many privileges and advantages which other ages and nations have been strangers to." Among these modern privileges is "*liberty of enquiry* into matters of *religion*."

Though expressing an unorthodox religious opinion "may be contrary to the *laws* of this *kingdom*" and though some "*wish* to see the laws rigorously executed upon their neighbours," such extremists "are under a proper and happy *restraint*, by the just and wise administration of the present government" (p. 422).

Chubb argues that "nothing can be more *unjust* or *unreasonably assuming*" than for one person "to *direct* and *govern* the understandings and consciences of others in matters of religion; that is, in matters relating to the favour of God." This is because "religion is purely *personal*, and every man must be answerable for himself to *God*." It follows that every person has "a *right* to judge for himself in all matters pertaining thereto." From this it must also follow that "it must be *just* and *reasonable* in our governours, to *indulge* their subjects in the enjoyment of that right" (p. 422). Though Chubb affirmed that religious convictions were "personal" matters which could not be judged erroneous, he nevertheless was willing to label Christianity "absurd" because it is "repugnant to the *nature* and to the *truth* of things" (Chubb 1748, p. 14).

Herbert Randolph's Legal Punishments Considered

To those, like Herbert Randolph, who believed that Christianity was at stake in the Deist controversy, trying and punishing Deists was proper and biblical. Randolph, rector of Deal in Kent, preached his sermon *Legal Punishments Considered* the week of Woolston's trial in 1729. Randolph argues the dangers of leaving writers like Woolston unpunished and the necessity of trials and punishments for blasphemy. Woolston and others had engaged in "*daring insults*" to "our most holy Religion," and these had elicited "repeated warnings and Admonitions from the Pulpit." But the warnings had been largely ineffectual, and, Randolph adds, "it is high time for all who have any Zeal or Love for it to rise up in [Christianity's] Defense." Nothing less than the survival of Christianity is at stake: "It is no longer a Secret that a Design has been carrying on by various Arts and under different Disguises, to subvert the whole of Christianity" (dedication).

Randolph asserts a conspiracy in the Deists' efforts to undermine Christianity. "A Club of men by their joint Endeavours undertook to propagate infidelity." These writers employ "prophane Raillery" and "an unworthy Treatment of every thing that is sacred abounds in their Writings." They thus appeal to "the unthinking Part of Mankind," with whom "Banter weighs more than Argument." Deists know, moreover, "that the most important truths may be ridiculed tho' they cannot be confuted." Randolph adds:

Their whole aim seems to be to destroy the *Established Faith* without building any thing in its Room; . . . All their Endeavor therefore is to cavil at, and asperse the miracles and Doctrines of *Christianity*, and make Men Infidels, either by running down the evidences of *Revealed Religion*, or which amounts to the same thing, by introducing an universal *Libertinism* in practice. (dedication)

Randolph is particularly concerned with the relationship between audience and style. Tindal and Collins commended ridicule as accessible to the common reader; Randolph sees the approach as dangerous because of its capacity to mislead that same reader. Clever people employ raillery when they lack arguments or when the ideas they are contesting "cannot be confuted." Woolston's work, for instance, "was recommended by lively strokes of Humour, and an Air of Gaiety and Triumph ran through the whole" (dedication).

Randolph's principal biblical support for legal action against the Deists is Ezra 7:26: "Whoever will not do the Law of thy God and the Law of the King, let Judgment be executed speedily upon him; whether it be unto Death, or to Banishment, or to Confiscation of Goods, or to imprisonment." Randolph emphasizes the crucial point that "the *Law of God and the Law of the King* are here conjoined together." He cites the great legal authority of the day, Sir Edward Coke, as supporting the view that the Bible provided warrant for laws against treason. Coke, "the great Oracle of our Law" has shown "that all the Punishments inflicted by the law on Traitors may be originally deduced from *Scripture*" (p. 3). The maintenance of civil society itself requires mental submission to laws and regulations. Moreover, a crime and its punishment must match one another in severity. As scripture provides the very groundwork of social order, "the Authority vested in the Magistrate is fixed upon a strong and immoveable Foundation." Citizens of a Christian nation must submit to magistrates as God's appointed agents in order to maintain harmony in a diverse human world that reflects the diversity of the created order itself. "God who is the author of Peace and Order, and not of Anarchy and Confusion, hath thus made one Man to differ from another, and by a due subordination of Persons as well as Things, hath so regulated and diversified the several parts of the Universe, as might best contribute to the Beauty and Conversation of the whole" (p. 7).

In opposition to Chubb's argument that legal conventions dictate which acts are crimes, Randolph affirms that the criminality of acts *precedes* their indictability under law. Thus, religious law is natural and not conventional. "All *Punishment*, if Just," he reasons, "must be the *Punishment* of some *Crime*." Moreover, "to suppose no Action Criminal, till it was made punishable, would be as absurd, as to suppose no Object Visible prior to that Sense which perceives it." Human laws, then, are not arbitrary, but are "founded upon Reason" which is itself rooted in "the Transcript of Eternal Truth." Thus, "it follows that Mens Actions are not therefore Right or Wrong, Just or Unjust, because commanded or forbidden; but are therefore commanded or forbidden, because of their inherent Rectitude or Obliquity" (p. 9).

Who, then, were the real advocates of natural religion and law in the Deist controversy? The Deists claimed to be, though they argued that *actual* laws and religions were conventional. Randolph defended the Christian religion and the laws of England as natural, rejecting the Deists' cultural relativism as "absurd." Deist inconsistency on the point—that Law and Religion were natural, but that laws and religions were conventional—was weakly resolved by their master-trope of priestcraft. That is, all religions as practiced and virtually all laws as enacted represent priestly corruptions of a primitive religion of Reason. But, supposing this to be the case, then natural law and religion are evident only to the Deists themselves, and this in spite of their insistence on the universality of human access to the religion of reason.

Continuing to develop his theory of law, Randolph argues that "*Human Laws* are but a kind of *Superstructure* built upon the Divine; and whatever tends to weaken or diminish the sacred Authority of Religion takes away from the very *Basis* on which they stand." To attack religion, then, is to attack the basis of civil law and to encourage anarchy. Thus, Randolph announces a theme that raises the ante on the charge of blasphemy: "The Interests of Religion and Government are one: They have both the same Origin, the Ordinance of God" (p. 15). Moreover, it is only "the Fear of God" that is "the Sanction of all human Ordinances" (p. 14). To undermine religion weakens the foundation of civil law and society, while at the same time removing the fundamental motive for compliance with civil law—fear of God.

Randolph develops his theory of the relationship between civil and religious authority in some detail. While both share a common source in divine mandate, their functions are rather complementary than identical. "It is the Business of the one to teach Men the Principles of Gentleness, Meekness and Temperance, and of the other, to Countenance and secure them in the practice of such things against which, as the Apostle tells us, there is no Law." Religious authority "is concerned to shew men the evil Tendency of Vice," while the work of civil authority is "to make them feel it." Finally, lest there be any doubt as to Randolph's point, "the one denounces against Sinners and *Judgment* to come, and the other gives them in this World a Foretaste and Earnest of that Judgment" (p. 15). Randolph contrasts a more biblical past when "scorners" were punished to the libertine present. "There was a Time indeed of *Godly Discipline* when notorious Offenders were put to *open Penance* for their Crimes, and our Liturgy teaches us to *wish* that time may be *restored*" (p. 16).

Randolph asserts that there are many benefits in punishing scoffers. Some are personal, as the book of Proverbs suggests: "When the scorner is punished the simple is made wise (Proverbs 21:11)." Other benefits are social, as punishments prevent immoral behavior and staunch the flow of published blasphemies better than do written responses to skeptics. "The most *pathetical Discourses* would be but empty and vain Words, and the most *rational Arguments* insufficient to stop the Current of Vice, and prevent the *Overflowing of Ungodliness*, did not the *Civil Power* assist in our Endeavor, and repress the licentious and unruly, by making an example of the *incurable*." Ministers alone "can only *reprove, rebuke*, exhort with all *Longsuffering and Doctrine*; but 'tis the Magistrate who makes the hardened Sinners *believe and tremble*, and gives 'em the Demonstration they demand" (p. 16). Thus, force accomplishes a task that conscience is sometimes inadequate to finish. Of course, merely reading such warnings would be enough to intimidate some skeptical writers into quietude.

Society, then, would stand to benefit if "every Profligate Sinner would sensibly feel the evil Consequences of his Crime and stand self-excommunicated" (p. 16). The tacit acceptance of Deism implied in the State's failure to punish blasphemers poses a great threat to society. "Few will be convinced of the Heinousness of Vice, when they perceive, that, notwithstanding the Immorality of their actions, they can stand as fair in the Opinion of most Men as before" (p. 17).

If no public disgrace is connected with ridiculing the sacred, such profanity will continue. Public shame and physical pain are the only effective means of stopping irreligious talk. Legal punishments for crimes such as blasphemy have unfortunately been lost when most desperately needed. Returning to the temporal strategy, Randolph muses on the tragic irony "that those purer Ages which least needed such *Severities* could make use of 'em, and we who have the most pressing occasion for 'em are without 'em" (p. 17).

Randolph laments the passage of the Toleration Acts a generation earlier and more recent measures severely limiting corporal and capital punishments in blasphemy cases. The stocks were not unknown for such offenses in the 1720s, just not widely enough employed. Randolph calls for the *regular* use of such punishments for blasphemers and other immoral persons. "Many and excellent," Randolph concludes, "are the *Laws* which the Wisdom and Piety of our *Legislature* hath framed for the suppressing of Irreligion and *Profaneness*, of *Vice and Immorality*" (p. 17). England had the laws it needed to suppress blasphemy, though the magistrates did not enforce those laws with a regularity sufficient to discourage Deists and atheists from publishing their views.

Other Voices for Prosecution

Randolph's views were largely endorsed by John Entwick, who wrote his *The Evidence of Christianity* "with a true design to obstruct the present growth of infidelity" (title page). A legitimate portion of that obstruction is prosecution and punishment for blasphemers, whose wickedness is only ecouraged by tolerance. "When in our Days some favourers of the ancient *Arians* dared to broach that impious Doctrine against the *LOGOS*, the *Son* of God, and they suffered to pass unpunish'd, what could we expect would follow from such a Toleration, than what we have lately seen come to pass" (preface). Failure to prosecute Whiston in 1710, that is, brought us his more dangerous disciple Woolston in 1727. The clergy as good shepherds must protect their flocks from these "modern Wolves" who, "under a religious Disguise, endeavor to divest Christianity of all truth or credit." Exploring a different metaphor of protection, Entwick writes that "it's *necessary* for, and incumbent upon, the Pastor of *Christ's* Church to defend his Spouse" (pp. x, xi). Clergy, then, are male defenders of the female Church's honor against a lecherous, rapacious pursuer. And in order to protect her it may be necessary to control her by restricting what she may read.

Bishop Gibson was right to push for the trial of Woolston and to speak and write forcefully for the prosecution of the Deists generally. Blasphemers are enemies of national security, "which makes the checking and suppressing of them here as much as possibly to be, truly a *National* Concern" (Gibson 1728, p. 2). The suppression of irreverence is, then, as essential as protecting national borders. Deism threatens the social fabric by making citizens "easy in their Vices" and by "deliver[ing] them from restraints of Conscience." Thus, Deists consciously pursue these goals by "undermining all Religion, and promoting Atheism and all Infidelity, and what adds to the Danger, by doing it under specious Colours and Preferences of several kinds" (Gibson 1728, p. 3). The Deists' deceptiveness in promoting unbelief and immorality made it all the more necessary to stop them by prosecution, as the general reading public was often unable to discriminate between true religious sentiments and Deistic dissembling.

In his sermon *A Preservative Against the Growing Infidelity and Apostacy of the Present Age*, William Tilly lashed out at Woolston personally as "a most contemptible *miscreant*, of no worth, value, regard, or consideration." And yet, "in a loose and degenerate age," he has had influence "through the fault or folly of others" who failed to stop him. His influence does not come by way of "his own light, empty, frothy, foul, insolent, impious, and infamous" writings, though these do sometimes sway "unlearn'd, ignorant, and unstable souls towards their own destruction." Prosecuting Deists shows "the High Wisdom and Justice of our laws" and that "those Great and Good men that are set over them, have thought it fit and necessary to give a severe and seasonable rebuke, to our common and greatest comfort."

Vigorous prosecution is the only remedy for Deism. "Tis to be hoped," writes Tilly, "that none of these ill men hereafter will ever find our Laws too slack, or those that guard them too remiss" to provide a "timely check and reprehension" against such "outrageous, impious insolence" that "stands in defiance of all authority both Sacred and Civil." No Deist's soul should be allowed to "proudly and foolishly conclud[e] with it self, Our tongue is our own, who is Lord over us?" (Tilly 1729, p. 6).[2] One's words are not one's own to control when those words are directed profanely against the Church. Tilly, like Gibson, strategically links the security of the state to that of the Church, a maneuver that became more common following Woolston's trial. Tilly is forthright in joining the two concerns and thus fusing the duties of a Christian with those of an Englishman. "For what call or cry can be louder, or more piercing in the ears of an *Englishman* than this, that his Church and Constitution are in danger?" (p. xiv).

Bishop Richard Smalbroke exhorted the Society for the Reformation of Manners to oppose the "open Contempt and Defiance of [religion] by too great Numbers among us." Smalbroke finds that the "too free and excessive Ridicule of Superstition" has led to "a Burlesque of everything that is Serious and Important, and even of *Prophecy* and *Miracles* themselves, and particularly those of our Blessed Lord, though they are the great standing Proofs of the Christian Religion. And I am sorry," he adds, "I am obliged to observe, in a Christian Country, that our common Christianity was never more profoundly abused and reviled, both in the grave and the buffoon sorts of Ridicule, than it is at present" (Smalbroke 1728, p. 11).

Clearly, blasphemy's most painful barb was ridicule. Once this discursive possibility had been introduced into the arena of religious debate, its extension to criticism of Christianity itself was inevitable. Smalbroke and other Church leaders, then, faced a dilemma. Publicly committed to the free discussion of ideas, including religious ideas, they nevertheless found certain rhetorical practices dangerous. The open, public ridiculing of Christianity occurring in England in the 1720s was "without precedent any where, and is not to be paralleled in any other Nation in the World." But, wasn't England a land that prided itself on the freedom of its subjects? Perhaps, but certain limitations on discourse must still obtain. The "Liberty" enjoyed by citizens of "a free Country" allows "a sedate and calm way of reasoning upon any Religious Subject" and may even protect the right to "propos[e] Doubts and Objections with a just decency; in order to receive serious Answers and farther Satisfaction." However, such liberty should never lead one to conclude that the civil authorities "will allow, with Impunity, a set of distinguish'd Infidels to insult and treat with greatest contempt and scorn the most sacred and important Truths, that are openly professed by the whole Body of the People, of whatever Denomination" (Smalbroke 1728, p. 12). Free expression does not, anywhere in the world, imply that a small, dangerous minority can threaten the nation's stability. In such cases, punishments are entirely appropriate, even necessary, to preserve the Kingdom itself. No land other than England would have allowed itself to be brought to such an impasse by granting such extravagant rights to its citizens.

The English people are too tolerant, in Smalbroke's opinion. They are "sunk into a spiritual Lethargy," when they "can hear with Patience the shocking Blasphemies of the Tribe of Infidels." The danger posed by blasphemers is not merely that the Bible would be discredited but that public morals and clerical authority would both thus be undermined.

The general public is ill-equipped to defend itself against spiritual de-ceivers, and "nothing is more evident than that an avowed Immorality is the natural Consequence of shocking the Faith of unlearned, weak, and incompetent Judges of profane and impious Writings." The vulgar-ity of Deist rhetoric is "*the language of the Fiends*," and it "does so prevail, as to constitute not only the Expletive but the Ornamental part of Dis-course of the Vulgar among us, and that in the open Streets of this City" (pp. 15, 16). People were starting to talk like Deists, and the language of Deism was deemed even more dangerous than its theological content. When one considered the risks posed by allowing blasphemers to write and publish freely— including possibly losing an ordered, Christian society— prosecution was both reasonable and expedient. State enemies like the Deists "very properly fall under the Execution of Justice by the legal as well as pious Zeal of the Magistrate" in the "Vindication of the Honour of an affronted God" (p. 17).

Bishop Warburton and Others Against Prosecution

Of course, opinion on questions of press restriction and the related issue of prosecution for blasphemy was mixed, even within the Church. In the opening of the first book of his *Divine Legation of Moses*, Bishop Warburton added an epistle entitled "To the Free-Thinkers." Warburton warns Deists, I "neither love your cause, nor fear the Abilities that sup-port it." He sneers at those who herald the Deists "with all the applause due to the Inventers of the Arts of Life, or the deliverers of oppressed and injured Nations." And, while Warburton is concerned with the pres-ervation of even the Deists' liberties, he holds that "the glorious liberty of the Gospel is forgot amidst our Clamour against a pretended Ecclesi-astical Tyrrany" (p. ii).

Nevertheless, Warburton opposes restrictions on free expression. "Mistake me not," he writes, "here are no Insinuations against Liberty," for if skepticism has flourished in Britain, it is not the fault of a free press. In a telling metaphor, Warburton urges that a free press can actu-ally shape the ideas whose expression it facilitates. "For surely, what-ever be the Cause [of Deism's rise], it would be unjust to ascribe it to Freedom of the Press; which, though it be the Midwife, as it were, to these Monsters of the Brain; yet, at the same time that it facilitates the Birth, it lends a *forming* Hand to the Issue" (p. ii). Warburton's argument is pragmatic: liberty of the press is less dangerous than are restrictions and prosecutions. At least when skeptics are allowed to advance their ideas openly, their ideas are moderated by the accountability accompanying responsible public debate. It is interesting that Warburton the bishop does not argue from scriptural bases in making his case for a free press but rather from democratic values.

Warburton does not wish his adversaries "disarmed" by the law; he intends to "put myself on the same footing with you, and would claim no Privilege that was not enjoyed in common" (p. iii). Do the Deists not, he argues, already enjoy a substantial freedom to write and publish their ideas? Though Deists complain that they are being denied freedom of the press, they do so in print. Is this not self-contradiction? Warburton notes that two highly influential Deist pamphlets have "already passed often enough through the Press, to reach the Hands of all the Clergymen in *Great Britain* and *Ireland*." Warburton thus upbraids the Deists for "the poor thread-bare Cant of the Want of Liberty" (pp. v, vii).

Other writers also opposed religious prosecution. Jonathan Jones wrote in 1730 that liberty to express one's views was inherent to British citizenship. It is "an Insult upon the *British* Nation, that any Bishop or Churchman Whatsoever, should *dare* to *prescribe us laws, or limit our liberties*," a reference to Gibson's pursuit of Woolston. British subjects would not have stood for such abuses a century earlier. "A proceeding like this would have procured an *Impeachment* in former times, and Arch-Bishop *Laud* was brought to the Scaffold, for Offenses much less injurious to his Country" (p. 11). The temporal strategy appears now on the side of free expression. Jones, like Randolph, invokes an earlier day as having exhibited a truer sense of discursive justice. But, Jones's "earlier time" was an era in which Britons enjoyed greater liberty of speech. He also rejects the common Orthodox distinction between "serious argument" and "buffoonery." This supposed "real *Difference* between *Arguments* and *Buffoonery*," which Orthodox writers employed in the effort to designate the *types* of religious writing that should be restricted, represents for Jones "only *a nominal* difference" (p. 13).

Tindal and the Possibility of Blasphemy

Matthew Tindal's *An Address to the Inhabitants of the Two Great Cities of London and Westminster*, a response to and imitation of Bishop Gibson's *Pastoral Letter*, also condemns "the wicked methods taken to hinder men from thinking freely themselves, and as freely communicating their thoughts" (p. A2). Tindal condemns Gibson's strenuous assaults on blasphemy as "the wicked methods taken to hinder men from thinking freely themselves, and as freely communicating their thoughts." He then asks ironically whether a man of such "violent Temper" should be "placed at the head of the Clergy?" (p. 16).

Tindal argues that the charge of "Blasphemy, and bringing Opinions to the Test of Ridicule," are "the grand Pretense for Persecution" (pp. 21–22). The two—blasphemy and ridicule—are virtually synonymous for the clergy, revealing that rhetorical *manner* of Deist polemic is the real issue at stake in the controversy, not Deist theology. Thus, there is no material basis for the charge of blasphemy beyond a difference over language.

Can there be, then, an activity defined as "blasphemy" which has a material basis, that is, which is more than a difference over language? Tindal thinks not, for blasphemy *per se*—the "vilifying" of God—does not occur. That one could offend God by being honest in one's religious opinions is contradictory. Thus, prosecutions for blasphemy are absurd. Tindal reasons that "if *Blasphemy* consists in an Intention to vilify that being, a Man acknowledges to be his GOD," then it is "absurd . . . to punish Men as Blasphemers." After all, "such Notions, as they, out of an Intention to do Reverence to the Deity, think themselves obliged to profess . . . must make them acceptable to a Being who requires no Impossibilities" (pp. 21–22). By definition, then, blasphemy is not possible. It is only an instance of one person's religious expression offending that of another person who happens to hold power.

Hoisting Gibson on His Own Petard

Bishop Gibson often affirmed the right of free expression on religious questions, but argued against a right to publish irreverence under the guise of free thought. As the Church's most vocal polemicist on the issue, Gibson was a lightning rod for controversy over expressive freedoms in the period between 1729 and 1745. In 1742 a cleverly edited collection of his arguments on freedom of religious expression appeared. Its editor remaining anonymous, the document was entitled *Pastoral Politicks. or, The Political Principles avow'd and maintain'd by Edmund Gibson, D. D.* The work adhered closely to Gibson's own words in published materials, though his arguments were carefully selected and arranged for rhetorical advantage. The passages in the book are *"Faithfully extracted from his Lordship's WRITINGS; and now published as a seasonable Admonition to our Modern Patriots and their Adherents."* The goal of *Pastoral Politicks* is to present Gibson as an ardent opponent of freedom of expression who has constructed an elaborate and biblically justified case against free speech and free thought. Thus, Gibson is refuted by his own testimony and appears guilty of the same crime of disguising his true beliefs with which he had charged leading Deists.

Gibson is quoted as attributing all desire for free thought and expression to sins such as envy, pride, ambition, and "interest." He also argues that the case for individual freedoms is always advanced on the basis of concern for the good of the governed:

> Now the *pretended* Motives to the Censuring of Government, are generally the same in all Ages; a mighty Concern for the Publick Good, and an Abhorence of Measures and Designs of the present Administration, with a specious Resolution to protect the people from some terrible danger that is coming upon them. And these, without doubt, are excellently calculated for the ends of Ambition and Popularity. (p. 4)

This subtle satire develops by carefully selecting passages from Gibson's own public statements.

Gibson next argues that freedom of expression is unnatural. "This practice [of complete freedom of expression] is contrary to *Reason* as it inverts the natural *Course* and Order of things: According to which, the Prince as the Fountain of Authority, is to derive Justice and Judgment to his Subjects by the Hands of the Ministers" (p. 10). Subjects of a monarch must be limited in what they can say, whether about the crown, the state, or the faith on which the state is built. "But if every private Subject" may take such liberties, the end would be anarchy. What is needed is a "Reverent and Religious regard to authority" (p. 19). To attack the Church is to attack the state, and "every such representation is a real wound to the Honour of the Prince himself" (p. 21). This claim, as we have seen, was at the heart of the blasphemy controversy, and the charge of blasphemy was as much a political weapon as a tool of religious restraint.

Ilive on a Free Press

Jacob Ilive, a Deist and the subject of chapter 9, was throughout his life a vigorous advocate of freedom of the press, an issue in which he had a vested interest as a printer. He was invited to speak to a meeting of master-printers in 1750, after his career as a Deist polemicist was well established. In this brief address, Ilive proclaims the need for printers freely to publish all sorts of materials and messages. In fact, were it not for printers, the progress of humankind would be stopped dead. A free press is the principal engine of religious advancement. "It is plain from the many pious and good Books, Comments, Expositions, Manuals and the like, the *Press* daily and hourly as it were, exhibits to the World, that we are almost become the *sole* Promoters of [religion] and in this degenerate Age, one of its *main Supporters*" (Ilive 1750, p. 4). The statement would have struck many in the Church as ironic, for their battle with heterodoxy had been waged in large measure against tradesmen like Ilive, many of them printers, who had disseminated exotic religious notions and turned religious debate into a public sport.

There have been frequent "Attempts to restrain the *Liberty* of the Press" in Britain, none of which has succeeded. "And it is greatly to be hoped never will; but if it should ever be restrain'd, it ought, it must be look'd on by all wise and good Men, as one of the *greatest Evils* that can possibly befall a free and brave people" (p. 6). The Deists' interest in freedom of the press was largely an interest ensuring freedom of religious inquiry and expression. Press freedom was only secondarily a commitment to a broader political ideal in the service of democracy.

A vigorous debate over free religious expression, religious tolerance, and prosecution for religious crimes was one important consequence of the Deists' case against revelation. Deists protested that their rights of expression were violated by threats, censure, and prosecutions. It is true that the only trials for blasphemy in the eighteenth century were of Deists. But, despite official efforts at suppression, free expression survived by what one anonymous author referred to as "the Spirit of Opposition, which lived long before Christianity, and can easily subsist without it" (*A Modest Address to the Wicked Authors of the Present Age*, p. 24). Would England survive as a Christian nation if Deists like Woolston and Tindal could freely challenge the limits of decent and respectful argument in their efforts to undermine scriptural revelation? The same writer asked whether an "indifferent Foreigner" with access to "the Trumpery lately written by Tindal, Toland, Morgan, the Authors of The Fable of the Bees [Mandeville], the Resurrection of Jesus considered, Christianity not founded on Argument, and forty more," would "imagine the Gospel to be our Rule of Faith, and to be confirmed by Parliament?" (p. 15).

But, as we have seen, the contest over free expression was not principally about the specific theological content of works like Tindal's *Chris-*

tianity as Old as the Creation, Woolston's *Discourses*, or Annet's *Resurrection Considered*. Rather, the debate about blasphemy, free expression, and prosecution for crimes of the pen centered on the kind of language one could employ in religious disputes, on the sorts of things that could be said about religion. This early debate over free expression in England was not a debate about the content of Christian theology, nor was it a battle over the existence of a general right to free speech for British subjects. Rather, the debate explored the personal, social, and legal limits of the practice of *religious* discourse. To the Deist mind, if a right to free religious discourse could be established, all other social reforms would follow. Critical religious thought, freely expressed and tested in public debate, was the *sine qua non* of reformation, of the individual, of religion, of politics, and eventually of society.

But, of course, the interests of the state were inseparable from this question of religious rhetoric. The Crown's own mandate was derived from scripture, and the king was God's representative on earth. If Deists were allowed to speak irreverently of God, the state itself was threatened. In addition, how people wrote, spoke, and thought about God was indistinguishable from how they wrote, spoke, and thought about the Sovereign. Thus, as for the Deists, so for officials of Church and State: religious expression was the key to social and political harmony. Respectful discussion of religious topics among qualified advocates was acceptable within limits suggested by tradition, decorum, and orthodoxy. Poisonous, blasphemous, irreverent banter from irresponsible popular advocates like the Deists, however, threatened the very foundations of English society by questioning the source of government authority and by disturbing the public mind with doubts and wild fancies.

Deists maintained throughout the long controversy that the right to say what they thought was no different from their right to think freely in the first place. To restrict expression was to restrict rational inquiry, and to prosecute and punish authors for the crime of expression was indistinguishable from punishing a man for asking himself honest questions. God would not punish earnest inquiry, so why should the state? Moreover, free religious inquiry was both the duty of the truly religious person and the engine driving the development of civilization. Thus, prosecution by the Church and State for free-thinking amounted to punishing people for obedience to God and service to humankind. Could the citizens of any nation that allowed such prosecutions, such limits on thought and speech, be truly free?

Chapter Six

Peter Annet:
Radical Deism in the 1740s

[A]t the trumpet of reason the dead shall rise. Before that bar all
shall come to judgment: and it shall be known who are, and who
are not sinners and saints, infidels and true believers. The veil of the
temple, the curtain, the covering of the Holy of Holies, shall be rent,
and we will boldly look therein. Mystery, Bablyon, the great, shall
be searched: the mother of harlots displayed, and the abominations
of the earth exposed. . . . We shall espouse the philosophy founded
on nature, and such philosophy will be found to be the basis of true
religion.

Peter Annet, Free Inquirer

Radical English Deism made its most significant mark on British
religious and social life in the 1720s. Writers such as Collins and Woolston
pressed the case for skepticism and the rejection of orthodox Christianity throughout the decade. Public and even clerical receptiveness to some
elements of Deism alarmed both the conservative clergy and the faithful laity. Action had to be taken to oppose writers who threatened not
only belief but social and political stability as well. A telling blow against
radical Deism was delivered in 1729 when Woolston was successfully
tried for blasphemy.

But radical, popular Deism did not die with Woolston. Nor did the
brilliant apologetic works, including Butler's *Analogy*, William Law's
The Case of Reason, Berkeley's *Alciphron*, and Thomas Sherlock's *Tyral of
the Witnesses*, assure Deism's demise. Deism was not, as Clark asserts,
"a spent force" by the 1740s (Clark 1985, pp. 280–81). Instead, the Deistic challenge was mounted anew in the 1740s by a writer of peculiar
power and courage who dared to challenge the best of the Christian
apologists including Sherlock and Berkeley. This writer, a schoolmaster
from the provinces, revived the spirit of Woolston a decade after his
death and again aroused the Church to find a solution for Deism in a
blasphemy trial.

Annet's Life

Peter Annet was born in Liverpool in 1693, just three years before the publication of Toland's *Christianity Not Mysterious*.[1] If Toland (1670–1722), who published his most controversial work before he was thirty, represents the first generation of popular Deists in England and Woolston (1670–1731), whose most damaging works appeared after he was fifty, the second, then Annet (1693–1769), writing in the 1740s, is the most important member of a third generation of British Deists. The careers of these three writers, stretching from 1695 to 1765, provide some indication of the duration and severity of the Deist challenge to British Christianity.

Annet trained for the dissenting ministry. He was, then, like Woolston, a disaffected Christian minister turned Deist. He worked for a time as a schoolmaster and developed a widely used system of shorthand. His first Deistic statement came in two lectures delivered in London on January 25 and February 1, 1738. These talks were published in 1739, ten years after Woolston's trial, as the tract *Judging for Ourselves*.

Annet was a controversialist first and a theologian only second. The subtitle of this first publication announces this fact: *Address'd to the new sect of Methodists, all Faith Mongers, and bigots, with a poem to the Rev. Mr. Whitefield*. But Annet was not merely judging for himself, he was answering what he took to be the religious bigotry of the revivalists. The strategy Annet chose for this work is significant; he professes "not to set up any *new* Religion, but to illustrate the *old* which was from the Beginning . . ." (p. 1). Annet thus rehearses the Deist trope that the original "Christian" faith began with the human race itself and was later corrupted into the unrecognizable forms of established religions. Annet quotes the Bible frequently, as did many Deists, though his interpretation is never orthodox. But the orthodoxy of one's interpretation of scripture is irrelevant, for "it is all Mens natural Right to *think*, and *judge freely* for themselves, and *freely to declare their judgment*" (p. 5). There is no theological orthodoxy validated by authority, only individual readers consulting reason to determine the content of true religion.

Of course, priests are so threatened by such freethinking about faith that they try to prevent it. Annet asks, "What Reason can be given for the violent Outcries we meet with against the use of this Liberty" to interpret the Bible as one sees fit? The reason is "the Enjoyment of this Right is so destructive to *Priestcraft*, that it is impossible these two can stand together; they are irreconcilable as *Light* and *Darkness*, as *God* and *Mammon*; tis the Axe that is laid to the Root of that accursed Tree" (p. 5).

Why, then, do *not* all people recognize the truth of Deism and the virtues of free thought? Because "the faculties of the soul [are] born *down* by the Gravity of *Education, Tradition,* and *Authority* defended by Chimerical Fears and tremendious [*sic*] Horrours of imagining Dangers, and render'd weak and languid thro' misuse" (p. 13). Thus, the Indian Chief discussed in chapter 2 was a Deist because his reason had never been infected by priestly education. He was a freethinking man in a state of nature who had arrived at both Deist theology and vocabulary. The Deists alone had, by the careful use of reason and the judicious use of ridicule, seen through the fog of priestcraft. They now had the task of leading humankind to light.

Annet's Early Attacks

In 1743 Annet attacked Bishop Sherlock and other religious leaders in print, an act for which he lost his teaching position. He moved to London, where he joined the Robin Hood debating society, meeting at the Robin Hood and Little John Inn in Essex Street, Strand. Richard Lewis, a noteworthy member of this group, made Annet a principal in his *The Robin Hood Society: a Satire* in 1756. Annet, like Woolston, arrived in London with a score to settle with the clergy. He wrote voluminously, anonymously, and often pseudonymously in the 1740s.

Annet's second work appears to have been *The History of Joseph Considered* (1744), an attack on the character of the biblical figure who became prime minister of Egypt. This work was a response to Samuel Chandler's *Defense of the Prime Ministry and Character of Joseph.* Here Annet reveals a penchant for harsh *ad hominem* in the vein of Woolston and of certain of the Orthodox apologists, as well. He attacks Chandler for having the "impertinent and trifling character of a pedant" (p. 9). Annet also defends historical criticism of the Bible by asking whether "an Enquiry into the Truth, or true Sense of ancient History" amounts to "a kind of Sacrilege, as criminal as Profaning the Mystery of the Heathen Gods was with *Pagans*?" (p. 11). In the dialogue which follows, Dr. Chandler is questioned about the life of Joseph by both the Moral Philosopher and Mercius Philalethes. In 118 pages every aspect of Joseph's life is examined for character flaws, deceptions, and immoralities.

In similar fashion, Annet published in the early 1740s *The History*

and Character of St. Paul, Examined. Critical scrutiny of the lives of biblical personalities such as Joseph, Paul, Moses, David, and even Jesus himself characterizes Annet's writing. Under the name W. Stilton, Horologist,
Annet published a scandalous attack on the life and character of King
David in a thirty-eight-page pamphlet entitled *A View of the Life of King
David.* David's brutalities, deceptions, and immoralities are explored with
relish and in salacious detail. Annet also published around this time an
answer to Lord Lyttleton's *Observations on the Conversion and Apostleship
of St. Paul* (1747).

Annet is said by Voltaire also to have been the author of a later anonymous treatment of the life of David entitled *The Life of David, or The History of the Man After God's Own Heart,* a work with anti-Semitic overtones.
A French translation of Annet's work on Saul and David, probably translated by d'Holbach, appeared in London in 1761. The same work was
republished again in 1768, attesting to its popularity with French readers. *The History of the Man After God's Own Heart* was also published in
America as late as 1796, along with a work by John Fellows entitled
Reasons for Scepticism. Further evidence of Annet's acceptance in France
is the publication in 1770 of *Examen Critiques de la Vie & des Ouvrages de
Saint Paul, Avec une Dissertation sur Saint Pierre.*

Character attack was among Annet's preferred strategies. The
apostles were the "most unnecessary parcel of fools" (*The Resurrection of
Jesus . . .,* p. 9). Of Peter, and Christ's proclamation that he would be the
foundation of the Church, Annet muses:

> Tho Parsons may have a particular Affection for *Peter,* to whom it
> was said with a most emphatical Justness; Thou art Peter (Sc. an *ig-
> norant* Fisherman) and upon that Rock will I build my Church; upon
> skulls as thick as Thine, will I erect the Edifice of Religion; its proper
> Foundation, as 'tis like to be its sole Support. RELIGION HAS FIXED
> ITS ONLY SEAT, AND ITS ONLY ROCK, THE ROCK OF IGNO-
> RANCE. (p. 9)

Similarly, in *The History and Character of St. Paul,* Annet asks, "What authority have we, Theophilus, for the truth of the scriptures, but the scriptures themselves? Can any history prove itself? Were not the Christian
writers in the early ages of Christianity notorious for lies and forgeries?" (p. 11). The charge of madness, often leveled at leading Deists, is
advanced by Annet against Paul, who "acted with as much Madness
against the Priests as he had acted for them" (p. 6).

The *ad hominem* strategy is a means to a more consequential end, however. If the character of St. Paul, for instance, can successfully be called in question, then Christianity itself, which he had such an important part in shaping, is similarly put under a cloud of doubt. "The religion of him that stands on St. *Paul*," writes Annet, "must fall with him." He continues: "Divinity, law, and physic, are only rightly founded on the nature, reason and circumstances of things, all besides is enthusiasm, tyranny, and imposture" (p. 106). Found your religion on the rock of reason, and it will stand; found it on the shifting sand of a Paul, a David, or a Moses, and it will fall.[2]

Annet's most important work, *The Resurrection of Jesus Considered by a Moral Philosopher*, is an answer to Sherlock's landmark *Tryal of the Witnesses to the Resurrection of Jesus Christ* (1729), itself a response to criticisms of Woolston's trial.[3] Annet's sharp and astute condemnation of Sherlock and the biblical evidences for the Resurrection made the work instantly controversial. A second edition, keyed directly to the dialogue in Sherlock's *Tryal*, appeared within months of the first. A reader with both works could easily compare Sherlock's claims with Annet's rebuttals.

Annet ridiculed every aspect of the Resurrection accounts. For instance, he wondered about the number of days Jesus spent in the tomb. Buried on Friday afternoon, Jesus allegedly was not in his tomb at dawn on Sunday, and thus the prophecies of a three-day burial seemed to be at odds with the narrative. Annet lampooned efforts to reconcile the inconsistency by an analogy to the mathematics of trinitarianism. "Those who can work miracles in words," he taunts, "can as easily do it in numbers." Nor should one wonder that "such mystical accountants, who can make three to be one, and one to be three . . . should make one and a half to be three, which comes nearer the mark" (pp. 19–20). Annet also mocked inconsistencies in the story of the guard placed at Jesus' tomb, asking: "What judgement can we form of the watch?" No person of "common sense" can imagine that "the pharisees should be alarmed about the resurrection of Jesus, if they never heard anything more of it than has been mentioned; and that the disciples, to whom it is said to have been plainly and repeatedly foretold, should know nothing of the matter" (p. 24).

Treating the four Evangelists as rival witnesses, Annet reveals several contradictions among biblical accounts of the Resurrection. He notes, for example, that "in St. Matthew Jesus is reported to give them that sign which they make nothing of, and in St. Mark to give them no sign at all." He asks at another point, "Why do these evangelists tell different stories? Matthew one about guarding and sealing the sepulchre; St. Mark and St. Luke another which shews it was neither guarded nor sealed; St. John to the same purpose, but different from both? Who can know the truth of these disagreeing historians?" (p. 27). Annet's strategy is to set numerous such problems side by side, treating them as evidence of the general inconsistency, and thus unreliability, of the accounts. A reasonable reader demands a precise, clear, consistent reporting of events. In the biblical accounts such a reader finds inconsistencies, ambiguities, and contradictions.

Another response to his critics, *The Resurrection Reconsidered*, was published in 1744. These works were answered many times in pamphlets such as *The Evidence of the Resurrection Cleared from the Exceptions of a Late Pamphlet Entitled The Resurrection of Jesus Considered by a Moral Philosopher; in Answer to the Tryal of the Witnesses*. Responses to Annet followed Sherlock's model of sifting the biblical evidence and relied on a close reading of the New Testament miracles accounts along the lines of a legal brief. Gilbert West was Annet's most thorough respondent. His 310-page *Observations on the History and Evidence of the Resurrection of Jesus Christ* was published in 1747, three years after Annet's flurry of attacks on the Resurrection. West suggests that, as a layman, he may be better able to speak to those in the public suspicious of the clergy. He engages in a minute comparison of the Resurrection accounts, arguing that the minor differences among accounts actually suggest their veracity and reliability. Nor were the inconsistencies impossible to explain or reconcile in a plausible if not entirely convincing fashion. The very inconsistencies Annet highlighted were one proof that the biblical narratives were authentic independent accounts—one would expect perfect agreement among four witnesses only in a blatant forgery.

Annet was confident that he had disproved the Resurrection and thus discredited the clergy. He does not intend "to lengthen out a Subject, that may be finished in a Twelve-penny pamphlet, to make the publick pay Two Shillings." To come to the point, then, "The *No-Resurrection* being proved, as satisfactorily, as a Negative can be proved, to all, that will make the least use of their Reason, it is to be hoped, we shall hiss Parsons off the stage" (Annet, *The Ressurection of Jesus Demonstrated to have No Proof.* p. 9). Clerics will take flight in the face of Annet's assault on them and their superstitious props. "How the Birds of Night fly chattering about since the day has broken upon them;

what haste they make to shelter in an ill-built House that is tumbling upon their Heads" (p. 8).

In his several works of the 1740s, Annet repeatedly employed the method of identifying inconsistencies in and among biblical texts. In *The Resurrection Defenders Stripped of all Defense,* a supplement to *The Resurrection Reconsidered,* he marshals a series of biblical contradictions. Even relatively inconsequential textual discrepancies are illuminated. For example:

> Permit me, Sir, to remark how little these historians regarded exactness in their narrations: I observe they don't agree exactly in the words of the title over the cross, that all Jerusalem might read; for tis according to
> St. Matthew, This is Jesus the King of the Jews
> St. Mark, the King of the Jews
> St. Luke, This is the king of the Jews
> St. John, Jesus of Nazareth the King of the Jews. (p. 70)

Annet's assault on the Resurrection was answered by a number of apologists. The author of *The Evidence of the Resurrection Clear'd from the Exception of a late Pamphlet entitled, The Resurrection of Jesus Consider'd by a moral philosopher* took Annet to task immediately for pretending to be a Christian while at the same time dismantling the miracles. "Some have pretended Friendship to the Gospel, that they might the more successfully undermine the foundation of it" (p. 2). This author argues that any critic who decides ahead of time that all miracles are "absurdity to common sense and understanding, and contrary to the Attributes of God" is probably not a fair judge of the authenticity of any particular miracle (p. 3).

The author of *Evidence Clear'd* is repulsed by Annet and his argument, as any sincere Christian would have to be. "The Faith which the Gospel proposes in *Christ Jesus,* the ever blessed Son of God, and the only Name under Heaven by which we may be saved, is here with an astonishing Degree of impiety, called 'a divine Hag with Pious Witchcrafts.' Unhappy Man! What could he mean by this? I pity him from my heart" (pp. 3–4). In a manner reminiscent of Bishop Gibson's warnings to his parishioners not to be deceived by Woolston, this author cautions his readers that "Every serious Man will read these Passages with abhorance." Moreover, Annet's works "are a Warning to every Reader to be upon his Guard against the Representations made of the Doctrines of the Gospel, and the Evidences of Christianity, by so determined, and so inveterate an enemy to both" (p. 4). Thus, Christian apologists cast themselves in the role of critical mediators standing between Deistic impieties and the Christian public.

If "the *plain fact* reported" be "contradictory to the constant course of nature," Annet asks, "should I renounce the evidence?" (Annet, *Resurrection of Jesus Considered,* 3d ed., p. 73). His *a priori* rejection of miracles was thoroughgoing, Annet asserting that he would doubt even his own senses if they reported something contrary to the known course of nature. This is a response to the Christian argument that witnesses to the biblical miracles could not have been mistaken about events they had seen with their own eyes. But, says Annet, if he would not believe his own eyes in such a case, *a fortiori* he would reject testimony regarding a miracle from others. "If a stone appeared to roll up a hill of its own accord to my sight, I should think I had reason to doubt the veracity of my eyesight. . . . Therefore, I cannot admit the like fact on the evidence of others" (p. 74). To believe such an event possible "violates this maxim; that nature is steady and uniform in her operations" (p. 75). To accept one's own sense impressions or the testimony of others as adequate evidence for a miracle is to give up the possibility of a rational universe under the direction of natural laws. Annet summarized his theory of miracle testimony:

> That testimony cannot be credible which relates incredible things; therefore the relaters of such have not an equal right to be believed, as those that relate any other historical facts. . . . I ought to have extraordinary evidence, to induce me to believe extraordinary things, that are supernatural, which cannot be so credible as ordinary things which are natural. (p. 71)

Annet attacked the miracle of the virgin birth of Christ in *The Miraculous Conception.* Annet wished to undermine the "miraculous conception" as a foundational Christian miracle, much the way he had sought to destroy the credibility of the Resurrection. He ridiculed both the notion of a virgin giving birth and any reader gullible enough to believe such a story:

> But all this happened "before they came together"; this assertion was made for the open-mouthed, wide throated, credulous, ignorant people, to whom this gospel was addressed, and for their successors.

... Cavillers may talk themselves blind, learned doctors may preach themselves hoarse, commentators may write "so many books that the world would not contain them," they will never be able to make anything of the story than that a poor, ignorant, credulous man, dreamed in his sleep that an angel had been talking nonsense to him. (pp. 10–12)

Following Woolston's strategy of arguing from the opinions of the Patristics, Annet points out early in another treatise on the virgin birth entitled *The Conception of Jesus Considered as the Foundation of the Christian Religion* that Athenasius "does not attribute the Incarnation of Christ to the Operation of the Holy Ghost, as the Authors of the *Apostolick* and *Nicene Creeds* have done . . ." (p. 7). The whole notion of a virgin conception is more similar to pagan mythology than to Christian theology, Annet argues. He thus attributes the story to the priestcraft of Christian leaders and asks regarding earlier pagan writers: "What did these Men that liv'd in a State of Darkness more to enslave Mankind, than the Priests of the several *Christian* Countries that pretend to hold forth the Light of the Gospel?" (p. 11). To make belief in a virgin birth a qualification for membership in the body of Christ is to make the rejection of reason a condition of belief and thus to exclude reasonable people from the hope of salvation. "Such is the Foundation of Faith, and if the believing of this is necessary to Salvation, how deplorable a State is theirs to whose Reason it is repugnant" (p. 87).

The first editions of *The Resurrection of Jesus Considered* and *The Conception of Jesus Considered*, as even their titles imply, appear to have been companion volumes published the same year (1744), printed at Annet's own expense and presented in similar formats. Each book opens with the relevant biblical passages set out for easy reference and then proceeds to a close critical analysis of these texts. It is likely that Annet had identified these two miracles as the twin props on which all of Christianity was built and sought to undermine each in the hopes that the superstructure would then fall.

Annet continued to publish provocative attacks on miracles throughout the 1740s. In *Supernaturals Examined* (1747), Annet argues in response to Gilbert West's *On the History and Evidences of the Resurrection of Christ* and Mr. Jackson's *Letter to Deists* that all miracles must be rejected by reasonable people. He also argues against the very idea of a divine revelation containing truths not evident to reason. Annet thus represents a pure strain of English Deism in midcentury. His argument is indistinguishale at points from those of Shaftesbury or Collins. As the "Religion of Nature" emerges from the "natural Relations and Circumstances of Things," the only persons who discover it are those willing to "set aside all *supernatural Revelation*, and the Need of it." Simply put, there is "no Revelation from God, of Doctrines and Duties for Man's belief and Obedience, but such as not only have, but *appear* to have their Foundation in Reason and Nature" (p. 181).

Annet is said by one of his biographers to have been "the forerunner of Thomas Paine" (Twyman, p. 2). Certainly the two writers exhibit similarities: each rejects revealed religion in the strongest terms, advocates freedom of expression and religious inquiry, and advocates social reforms. In *Social Bliss Considered* (1749), for instance, he argued that divorce should not be denied when it is desired. In developing his position on moral and social issues, Annet drew on the cultural relativism that marked Deism. "The Ceremonies of Marriage," he writes, "are various among various Nations and People; but whatsoever they are, they are but Ceremonies, which law and Custom only make necessary, and are the least part of Matrimony . . ." (preface). Marriages of conscience are not offensive to God, who has no interest in local marriage customs.

Annet's moral views met with sharp opposition from one respondent who satirized the suggestion that freedom from religious restraint would benefit English society. "One great Advantage proposed by the abolishing of *Christianity*," suggests the respondent, is "that it would very much enlarge and establish Liberty of Conscience, that great Bulwark of our Nation, and of the Protestant Religion, notwithstanding all the good intentions of the Legislature." Annet is accosted as one of the "Great Wits" who "love to be free with the highest Objects; and if they cannot be allowed a God to *revile* and *renounce*, they will opt to speak evil of Dignities, abuse the Government, and reflect upon the ministry" (H. F., p. 13). Again the notions of free religious inquiry and political radicalism are linked in Deist polemic, in much the same way that blasphemy and treason were linked in the Christian case.

Annet's Free Inquirer

During the early 1760s, following a period of relative inactivity during the 1750s, Annet began publishing the periodical which would lead directly to his trial and imprisonment. *The Free Inquirer* was only issued nine times in 1761, but the mood of Church and state under the young George III was not favorable for freedom of the press. At the age of twenty-two, George succeeded his grandfather, who had died suddenly at Kensington on October 25, 1760. Within two years of taking the throne, and probably under the influence of advisors such as Lord North, George sought indictments against several dozen periodicals. Annet's *Free Inquirer* was one.

Annet sounded some familiar Deist themes in the *Inquirer*. In number 1, issued on October 17, 1761, he writes of reason as "God incarnate," a heretical if not a blasphemous claim. Annet's style is popular in the *Inquirer*, and his metaphors patent:

> [R]eason is a divine faculty, it is the divinity operating within us, it is God incarnate; and it is the army of this Lord of Hosts, that we, the Free Inquirers, enter volunteers to encounter error and imposition, wherever they appear. The weapons of the warfare are not carnal, but spiritual; and will prove mighty in pulling down their strongholds, and in treading Satan under our feet. (p. 3)

Annet consistently works with familiar biblical passages, as here, though reinterpreting them in a counter-scriptural manner. Such imitation of scripture was common in Deist rhetoric, frustrating opponents who could only claim the passages had been misused. The implied assertion in this strategy is that the ambiguous nature of biblical claims makes them subject to all manner of application and interpretation. No one, and especially not priests, has a final say as regards appropriate exegesis.

Continuing to develop the theme of reason's authority, Annet exploits a series of eschatalogical images in which reason takes the place of Christ. Reason is "that authority which we are determined to advance above all other authorities" and is "the authority of God." Deism will "bring to light the hidden works of darkness, ransack all nature to find out truth, and drive falsity to the bottomless pit." In a remarkable flourish, Annet adopts apocalyptic imagery of Revelation to describe the role of reason in judging humankind:

> At the trumpet of reason the dead shall rise. Before that bar all shall come to judgment: and it shall be known who are, and who are not sinners and saints, infidels and true believers. The veil of the temple, the curtain, the covering of the Holy of Holies, shall be rent, and we will boldly look therein. Mystery, *Bablyon*, the great, shall be searched: the mother of harlots displayed, and the abominations of the earth

exposed. . . . We shall espouse the philosophy founded on nature, and such philosophy will be found to be the basis of true religion. (pp. 3–4)

Reason takes the place of Christ in the final judgment, and "religion, however rebellious against Reason, however untractable it may have been made, shall be compelled to submit to the examination of common sense, and yield to the divine authority of Reason" (p. 4). Reason, then, supplants each member of the trinity. Like the Father, it is "that authority . . . above all other authorities." Like the Son, it is "God incarnate" who will judge the quick and the dead. And, like the Holy Spirit, reason is "the divinity operating within us." Such claims were advanced in the inaugural volume of *The Free Inquirer* and set Annet on a collision course with the authorities.

Annet's strategy in *The Free Inquirer* shifts markedly, however, from the Woolstonesque provocation of *The Resurrection Considered* to a measured invitation to the pleasant and constructive use of one's reason. Annet envisioned an amateur intellectual's magazine with essays on a variety of religious and social topics rather than a pamphleteer's caustic broadside. The ideal space for reading *The Free Inquirer* is the privacy of one's home rather than with the gathered public in a coffeehouse.

The mode of consumption differs as well from the works of the 1740s. *The Free Inquirer* is offered for the nourishment of quiet contemplation and "entertainment" rather than as the fodder of public debate. Annet promises readers, for instance, essays on "such subjects as will exercise and improve the understanding" which will be "dedicated to the amusement of the intellect, or the day of retirement from the fatigues of business" (p. 8). Thus, reason is stimulated and improved through a regular periodical read at the leisure of mature persons. "To excite and entertain the mind is the design of this paper; let our readers examine, ponder, and judge all things for themselves, all who have arrived to years of consideration and discretion" (p. 6).

Consummate and flamboyant rhetorician that he was, Annet warns his readers against the rhetorical art. "The wise *Athenians*," he notes, "were so sensible of the evil of countenancing the art of rhetoric, that it was corporally dangerous for the specious orator to attempt amusing the high court *Areopagus* with a licentious display of his abilities." Annet shares, or so he says, "a like sense of the mischievous tendency of luxurious language," and so he also will "disclaim all assistance from it." His desire is "not to *persuade* but to *convince*, not to *declaim* but to *demon-*

strate.—Strictly adhering to the Apostle's advice, in our motto, at the beginning of the paper [prove all things]" (p. 8). Though these protestations are true to the Deists' stated suspicion of high-flown language, especially the language of priests, they seem disingenuous from a writer renowned for his skillful use of a veritable arsenal of rhetorical devices.

In keeping with his announced shift from the public to the private sphere for this new assault on Christianity, Annet's intended audience for *The Free Inquirer* included women. Freethinking, he argues in the inaugural volume, benefits women as well as men. His "intention is not to entertain men only, but the fair sex also; both are comprehended in the term mankind; and both equally entitled to regard." To women he will "pay all due respect without flattery which makes them fools; and without deceit, which betrays them into error and misfortune." Women, "by learning to think," gain an "inward beauty [that] will enhance the outward," which "will shine through it, and make their looks still more lovely" (p. 6).

Apparently Annet viewed the time as ripe for appealing to women as potential adherents to Deism. Early in the century Deism had had some female devotees. Queen Caroline, wife of George II, for instance, had apparently been part of a freethinking group. But Deist authors prior to Annet did not specifically direct their arguments to women. By mid-century, women had gained greater access to education and a somewhat expanded role in British society, and Annet was quick to recognize the rhetorical significance of such developments. But, regardless of the presence of a sizeable new audience of potential freethinkers, Annet lamented in a later volume of *The Free Inquirer* that "the thinking part of mankind are still but comparatively few" (October 24, 1761, p. 9).

Rhetorical innovations such as recasting the medium and the audience for Deism notwithstanding, much of Annet's case against revelation was stale by 1761. The Deist vision of an emancipated human reason had been played out in widely accessible publications for more than fifty years, and the English reading public was becoming jaded to what had once been scandalous irreverence. Nevertheless, like the true believer he was, Annet continued to ring the changes of rational inquiry in religion. "Our aim," he writes, "is to pull off the mask of sanctity from wolves in sheep's clothing; and shew, that a saint without virtue, is a hypocrite; that absurdities are not divine mysteries; and that the professed believer of such, is inebriated with nonsense and intoxicates his understanding" (October 17, 1761, p. 7). Here are all of the old themes of

Deism's earliest heroes rehearsed a generation after the passing of Woolston and fifty years after the publication of Shaftesbury's *Characteristics*.

Throughout his life Annet maintained the ruse of adhering to Christianity by invoking the early Deist *topos* of a primitive religion of reason and nature that is *true* Christianity. He affirms "that Christianity is not created in the moveable sands, which winds and waves may blow down and wash away; but that it is built *on a rock;* on the rock of Nature." Moreover, he argues that Christianity "was before Judaism, and is independent of it; in short, that true Christianity is as old as the Creation." He cites as evidence of this proposition Jesus' own claim that "Before Abraham was, I am." Abraham is reported to have been glad when he saw the day of Jesus. "What day did Abraham see?" asks Annet. "The light of Christ. He saw the doctrine of Jesus, which was day-light to his understanding, and he rejoiced in that day" (October 31, 1761, p. 20). Clearly Jesus could not have been referring to himself in these passages, reasons Annet, so he must thus have been referring to reason, the principle of all true religion.

Annet, like Woolston, freely reinterpreted crucial biblical accounts to support the Deistic view. Of particular interest to several important Deists was the Genesis account of the fall from grace of Adam and Eve. Annet writes in the November 3, 1761, issue of *The Free Inquirer* that the "fall" of Adam and Eve was to their advantage, as even God admitted. As a result of their fall they gained reason, knowing the difference between good and evil and becoming like God in their rational capacities. The Fall, then, far from injuring reason as Christian advocates like William Law had argued, actually improved human reason. Moses, the supposed author of Genesis, misconstrued the actual events in the garden of Eden and thus posited a monstrous God who would punish people for thinking. "Thus tyrannical, thus wrathful, and thus revengeful, does Moses represent the all beneficent God" (pp. 21–22).

Annet also attributes to Moses a polytheistic view, since he believed in a council of Gods. Seeing this claim as an opportunity to attack the integrity of scripture generally, Annet adds that this belief of Moses' may have been mistakenly attributed to him. "But I hope this to be ascribed to the ignorance of translators, blunders of copiers, or insertions of interpolators" (p. 22). Even if Moses is a monotheist, he believed in a limited, anthropomorphic God with emotions such as jealousy, caprice, and anger.

Annet is harshly critical of the Jews and their leaders, Abraham,

Moses, Joseph, and David. His criticism is extended to the whole of the ancient Jews, whom Annet refers to as "ignorant people" who credulously accepted whatever "wonders" their leaders might concoct for their consumption and who "easily report and assert, as truth, what they believe" (p. 27). Moses is Annet's principal target in *The Free Inquirer*, but in attacking Moses and his record of Jewish history, Annet condemns the foundational documents of both Judaism and Christianity—the Pentateuch. If the portrait of God painted by the author or authors of Genesis, Exodus, Leviticus, Numbers, and Deuteronomy is the concoction of ambitious and superstitious writers intent on duping a gullible tribe, then both Judaism and Christianity are largely in error in what they assert about God. This was without doubt the Deist view, though one they typically advanced indirectly so as to avoid prosecution and to insinuate their views into a public inclined to find the Bible credible.

Two important *a priori* commitments informed Annet's criticism of the books of Moses. First, rational religion must be universal. It thus may not give privilege to one faith over another. Second, reasonable religion does not involve irrational and superstitious elements such as miracle, mystery, sin, guilt, an emotional deity, or divine judgment. With these principles guiding his hermeneutic, Annet approached the biblical documents. Where those documents did not confirm rational religion, he drew upon a number of strategies for diminishing the texts: 1. Their authors were motivated by political ambition in what they taught their people about God; 2. The texts were written by ignorant and superstitious people; 3. The original documents had been heavily edited and otherwise tampered with over the centuries; 4. The texts reflect widespread misunderstanding of ancient people about God; 5. Many of the stories contained in the documents are pure fabrications; 6. The documents were written to advance the status of a particular tribe. These are the interpretive possibilities available to the rational critic when encountering mystery, miracle, superstition, acts of divine judgment, or the claim to a special revelation.

Of what value, then, are these or any other ancient religious documents? Annet's answer is clear: they are of no value whatever. The textual critic's job, then, is to subject them to corrosive criticism that reveals them as fraudulent. Only in this way is their influence erased from the public mind. Such important critical work, and *only* such work, clears the way for rational religious thought.

Annet's criticism is founded on a prominent Deistic hypothesis that the major world religions grew out of struggles for political power in ancient communities. Ancient priests used spiritual coercion to control their tribes or nations, usually claiming both a revelation from God, and miracles to confirm that revelation. Thus, all revealed religion had its origins in political tyranny and thus such religion cannot contribute to spiritual liberation. In number 6 of *The Free Inquirer,* published on November 21, 1761, Annet argues that "men drove to religion by terrifying motives, whether they be that of hell fire, or worldly fire, only have a force put upon their nature." Thus, religion as practiced can "have no influence to plant the love of truth and virtue" in human hearts. Religion that is "founded on bribery and punishment," Annet adds, "must be false religion" (p. 67). Following this line of argument, Annet also condemns "the establishment of a religion by the laws of men," that is, all state religions. Annet's rationale for the separation of Church and state, then, is rooted in the assumption that legislated religion is always spiritual coercion and thus always false religion.

Annet pleads only for the "rights of Conscience," which, he adds, "not wisdom in any state, but the tyranny of priestcraft, ever 'judged necessary to restrain'" (November 28, 1761, p. 71). Freedom of religious inquiry is linked to the freedom to question civil authority. Deists like Annet consistently advocated the trinity of liberties: free speech, a free press, and free thought. All three had been stifled by both religious and governmental hierarchies. The key to loosening the grip of government was to assault the authority of religion. State tyranny is founded on spiritual tyranny and is perpetuated by priests who benefit from maintaining the governmental status quo. American colonial writers were greatly influenced by Deists like Annet as they pleaded for the liberties of press, thought, and religion. But the key to all other liberties was the liberty of religious inquiry.

Ridiculing Miracle

The one element that supported revealed religion and the whole superstructure of governmental and religious authority was miracle. The rejection of miracle was true north on the compass of Deist rhetoric. No matter which way the discussion turned—to social conventions, freedom of the press, speculative theology—it eventually returned to miracle. Belief in miracle made the belief of any other sort of nonsense possible and eventuated ultimately in establishing the power of king and bishop. Only rational criticism and ridicule restore sense to one duped into belief in miracles, "for when once a man's brains are miraculously turned, it is not in the power of nature to restore him to his right senses. He that is lost in the woods and wilds of faith, can never find his way out" (p. 77). Annet offers himself as a guide to those lost and disoriented by believing miracles. Once an individual had been disabused of this superstitious faith in miracle, all other rational liberties were possible.

If miracle is ever at the center of the Deist argument, ridicule is ever the center of their critical method. And Annet was one of ridicule's most accomplished practitioners. His lengthy lampooning of the Mosaic plagues of Egypt demonstrated his relish for the approach. The whole story is made to appear as the most ludicrous nonsense. A brief excerpt from his treatment of the plague of frogs communicates some of the flavor of the whole analysis:

> Look there! Now Aaron stretches out his wand over the waters of Egypt, and the subsided blood is turned into frogs. See how they come leaping out of the waters, croaking in prodigious multitudes, so that, "they cover all the land of" Egypt! Look, look again! Pharaoh's magicians do the same: they are at the frog making work too. So, so, there will be frogs enough. . . . Had this frog miracle been done in France, the people would have thought the plague a blessing. Every house might have had rich fricasses, without going out of their doors frog-hunting. The Hebrews, one may suppose, ragooed them with their garlic and onions, and made a dainty mess. (December 5, 1761, pp. 79–80)

As the publisher of a periodical, Annet engaged the power of ridicule to attract readers as much as to make his polemical points. The comical and argumentative functions of such ridicule are often confused as here, where the last two sentences add nothing to the "argument" from ridicule but would delight many of his readers who held the detested French to have strange culinary tastes. Annet was not above puns and other strained comic devices to keep his readers' interest. "But in the next miracle, which was a lousy one, Moses out did them. You must take out your optic glass to discern them. They are very little creatures." Annet employed this pun on "lousy" repeatedly, along with a similarly crowd-pleasing play on fingers and scratching. "See! Pharaoh's magicians try to make lice, but they cannot: Therefore they told the King that this lousy miracle was done, by the finger of God: but the King without intreating him to kill them with his thumb, scratched himself again, though it makes one itch to think of it" (p. 80).

Annet's *Inquirer* lived up to its claim to being an entertaining publication. But these and other passages were also intended to exhibit the free exercise of unfettered reason. Such criticism of revealed religion would lead Annet's readers to truth and spiritual liberation, the periodical's other purpose. Annet seeks to awaken "reason, enlightened by the nature of things" (*Lectures,* number 12, p. 123). He equated inner light with Christ: "This inward illumination is man's only true light from God; 'tis the only begotten son of God, the God incarnate, or God humanized" (number 11, p. 113). In this way, Annet's underlying theological commitments place him in the religious tradition of inner illumination which would include Quakerism, Rosicrucianism, New Thought, and Christian Science.

Annet's Blasphemy Trial

Annet's trial for blasphemy was not, interestingly enough, precipitated by his harsh criticisms of crucial miracles in the 1740s. Rather, the *Free Inquirer* led directly to his prosecution before the King's Bench in the Michaelmas Term of 1762. Annet was sixty-nine years old at the time of his trial, but this fact did not prevent his serving time in the public stocks. No doubt Annet's earlier publications contributed to the severity of his punishment, though the official charges against him focused on the nine issues of the *Free Inquirer* published between October 17 and December 12, 1761. Of particular concern was his "A Review of the Life and Doctrines of Moses, the Celebrated Legislator of the Hebrews," which formed the contents of numbers 3, 4, 5, 8, and 9 and is "a veritable masterpiece" in the opinion of one commentator (Twyman, p. 11).

The 1760s were hard times for the publishers of "seditious" periodicals in Britain, with dozens of publications being subjected to official sanction.[4] Annet's ridiculing of sacred ideas, persons, and texts was his, as Woolston's, actual crime. He was "tried for 'Blasphemous Libel,' the information [warrant for his arrest] stating that he had ridiculed the Holy Scriptures in the Free Enquirer." Annet was convicted of blasphemy, and sentenced to

one month's imprisonment in Newgate—to stand twice in the Pillory—once at Charing Cross and once at the exchange, with a label "For Blasphemy" attached to him—then to undergo a year's *hard labour* in Bridewell, to pay a fine of 6s. 8d., also to find securities, himself in 100 pounds and the securities in 50 pounds each, for his good behaviour for the rest of his life. (Twyman, p. 11)

Though Annet had turned seventy by the time the sentence was handed down, the harsh penalty was "rigidly enforced." He stood in the pillory on December 14, 1762.[5] The National Secular Society's Almanack of 1877 recorded a contemporary report of Annet's experience in prison: "He has suffered already a month's imprisonment in gaol, perhaps the worst in the world, among thieves, highwaymen, murderers, etc., and where it is next to a miracle that a man broken down by seventy years could exist so long." The editors of the Almanack lament "That such an infamous sentence should have been inflicted on a feeble old man, against whose character for honesty and benevolence, malice itself had never breathed a whisper, was a disgrace to the eighteenth century and to the laws of England" (quoted in Twyman, pp. 12–13).

But even a few of Annet's sympathizers felt that he had overstepped the bounds of just debate in his assault on both scripture and the character of biblical characters. In his *Life and Times of Oliver Goldsmith*, John Forster reports Goldsmith's reflections on his experiences with the Robin Hood debating society, of which Annet was a prominent member:

One of the members of this Robin Hood was Peter Annet, a man, who, though ingenious and deserving in other respects, became unhappily notorious by a kind of fanatic crusade against the Bible, for which (publishing weekly papers against the Book of Genesis) he stood twice in the pillory, and was now undergoing imprisonment in the King's Bench. (quoted in Twyman, p. 13)

Annet survived his ordeal in prison, "wrecked in bodily health, but his mind as clear, alert and active as ever" (Twyman, p. 14). He took up residence in the vicinity of St. George's Gardens in London upon his release. Returning to teaching, he accepted a few young students. However, these were eventually removed from his care by parents concerned that their children were being taught to doubt the Bible. Annet authored during his seventies "a child's book on grammar," which attracted the interest of some publishers. However, his trial had made his name infamous, and even with Goldsmith's intervention no publisher would take the book. Annet also edited a volume of his tracts in 1768—*A Collection of the Tracts of a Certain Free Enquirer, Noted for his Sufferings for his Opinions.* He died while editing a second volume, on January 18, 1769, at the age of seventy-six. J. M. Robertson writes that Annet was "practically the first who sought to reach the multitude; and his punishment expressed the special resentment aroused in the governing classes to such a policy" (quoted in Twyman, p. 3).

Chapter Seven

Reason, Revelation, and Miracle: The Christian Response

When these Truths are delivered in a plain and intelligible Manner, and the Reasons of them from Scripture, made as sensible as possible, the Preacher cannot err, nor his Hearers go away unedified.
John Waugh, *A Charge Delivered to The Clergy* (p. 13)

Among the most important issues separating Deist and Christian writers in their eighteenth-century debate were the status of reason, the necessity of revelation, and the need for miracles to establish one revelation as supreme. This chapter examines the Orthodox response to Deism on these crucial and connected matters. Chapter 8 considers the closely related development by Christian apologists of a method for arguing the authenticity of the Christian miracles. We will begin by considering the clash over reason and the rhetorical problems this difficult topic posed both opponents and defenders of revelation.

Thomas Chubb and His Respondents on Reason

Thomas Chubb, like the other Deists, expressed a profound trust in the operations of human reason, particularly as regards religious questions. The Deists tended either to reject or to reinterpret the Fall. Some claimed, as did Annet, that the fall of Adam and Eve was a beneficial event that elevated human reasoning to a divine level. Others, like Chubb, argued that the Fall did no harm to human reason. Thus, for Chubb, "reason *is* a sufficient guide in matters of religion." Moreover, reason "is *sufficient* (notwithstanding *Adam's* misscarriage) to answer the purposes for which it was intended, *viz.* to guide men to, and engage them in the practice of their duty here, and to bring them to *happiness* hereafter" (Chubb 1731, p. 10). It would have been unjust of God to allow reason to be injured in the Fall, for "our species was no way *accessory* to *Adam's* transgression." Chubb traced the problem of reason's failure to the "*superstition* and *idolatry*" of religion which hobbled the faculty (p. 7).

In *An Enquiry into the Grounds and Reasons* (1732), Chubb argues that reason is "to every individual of our species who is answerable to God for his actions, under any or all the most disadvantageous circumstances he can possibly fall into, whether he resides in *China* or the *Cape of Good-Hope,* a sufficient guide in matters of religion" (p. 53). Several Christian writers sought to refute Chubb's case for reason. Anthony Bliss called Chubb's arguments on the point "weak and inconclusive" (p. 2). The "morality of the Heathens" reveals that unaided reason does not discover that we are "to forgive the most provoking Injuries, Love our enemies, to Worship God in Spirit and in Truth, &c." (p. 7). Pagan religions differ markedly from Christianity on such points. "I think I may very justly conclude that Mr. C. has been far from proving that Reason either *is* or *ought* to be sufficient in *any one* of these precepts," concludes Bliss. "You know well enough this Plea was first set on foot by the *Deists,* in order to prove [revelation] false by proving it useless" (p. 49). Thus, the comparative study of religions shows, not that reason is a universal guide to truth, but that a revelation from God is necessary. Human reason, left to its own devices, does not discover even the most fundamental Christian precepts, let alone doctrines such as the divinity of Christ or the trinitarian nature of God.

Other Orthodox writers also argued the limitations of reason. For Butler, reason is "the candle of the Lord within us." However, this candle "can afford no light where it does not shine; nor judge where it has no principle to judge upon." Thus, many divine truths "must appear liable to great objections," and we must be "incompetent judges" of them (p. 323). John Conybeare noted the "natural incapacity of a vast number of men in matters of strict reasoning" (Conybeare 1722, p. 17). Moreover, Deists labor under "unreasonable prejudices" when they assert "that whatever is incomprehensible by us is false. . . ." To take this position "is in effect to assert, that *all* truth is by us comprehensible, that we are capable of being equal to God in knowledge, and consequently, in every other perfection; since tis that where one perfection is in an infinite degree, there all others must be so too" (Conybeare 1723, p. 14).

James Edgcumbe argues in *Human Reason an Insufficient Guide in Matters of Religion and Morality* (1736) that reason, the "Noble distinguishing Faculty of our Nature," is, alas, weak and fallible (p. 3). Like other Orthodox writers, Edgcumbe found himself in the unenviable position of affirming the weakness of reason in elaborate arguments directed,

alas, to the reason of his readers. He thus notes that we readily acknowledge our ignorance in many arenas but that in "moral matters" most
people "think they are capable of determining for themselves, and therefore will not easily submit to Foreign decisions" (p. 4).

This "Pride and *Conceit* of Men" regarding their capacity to think
through moral issues is "the constant occasion of all those *Errors*, which
have been advanced in the Schemes of Particular Moralists" (p. 4). Even
in relatively straightforward practical matters reason is frequently wrong.
A *fortiori*, in that most elusive arena of religion, reason is almost certain
to lead us astray. There is not a single case in all of human history of a
society erecting "a competent Scheme of Religion and Morality, on the
mere Foot of Rational Principles only" (p. 11).

In response to the Deists' assertion of a universal religion of reason,
Edgcumbe advanced the Orthodox commonplace that there simply is
nothing even approaching universal agreement on religious matters. The
"Moral Writers both in ancient and Modern Times," he writes, "are frequently found to differ from one another in very essential points. Even
the common Fundamentals of Religion and Morality are not *clearly* and
indisputably settled by them." Each of these writers "drew up his particular system according to his own Notions," and all arrived at strikingly different conclusions. "They had all one and the same *Guide*, and
they all aimed at one and the same *End*, and as every End has its proper
Means, their *Guide*, if it had been a *sufficient* one, would have directed
them all the same *Way*" (p. 13).

Versions of Edgcumbe's argument were advanced repeatedly against
Chubb and other Deist writers who upheld the sufficiency of reason.
The argument for reason proved a genuine and perhaps fatal problem
for the Deists' general case, for it struck at their most fundamental tenet
in a decisive way. Reason did not lead human beings to the same, or
even similar, conclusions about religion. In response to this counterargument, Deists appealed to priestcraft. But the claim that all religious
differences could be put down to priestly conspiracy and corruption
seemed both far-fetched and suspiciously self-serving. The priestcraft
hypothesis condemned all religions but Deism.

Other Views of Reason

The author of *A Friendly Admonition to Mr. Chubb* (1727) takes a
slightly different tack from that of Edgcumbe. To write "such Expres-
sions against *Reason*," as had some apologists, may itself be "wicked."

On the other hand, to "exalt [reason] too high, and expect too much from it in Matters of Religion" is "the Error of *Mr. Chubb*" (p. 5). This author takes the moderate position that reason is weakened though not incapacitated by sin. Thus, revelation is important to teach us what reason can not, and miracles are provided to reason in order to confirm the one true revelation.

In his widely read *Moral Philosopher* (1738), Deist Thomas Morgan argued that "the reasonableness and fitness of doctrines" were ultimately to be decided by the "impartial consideration and judgment of reason" (p. x). John Chapman answered in his *Eusebius* the following year that revelation was necessary because the "principles and practices of mankind were so miserably depraved and corrupted as to want the light and assistance of revelation extremely" (p. 89). Chapman, then, stopped short of indicting reason itself, preferring instead to focus on corrupt human "principles and practices" that impede reason's activity.

Philip Doddridge also attempted to maintain a balance in the Christian perspective on the problem, arguing a relatively strong view of reason. "Can anyone indeed seriously think, that the noblest of our powers was intended only to the lowest and meanest purposes; to serve the little offices of moral life, and not to be consulted in the greatest concerns; those of immortality? Strange!" (*Perspicuity and Solidity of the Evidences*, p. 10). Strange, perhaps, but it seems there was no way of avoiding the fact that an Orthodoxy wed to revelation required a limited human reason. If reason could lead human beings to religious truth, why then was there any need for revelation?

Law Answers Tindal on Reason

The strongest refutation of the Deists on reason occurs in William Law's *The Case of Reason* (1731), a direct response to Tindal's *Christianity as Old as the Creation*. Law alone of the three great Christian apologists of the 1730s—Berkeley and Butler being the other two—has received relatively little attention from twentieth-century scholars.[1] This is not the result of insufficient talent or rhetorical force on the author's part. Leslie Stephen commented more than a century ago that "the question raised by [the works] of William Law, is how so vigorous a master of English and of reasoning should have sunk in such complete oblivion." Stephen adds that Law's "logical power shown in [his] controversial writings surpasses that of any contemporary author, unless Bentley be an exception" (volume 2, p. 133).[2] On Law's answer to Mandeville's *The Fable of*

the Bees, John Sterling writes: "I have never seen in our language a rational idea philosophy, as opposed to empiricism, stated with nearly the
same clearness, simplicity and force" (quoted in Harvey, p. 9). And
Roland Stromberg has called Law "without much doubt the finest religious writer of his age" (p. 101).

The full title of Law's work is *The Case of Reason or Natural Religion
Fairly and Fully Stated in Answer to a Book, Entitled Christianity as Old as
the Creation.* Law sought to refute Tindal, and his principal strategy was
to attack the Deists' conception of reason. "The infidelity which is now
openly declared for," writes Law, "pretends to support itself upon the
sufficiency, excellency, and absolute perfection of Reason, or Natural
Religion" (p. 57). Thus, all one need do to destroy Deism was to demonstrate that reason is not sufficient, excellent, or perfect.

Law pushes Deist assumptions to their logical breaking point. "If
the fitness of actions is founded in the nature of things, and persons,"
then "the rule by which [God] acts, must in many instances be entirely
inconceivable by us." For God to act according to his "divinely perfect
and incomprehensible nature," he must "necessarily act by a rule above
all human comprehension" (p. 62). Thus, one fundamental premise of
Deism—that unaided human reason can discover the nature of God—is
refuted by another, that God must act according to his own perfect and
infinite nature. Deism is self-contradicting.

Much of Law's argument rests on a series of analogies and contrasts.
The Deists themselves, according to Law, reasoned from a faulty analogy between human and divine knowledge. Thus, "to derive the wisdom and goodness of God" from "the relations of things, because our
wisdom and goodness is directed by them, is as weak and vain as to
found his knowledge upon sensation and reflection, because our rational knowledge is necessarily founded on them." The effort to constrain
God's reason or power on the basis of observations of nature is equally
unreasonable. When Tindal argues that God's "infinite wisdom" must
follow "the unalterable reason of things," he is making the same mistake as someone who reasons that God's creative work is "founded on
the unalterable nature of creatures." God cannot "be under any law at
all, any more than he can be under any authority at all" (pp. 82–83, 90).

Tindal's fundamental assertion that "God's laws" are "founded on
the eternal reason of things" is simply false. This is the same as to say
that God's existence is "founded on the eternal existence of things" or
that his "power is founded on the eternal capacities of things" (pp. 83–
84). Moreover, it may be true that "reason belongs to God and man, just

as power, life, and happiness belong to God and man." But the fact that happiness is common to God and man is not a proof that "our happiness [is] of the same kind and nature with God's" (p. 91). Some similarities between human and divine reason do not prove that the two are strictly analogous. "The truth of the matter is this; reason is in God and man, as power is in God and man." And as God's power "has some degree of likeness to human power, yet with an infinite difference from it; so that perfection which we call reason in God, has some degree of likeness to reason as it is in man, yet is infinitely and beyond all conception different from it" (pp. 91–92). We are not even capable of adequately accounting for our own highly fallible ability to reason. Human reason "is so small, and we enjoy it in so imperfect a manner, that we can scare, think or talk intelligibly of it, or so much as define our own faculties of reasoning" (p. 92).

But Law argued well beyond the assertion that human reason is limited and that it thus cannot be analogous to divine reason. Our faculty of reason is deeply flawed by the fall into sin. And "if man in a state of innocence" prior to the Fall "could have no pretence to set himself against divine revelation, and make his own reason the final judge of what God could, or could not reveal to him, much less has he any pretence for doing so in his present state of sin, ignorance and misery" (p. 61). Flawed reason cannot discover truth about God. The Deists in their faulty philosophy fail to take into account human "sin, and misery and ignorance" as evidence "of our own weakness." They thus follow the dictates of "guilty disordered reason" to suggest "methods of atoning for our guilt." This sort of pride renders them close to "the hardened state of those miserable spirits that make war with God" (p. 61). Human reason damaged by the Fall cannot provide us even the most basic religious truths and, in fact, rejects through pride the truth God has offered.

Law makes the additional point that reason includes the entire spectrum of human mental states, not just higher order cognitive operations. Thus, reason is solely responsible for all of the decisions we make. Though "common language" creates internal states such as "the blindness of our passions" or "the inconstancy of our tempers" or "the heat of our imagination" and contrasts these to "the coolness of our reason," all are reason. "In strictness of truth," writes Law, "everything that is done by us, is the action and operation of our reason, and is to be ascribed to it, as the sole faculty or principle from whence it proceeded and by which it is governed" (p. 129).

The Deists' universal human reason with access to divine truth is a phantom. Moreover, Deists cannot attribute differences from person to person—or religion to religion—to emotion, superstition, or prejudice. All is reason. "All the mutability of our tempers, the disorders of our passions, the corruption of our hearts, all the reveries of the imagination, all the contradictions and absurdities that are to be found in human life, and human opinions, are strictly and precisely the mutability, disorders, corruption, and absurdities of human reason" (p. 128).

Law takes up the specific consideration of human emotion as a test case of the Deists' notion of the universal agreement of human reason. The infinitely variable passions would be the same in every individual were the Deists' master hypothesis true. But, reasons Law, "as love is the same passion in all men, yet is infinitely different, as hatred is the same passion in all men, yet with infinite differences; so reason is the same faculty in all men, yet with infinite differences." There is no real distinction between reason and emotion for Law. "The distinction of our reason from our passions," Law holds, "is only a distinction in language, made at pleasure" (pp. 129, 130). Thus, vice as well as virtue is simply a fruit of reason.

In a summary passage which demonstrates his considerable rhetorical power, Law affirms:

It is not flattery that compliments vice in authority; it is not corruption that makes men prostitute their honor; it is not sensuality that plunges men into debauchery; it is not avarice that makes men sordid; it is not ambition that makes them restless; it is not bribery that makes men sell their consciences; it is not interest that makes them lie and cheat, and perjure themselves. What is it therefore? Why, it is that absolutely perfect faculty, which our author sets up as the unerring standard of all that is wise, holy and good; it is in his strong language, reason, the use of reason, human reason, that does all this. (p. 131)

If it is true that "all that is faithful, just and wise can only be attributed to that which is done by our reason," it is just as much the case that "all that is vain, false, and shameful, can only be imputed to any acts, as they are acts of reason" (p. 131).

So powerful was Law's case against reason that even his Christian colleagues were appalled. Law's argument led to mysticism, and his own mystical leanings were well known. In the words of M. Madan,

Law would direct Christians toward the "inward depth and ground of [the] heart," where the seeker may find "the devil, ready to take advantage" and to "instill his diabolical suggestions" (p. x).[3] But, interestingly, Law affirms that "reason always did, does, and ever will, govern rational creatures, in everything they determine, either in speculation or practice." We have no choice but to follow reason. "It is not a matter of duty for men to use their own reason, but of necessity; and it is as impossible to do otherwise," writes Law. To act without consulting reason would be as absurd as attempting "to think, without thinking upon something" (pp. 116, 117).

Law also held that revelation was essential for our moral guidance. How, then, is reason our only guide in matters of "speculation and practice"? The relationship here is the same as that between a human guide and a physical sign in the wilderness. The sign is available but the guide decides whether or not to heed it. Thus, the question is not whether we are to follow the guide of reason—we must—but whether our guide will heed the signs. "The dispute therefore betwixt Christians and unbelievers, concerning reason," Law argues, "is not, whether men are to use their own reason, any more than whether they are to use their own eyes." The real divisive issue in the controversy is "whether every man's reason must needs guide him by its own light, or must cease to guide him, as soon as it guides him by a light borrowed from revelation." Thus, the controversy arises over the question of when reason "is *best* followed . . . how it may be made our *safest guide?*" Revelation does not usurp the place of reason, which still makes both practical and moral decisions. But revelation provides needed assistance to reason in the decision-making process. "Christians oppose unbelievers, not because they reason, but because they reason *ill.*" Christians "receive revelation, not to suppress the natural power, but to give new and heavenly light to their reason; not to take away their right of judging for themselves, but to secure them from false judgments" (p. 116).

Deism hung by the slender thread of a conception of reason. Cut that thread, and Deism must fall. Law's argument against the Deistic conception of reason was built around four assertions. First, though we and God reason, human and divine reason are not analogous. God's reason, like his nature, is infinite and perfect. Second, human reason is deeply flawed by the Fall, and as a result, often unreliable. Third, "reason" includes *all* of the internal influences on human decision making, including the full range of passions. Fourth, reason is, nevertheless, our guide in decision making. As such, it must have the assistance of revelation. Leslie Stephen writes that Law has "scarcely left reason enough to serve as ballast" (volume 2, p. 136).[4] Perhaps, but the Deists' foundational doctrine of a universal reason leading reliably to religious truth is shattered by Law's inexorable logic.

Law on Miracles

Law's case for miracles was closely related to his case against reason. "The creation," he argues, "must of necessity be allowed to be the work of God" (p. 108). Our certainty on this point rests on an immediate and undeniable conviction from the nature of the evidence. Who else but God could be the author of such vast and intricate order? Law now reasons by analogy. In similar manner, a "course of miracles" has an immediate and undeniable impact on reason, producing a deep conviction as to source of the miracles. And, just as "the existence of things, is the highest and utmost evidence of God's having created them, and not to be tried by our judgments about the reasonableness and ends of their creation," Law reasons that "a course of plain, undeniable miracles, attesting the truth of a revelation, is the highest and utmost evidence of its coming from God, and not be tried by our judgments about the reasonableness of its doctrines" (pp. 109–10). Reason is instantly and undeniably impressed with the source both of natural order and of divine interruptions of that order.

But, having attacked the competence of reason earlier in his argument, how can Law now claim that reason can accurately judge either that nature or miracle proceeds from the mind of God? Law answers that we possess "a natural capacity of judging right of God, of finding out his perfections, and proving what is or is not worthy to be ascribed to him." Reason is specially equipped for judging the miraculous evidence that a revelation is of God. In fact, Law affirms unabashedly that reason cannot err in this regard, for the evidence of miracle is directed by the author of reason toward the end of convincing reason. "God can shew a revelation to proceed from him" (p. 100). To believe otherwise would be to place an unreasonable limitation on God's capacities. "If God has no ways of acting peculiar to himself, as to be a *sufficient* proof to human reason of his action; then no revelation can be sufficiently proved to be a divine, external revelation from God" (p. 107). Miracles are literally "undeniable evidence" (p. 100).

Reason is flawed, but also necessary to human decision making. God would not leave us without help in this desperate state. That help comes in the form of a revelation, but other "revelations" compete for our attention. God has thus endorsed one revelation by the undeniable proof of "a course of miracles." "The credibility of any external divine revelation . . . rests wholly upon such external evidence, as is sufficient proof of divine operation, or interposition" (p. 107). The biblical miracles immediately impress the reason God himself created with the fact that the biblical revelation is from God. The Christian miracles are God's own evidence to his creatures, and we can be fully confident they will achieve the purpose of proving the truth of Christianity. False miracles can never be undeniable, and thus we have only ourselves to blame if we are taken in by them.

Law's general conclusion is as uncompromising as is his general argument. "Christianity stands fully distinguished from all other religions, by the highest and most undeniable evidence; since it has all the proof that the highest state of miracles can give, and every other religion is without any support from them" (p. 112). Law accuses the Deists of ignoring the common experience of all people in all ages, the very evidence from which they claimed to be working in their pursuit of a universal religion of reason and nature. "These gentlemen," he writes, "only affirm such a sufficiency of light and reason to be natural to all men, as cannot be supported by a single instance of any one man, that ever lived, and is fully contradicted by the experience and history of every age since the creation of the world." He hopes that his own "inquiry about the perfection or imperfection, the strength or weakness, of reason in man as to matters of religion, rests wholly upon fact and experience." The Deists' "speculative reasoning" about religion and reason "are to be looked upon as idle, and visionary, as a sick man's dreams about health." Such arguments are "wholly to be rejected, as any speculative arguments that should pretend to prove, in spite of all the facts and experience, the immortality, and unalterable state of human bodies" (pp. 123–24).

Law eschewed his colleagues' careful search for biblical evidences. Though he "did not doubt the Bible," he did, in the words of Roland Stromberg, "doubt the wisdom of testing the authenticity of Christianity by Bible analysis." To treat religious belief "as a problem in evidence, was to play the deists' game" (p. 101). Thus, miracles are considered not as bits of evidence in an advocate's case but rather as immediate and indubitable communications from God. Thomas Sherlock, as we shall see in the next chapter, answered Deist criticism with evidentialism, a method of argument that relied on gathering and sifting a variety of evidences in support of miracles. Law saw such judicial debating of evidence as dangerous in the extreme. In the event that the available evidence is adequately answered by an opponent, what is left of the Christian case? Law preferred to argue that just as God created human reason, so God can provide reason with immediately convincing proof. Moreover, the method of sifting evidence allows the rational weaknesses of the advocate to enter the picture. The evidence of miracles speaks to whom it will speak, and with the authority of God. Was it wise of Christians, Law wondered, to suggest that the evidence might *not* be sufficient by examining it piece by piece before an undecided public?

Dodwell Satirizes Law

Law's choice to argue that reason is a "guilty, disordered" faculty rendered his case virtually useless, in fact, dangerous to the Christian cause. Other Christian writers completely avoided comment on *The Case of Reason*. Deist Henry Dodwell, however, capitalized on Christian ambivalence toward reason in his satirical and controversial *Christianity Not Founded on Argument* of 1741.

Dodwell's popular book elicited an instantaneous storm of protest. He satirized Law, Butler, and other Christian writers who argued reason's limitations. Affecting the voice of a sincere apologist in the school of Law, he writes that "if you do indeed intend to wave all religion till your reason is satisfied about it, know, that from the very moment of that resolution, so long you actually apostasize from Christianity, and renounce your baptismal-vow." The Christian who follows reason begins with a source other than revelation and follows a path that leads away from faith. "A strange method this is! To turn one's back upon religion in order to meet it, to discard it as a means to commence acquaintance" (pp. 5–6). Dodwell is imitating Law, who wrote in the *Case of Reason* that "claiming this authority" of testing God's doctrine "to our reason in opposition to the revealed wisdom of God, is not a frailty of flesh and blood, but that same spiritual pride which turned angels into apostate spirits" (p. 3). A reader might well wonder which writer—Law or Dodwell—is the satirist. Law's argument seemed a parody of Christian thought, a laughable exaggeration. Some mistook Dodwell for a sincere Orthodox apologist, and it is no wonder.

In his *Analogy*, Butler wrote that we are "incompetent judges" of many truths of scripture. Even on the most fundamental spiritual questions, "we are far from being able to judge what particular disposition of things would be most friendly and assistant to virtue" (p. 323). Dodwell mimics Butler in writing that "reason, or the intellectual faculty, could not possibly, both from its own nature and that of religion, be the principle intended by God to lead us into a true faith" (p. 7). Dodwell, like Law, concludes that reasoning about religion is hopeless and that, quoting St. Paul, "No man can say that Jesus is Lord but by the Holy Ghost" (p. 56).

Some readers did mistake Dodwell's intentions, but most Christian clergy were not taken in. By the end of the century Dodwell had received at least eighteen responses, with Philip Doddridge alone writing three and John Leland, two. By 1746, Benson, Leland, Mole, Mason, and Doddridge had all attempted to expose Dodwell's veiled attack, which meant, of course, fervently affirming that Christianity most certainly *is*, in some crucial respects, founded on argument. "Christ did propose the great doctrines he taught to examination," writes Doddridge. In addition, "the apostles did the same, urging (as their blessed master had done,) most cogent arguments in proof of them" (*Second Letter*, p. 4). Nevertheless, unless Christian writers admitted some strict limits to reason's ability to discern divine truth, there was was no apparent need for revelation and, correspondingly, none for miracles.

God, Nature, and Miracle in Christian Apologetic

Deist and Christian writers clashed over reason and revelation. They were also at odds over God's relationship to nature. Orthodox writers affirmed that God directed the course of nature freely and occasionally unpredictably. God's activities were certainly not bound by external forces such as "the reason of things." This notion violated fundamental components of Christian theology, such as God's sovereignty over nature. Moreover, if God intervenes miraculously in the material world, then normal historical methods should be sufficient for discovering and proving such interventions.

It is irrational to deny God's occasional interruptions of nature's normal course on *a priori* grounds. Hugh Farmer asks whether anyone would assert "that the almighty author of our frame is unable to repair disorders in it" or that "he, who with such exquisite skill formed the seeing eye and the hearing ear, cannot restore sight to the blind and hearing to the deaf" or that is it "impossible for him to raise the dead who every year renews the face of nature?" (p. 24). John Leng affirmed that the regular course of nature may, if God sees fit, "be as easily altered at any instant as continued" (p. 398).

"Nature is none other," Conybeare argued in 1722, "than the constant and uniform operation of the supreme being." Thus, "God may work a miracle by barely suspending his action on matter." In contrast to the Deists' law-bound universe, Conybeare envisioned a nature whose order was continuously imposed on it by a creator. "God, therefore, must have a power of producing innumerable other effects besides natural ones" (p. 14). Thomas Rutherforth argued in *The Credibility of Miracles Defended* that miracles "can be brought about by the immediate interposition of him, who established these laws" by which the universe runs and who "can over-rule them" (p. 11).

John Leng points out that Deists see nature's "motions preserved in a constant and regular course" and thus "imagine the course of nature to be something so fixed, as never, upon occasion, to admit of any change." But this is to reason as if the material world were "entirely independent [of] the will of God," having an "organized power of its own, which no intelligent being could either limit or control" (p. 397). Christians, on the other hand, hold that God established natural laws and can interrupt the order he imposes on nature at any time. Nature is not a reality parallel to God, and operating indpendently of him; it is a creation under divine control. Christians are not dualists, while many Deists are.

The system of nature is also too vast for our limited experience to comprehend. Thus, we may not reasonably rule out the possibility of extraordinary events based on experience. Our senses "inform us rightly what the usual course of things is," urges Sherlock. But when we conclude that things cannot be otherwise, we "outrun the information of our senses," the conclusion resting upon "prejudice," not reason (p. 64). Inhabitants of the tropics, to cite the most common illustration of the point, would, on the basis of their experience, conclude that "water can never freeze." Thus, "when men talk of the course of nature, they really talk of their own prejudices and imaginations" (p. 63).

William Samuel Powell argued that even the movements of the stars may not be eternally fixed. "That the motion of the heavenly bodies will be the same tomorrow as today, may be considered as almost certain. That it will meet with no interruption in a thousand ages, appears doubtful" (p. 95). Eclipses, black swans, comets, volcanoes, ice, and people with black skin were all advanced by Christian writers to demonstrate the irrationality of limiting nature to the scope of individual experience, which Deists did when they rejected miracles on the criterion of one's experience of nature's uniformity. Is it reasonable to hold that everything is "impossible or even improbable, that contradicts the notion men frame themselves of the course of nature?" (p. 63).

Similarly, William Adams argued that "uniform experience" would lead us to conclude that cutting an animal up into pieces could not produce more of the same. "Yet," he writes, "this sort of hydra has been discovered" (p. 26). Adams also notes that "the southern climates" would reject the notion of frost and that those never visiting "very cold climates" would not believe that a magnet loses its polarity there. John Douglas describes the unreasonableness of a man who "unfamiliar with the efficacy of cannon balls might reject as fictitious a report that a small metal ball could devastate a stone fortress" (p. 241n.). Richard Price wrote indignantly that

one cannot help being greatly disgusted with the inclination which shows itself in many persons to treat with contempt whatever they hear, be it ever so well attested, if it happens that they are not able to account for it, or that it does not coincide with their experience, just as if they knew all that can take place in nature. . . . (p. 443)

But, Christian apologists still faced the basic question of the Deist: Can one both believe in miracles and hold to a rational, predictable universe? Adams attempts to resolve the tension between Orthodox Christianity and an emerging scientism by arguing that miracles are, after all, quite rare and that "the concurring testimony of mankind to the course of nature is not contradicted by those who have experienced contrary appearances in a few instances." In fact, belief in miracle solves the intellectual problem posed by natural anomalies. "The idea of a miracle unites and reconciles these seeming differences" between nature's consistency and occasional alterations in its course. By supposing the anomaly in question to be miraculous, "the uniformity of nature is preserved, and the facts accounted for upon another principle entirely consistent with it" (p. 1). But if all unusual events are to be considered miracles, we would soon find ourselves awash in such sacred events and unable to conclude anything on the basis of any particular one.

If our ignorance of much of nature prevents our discarding miracles *a priori*, does this ignorance also prevent our identifying any particular event *as* miraculous? Theologian G. F. Wood comments that we are "driven to the somewhat paradoxical conclusion that we do not know enough of the limits of the natural order either to deny the possibility of miracles, or to identify one if it takes place" (p. 25). Thus, even on a Christian view of nature the value of miracles as evidence may still be called in question. And on the Christian view of a limited reason, reason's ability to assess either the evidence for a miracle or a miracle's value *as* evidence, may be doubtful.

The next chapter looks in greater detail at how Christian writers sought to address such problems in building their case for a reasonable, albeit revealed and miraclulous, Christianity.

Chapter Eight

Miracles and Method in Christian Apologetic

Who can help [being a skeptic], if the man will needs be distracted with pure ideal possibilities, without descending to plain facts and weighing the real evidence of things. The regular way is surely to consider not abstractly what is possible to happen, but what has actually happened in the case before us.

John Chapman, *Eusebius*

I am fully persuaded the method you condemn is reasonable. . . . Though [a prophet's] teaching never so reasonable a doctrine will not prove he comes from God, or, has an extraordinary commission from him to teach it: yet his teaching an unreasonable doctrine; his making God an encourager of vice, or discourager of virtue, is a greater evidence that he cannot come from God, than the doing of a miracle can be that he does.

Bishop Hoadley in response to Fleetwood

The Deists' consistent use of ridicule and attending strategies such as ribald insult of biblical figures and parody of biblical narratives, earned them the unyielding wrath of their enemies in the Church. "Decency and respect to the common sentiments of mankind," argued John Leng in 1717, "should make them forbear such unreasonable jesting." But Deists ardently defended their method as objective, rational criticism. Leng was unpersuaded. "No man of sense," he retorted, "ever treats that with ridicule which he does not either think contemptible, or design to make so" (p. 50). Conybeare wrote that "to be entirely careless is inexcusable, for it expresses a contempt for that being, whose will we are concerned to hear, as to obey" (Conybeare 1732, p. 427).

From Leng's Boyle lecture of 1717–1718 through Campbell's *Dissertation on Miracles* of 1762, Christian writers angrily denounced the Deists' method of ridicule. Just as Shaftesbury set the tone for later defenses of ridicule, so Leng provided a model for its repudiation. There can be no defense of "jesting upon [religion] or ridiculing it." Ridicule is inappropriate for treating "matters of great moment," a point repeated by nearly every apologist for miracles. "The common sentiments of mankind" are disregarded by the professedly universalist Deists when they ridicule religion (Leng, p. 50).

But attacking ridicule was a limited goal of Orthodox apologetic. A rival method was required that would vindicate miracles. Major intellectual figures such as Bishops Sherlock and Berkeley advocated evidentialism, which treated miracles as historical events and carefully sifted the evidence in their support. This chapter will explore both the response of Christian writers to the method of ridicule and efforts to develop an Orthodox method with miracles.

Warburton on Ridicule

Bishop William Warburton (1698–1779), a talented and tireless opponent of Deism, affirmed that the Deists were "a Sect of Anti Moralists who have *our Hobbes*, and the French Duke de la Rochfoucault for their leaders." By affirming the "Dignity of human Nature" they are "fatal enemies" to "Publick Liberty." Liberty must be constrained within boundaries that acknowledge the fallenness of the human soul. Warburton satirized "the rare Felicity of the Age that can afford to carry on such important Works with so much good Humour." What benefit can ridicule be when turned against the true Christian faith? "Seriously let it be as they say, that Ridicule and Satire are the Supplement of publick Laws; should not then, the Ends of both be the same, the Benefit of mankind?" Warburton reminds the Deists that Socrates "thought the laugh came too dear, when bought at the Expense of Probity: And therefore had it all out in the Improvement and Reform of Manners" (Warburton 1727, pp. 26, 28, 32, 33).

Warburton devoted the longest portion of his essay, "To the Free-Thinkers," to examining ridicule, one of the more sustained criticisms of the approach. He sharply condemns the use of this strategy "in religious Controversy" where "the great Cause of eternal Happiness" is at issue. When "Men and Angels [are] attending the issue of the Conflict" one should be loath to "find room for a merry story." The Deist "brings the Tidings of *Death,* and scatters around him the Poison of our *Hopes,* yet like the *dying Assassin,*" Belthazar Gerard who murdered the Prince of Orange, "we can laugh along with the mob, though our own agonies and despair concluded the entertainment" (Warburton 1738, p. viii).

Ridicule's success points up a problem with the popular audience for which the Deists wrote. "*Ridicule*," he writes to the Deists, "is become your favourite figure of Speech; and your writers have composed distinct Treatises to vindicate its use, and manifest its Utility." But, he adds, "to be fair with you, it must be owned, that this extravagant Disposition in the Reader, towards unreasonable Mirth, drives all Parties upon being witty where they can." Still, the fact remains that ridicule employed in the resolution of serious issues is inappropriate in religious controversy. "For what greater Affront to the Severity of Reason, the Sublimity of Truth, and the Sanctity of Religion, than to subject them to the impure Touch of every scurrilous Buffoon?" Deists must "learn the difference between the Attic Irony, and Elegance of Wit, and your intemperate Scurrility, and illiberal Banter" (p. ix).

By means of ridicule, Deists manipulate the common reader who cannot trace long arguments. The Deists' "low and mean . . . Buffoonery" is written at "the level of the People." By means of ridicule Deists "*lead captive, silly* Fellows, laden with *Sins, led away with divers Lust* who are as little solicitous, as capable of the point of argument, so they can but catch the point of Wit. Among such, and to such you write" (p. x). The bishop's own attitude toward "the People," particularly to the degree that it was shared by his colleagues, may have contributed to the appeal of the Deists' popular literature.

Finally, as for Shaftesbury's theoretical point that "what is deformed" is ridiculous, while "what is handsome and just is not," Warburton is unconvinced. It is entirely possible to "raise a laugh" among the vulgar by mocking beautiful and true things. The manner in which a topic is presented has much to do with its reception by an audience (p. xii ff). Warburton concludes by calling upon the Deists "to acknowledge this method to be the most Unfair and pernicious, that a sincere Searcher after Truth can be betrayed into." Rather than testing the truthfulness of ideas, ridicule's "natural Effect is to obscure the understanding, and make the heart dissolute" (p. xviii).

Orthodox Method: Evidences and Probabilities

The clash of Orthodox and Deist methods is memorably set out in George Berkeley's *Alciphron, or the Minute Philosopher*, published in 1732. A Christian in the dialogue calls the Deists "bigots" for "laying the greatest stress on points of the smallest moment" (p. 283). A reasonable investigator wishing "to make a wise judgement" about Christianity will "take a comprehensive view" of the religion, which includes examining its "principles, effects, and tendencies" and "its proof internal and external." Further, this careful investigator "will distinguish between the clear points and the obscure, the certain and the uncertain, the essential and the circumstantial." Rather than seeking demonstration on historical issues, "he will consider the different sorts of proof that belong to different things" and ask himself "where probability will suffice" to convince a reasonable person (pp. 283–84).

Most important from the Christian perspective, Berkeley's reasonable investigator will "proportion his pains and exactness to the importance of the inquiry," leaving aside "groundless prejudices" and silencing "passions," the earnest seeker after truth "will endeavour to untie knots as well as to tie them, and dwell rather on the light parts of things than the obscure," balancing "the force of his understanding with the difficulty of the subject" and "hear[ing] evidence on all sides." It is Berkeley's "sincere opinion" that the Christian religion "may well stand the test of such an inquiry" (pp. 283–84).

Other Orthodox writers also sought to combat ridicule with a serious approach to the evidences. Leng argued that the "miracles and the doctrines" of Christianity bear "more evident marks of truth than any other history whatever" (p. 437). Jesus' miracles are supported by "the best ground of assurance that any fact at such a distance is capable of" (pp. 435–436). Conybeare turned attention to the New Testament witnesses, arguing that "if we consider them only as witnesses to fact" we may "put them on the same foot as any other witnesses." Moreover, when viewed as historical events, miracles "do not require absolute infallibility to gain them credit" (p. 445). John Chapman held that the biblical miracles "carry all the evidence in this world, which a matter of fact can have," and a reasonable person "would believe a hundred other facts of consequence upon less evidence" (pp. 135–36). Abraham LeMoine argued that "miracles stand upon as good a foot of credibility as any other facts, of which public histories are composed" (p. 450).

Evidentialism, then, gained wide acceptance among Christian apologists. The unbiased investigator of miracles must, according to John Chapman, consider "the plain facts" and weigh "the real evidence of things" (p. 236). John Mason complained to Dodwell in 1743 that "you never yet have fairly collected all the evidence of Christianity, both external and internal, and set them in that full and impartial light" so as to "encounter them in all their force" (p. 16). And for John Leland, God had provided his "reasonable creatures [with] sufficient evidence to engage them to believe," evidence that "will actually have that effect on them, if it be not their own fault, and if they carefully attend to it with that disposition of mind that becomes them" (Leland 1754, p. 25). "The sum of all the probabilities for the truth of Christianity," according to Powell, would be impossible to calculate because of "the immensity of the numbers" (p. 99).

A survey of Orthodox apologetic from the 1720s through the 1760s reveals great Christian confidence in the method of weighing evidences. "They are afraid," Conybeare wrote of the Deists in 1722, "either of examining it all, or of admitting the most obvious truths" (*The Nature, Possibility, and Certainty of Miracles*, p. 4). "The miracles of the New Testament," wrote Price forty years later, "have many circumstances attending them which recommend them strongly to our good opinion, and which lay us under indispensable obligation to give the evidence for them a fair and patient examination" (p. 438). Sherlock's highly successful *The Tryal of the Witnesses* (1729) imagines a jury hearing the evidence for and against the resurrection. Each piece of evidence is carefully set out, every argument delivered with commensurate skill:

> *Judge:* What say you? Are the apostles guilty of giving false evidence in the case of the resurrection of Jesus, or not guilty?
> *Foreman:* Not guilty. (p. 60)

Sherlock's book was popular for a century, and the "Old Bailey" approach became the standard apologetic strategy. No one even attempted to answer Sherlock until Annet's *The Resurrection of Jesus Considered in Answer to the Tryal of the Witnesses* appeared in 1744.

Evidentialism contrasted favorably with Deist ridicule, which appeared careless by comparison. It also highlighted the strengths while minimizing the weaknesses of miracle evidence. That evidence was weak when construed as the individual pieces of particular miracle accounts, especially when attention was focused on inconsistencies in and among accounts. The evidence was considerably stronger when taken cumulatively as generally consistent support drawn from numerous independent sources. Evidentialism has never been abandoned by Christian advocates.

The method, however, rested on the debatable claim that miracles are simple historical events. Annet retorted that "a history of an extraordinary and uncommon kind, should have more than common proof" which might suffice for establishing "ordinary histories and reports." The "proofs given," he contends, "should be equal to the things proved, and the more momentous the affair is, [the more] certain and demonstrable should be the evidence" (Annet, *The Resurrection of Jesus Considered*, p. 9).[1] Thus, standard evidentiary requirements will not adequately establish a miracle report, particularly when that miracle is advanced to support an entire religion.

The Problem of Testimony

The New Testament miracles rest on a single type of evidence—the testimony of Jesus' disciples in the New Testament documents. Thus, Deists attacked testimony, and Christian writers sought to shore up its evidential status in response. Annet argued in *The Resurrection of Jesus Demonstrated to Have No Proof* that "a miracle is nothing to those, that don't see it." It is "not the miracle you believe, when tis told you, but a fellow," and this fellow "will certainly lie for his own interests." And when "the cause of religion" was at stake, lying was more common than usual (p. 7).

Christian writers affirmed the disciples' trustworthiness as eyewitnesses of the events they reported. For Berkeley, the disciples were "eye-witnesses, whom we cannot conceive tempted to impose upon us by any human motive whatsoever, inasmuch as they acted contrary to their interests, their prejudices, and the very principles in which they had been nursed and educated" (p. 222). When Deists argued that testimony for miracles contradicts uniform experience, Christian writers answered that testimony is often superior to experience or that the two are indistinguishable from one another. Thomas Rutherforth argued that sense impression and "the testimony of men who vouch the evidence of their senses" are really the same thing (p. 3). "I cannot, indeed, see with the eyes of other men," wrote William Adams, "but I can see that they have eyes." Thus, if a witness is known to be trustworthy, "I have nearly as good evidence for the fact as if I had seen it myself" (p. 27n.).

There is nothing that sense can prove which testimony cannot also prove. Moreover, testimony provides "positive" evidence of miracles, while experience can only provide "negative" evidence against them. Testimony is, according to Adams, "direct evidence to the existence or reality, not of similar facts, but of the fact itself." Moreover, testimony is rooted in a natural love of truth. Thus, "we find in ourselves that a love and reverence for the truth is natural to the mind of man" (pp. 43, 8).

Skeptics blasted the Orthodox view of miracles and testimony. According to Adams, these writers argue that testimony is "dark and doubtful," and we "go upon surer ground" when we argue from experience. Adams retorted that "the contrary . . . in almost every particular, is, I think, the truth" (p. 31). He recognized, of course, that much depends on circumstances and that, "as these circumstances vary, the evidence varies" (p. 10). Nevertheless, Adams affirms that "testimony is, for the most part, of much greater force to establish the truth of past facts than experience" (p. 25). Thus, testimony is sound evidence and can stand as reasonable proof of miracles in spite of the evidence from experience against them.

Vindicating Jesus' Miracles

The resurrection of Christ became the focus of much attention during the debate between the Deists and the Church. Woolston, Annet, and others had attacked this central Christian miracle in several popular works, and its defenders advanced their cases in reply with a vehemence and energy befitting an effort to save Christianity itself. In this section we will look more closely at a classic evidentialist defense of the Resurrection.

The anonymous author of *The Miracles of Jesus Vindicated* wrote in 1729 that "the Resurrection of *Jesus*" was "a Point of so great Importance, that the whole Weight of Christianity rests upon it." Any reader who considers the question of Jesus' resurrection "without Prejudice, may (it is hoped) be convinc'd of the Reality of the great Miracle, and be supply'd with a sufficient Answer to the several Objections lately rais'd against it" (p. 3).

This work, then, would train the layperson to answer Deist arguments against the Resurrection. First, the foundation of the biblical case for miracles must be established. The apostles' own evidence for Jesus' resurrection was sense perception. Thus, a dilemma: "If the account given us by the Apostles be False, it must have been, either because they were Deceived themselves, or because they knowingly Deceived Mankind." But, the apostles could not have been deceived about the Resurrection because, interestingly, they later received the gift of speaking in tongues. The apostles "could not possibly be mistaken" about having spoken in tongues at Pentacost, for the evidence they had was "the same Evidence" as they had "of their being Alive." And speaking in tongues was an experience which made sense only if the Resurrection had been true. Thus, "allowing that they were sure of This, it follows that they were Sure of *Jesus's* having been raised from the Dead, and of their having convers'd with him after his Resurrection" (p. 6). One cannot be mistaken about having had a conversation with a familiar person. The external experience of speaking to Jesus after his death is confirmed by the indubitable internal experience of speaking in tongues.

Thus, the apostles were not deceived about the Resurrection. Could they, however, have conspired to deceive their audience? Not likely, given the peculiar circumstance of Judas's betrayal of Jesus and his followers. "Is it not against all Reason and Experience that a Confederacy Among Wicked Men, when once broken thro' Treachery and Cowardice, should ever be renewed among the same persons and cemented again?" Moreover, "no Motive can be assigned" for the disciples' "Combining in such a Falsehood." It is, after all, "universally given up, that neither Grandeur, nor Riches, nor Pleasure, were what the Apostles aimed at; the marks of the contrary are too plain to be denied" (p. 7).

Concurrent testimony is stronger than that of an individual, particularly when it comes from people of high character. In addition, the disciples were willing to endure great hardships for their testimony. Thus, the testimony recorded in the New Testament is strong when standard tests are applied. This author summarizes the evidence from the apostles' testimony in a fashion that became part of the stock argument of Christian apologists. The apostles had suffered and died for their testimony that Jesus had risen from death:

> But above all things, it must be insisted upon as a Proof of their Sincerity, that the whole Number of the Apostles unanimously asserted this Fact of *Jesus's* Resurrection, and of their having seen him in all the Circumstances before related, in the midst of all kinds of Sufferings and Persecutions, even with their Dying breath, and when expiring under the Cruelest Tortures.

As "Death is the utmost Tryal, the surest Test which human Nature can be expos'd to," this author concludes that "this is naturally as Strong a Proof as a Fact is capable of" (p. 8).

The credibility of apostolic testimony was so crucial to the cases for and against the miracles that virtually every author in the controversy addressed the question. Deists debunked the apostles' credibility and character, the circumstances under which they observed miracles, their motives, and even their martyrdom. The argument from apostolic martyrdom to the reliability of their testimony had been anticipated early in the controversy by Deist Charles Blount. In his *Anima Mundi* of 1678 he sought to refute the argument by analogy to "the Aegyptians" who "died fighting for the Deity of Garlick, others for the Deity of Onyons." Thus, "a mistaken Martyrdom rather betrays the easiness of the party, than the truth of his cause" (Blount 1678, p. 48). Nevertheless, the author of *The Miracles of Jesus Vindicated* takes the evidentialist stance that "there is no Fact in Nature, than can be so well proved and supported" as Jesus' resurrection. That the apostles were themselves deceived is "impossible," while "to affirm that they were Deceivers" is also "to affirm a thing which is Morally impossible; i.e. Impossible in the highest degree" (p. 10).

Deists sometimes noted that Mary did not recognize Jesus at first, taking him to be the gardener. Surely this failure of recognition casts doubt on the identity of the individual the women met in the garden on Sunday morning. Not so, responds this author, rebutting the claim with an anecdote. "I met an old acquaintance t'other day in Westminster Hall," he writes, "whom I did not know at first; I was talking with him for some time, 'till at last recollecting my self I called him by his name, and we immediately knew each other. . . . Shall any one tell me now, that this man was *not* the old acquaintance that I took him to be, and use for his Argument, that I did not know him at First?" (p. 19).

It is certain that objections can and will be raised against the evidence for the Resurrection, but "will a wise man think a few Cavils sufficient to determine the Point against such evidence?" The cumulative weight of the evidence for the Resurrection is "so much Stronger" than are "the Objections to it" that there are "greater Difficulties to be met with in Disbelieving than in Believing" (p. 24).

Finally, the Deists' "religion of nature" is a poor substitute for Christianity. "If we give up Christianity, what Religion will they give us in the Room of it?" Because "Christianity is surely worth something . . . a Man would not part with it except to Advantage." So, what have the Deists offered "in the Room of it?" "Why, *The Golden Religion of Nature* is offer'd us in Exchange: but all is not *Gold* that glitters; it has been prov'd a thousand times, that Natural Religion is not sufficient for all our Wants. . . ."

The Deists themselves prove the failure of their recommended religion. The religion of nature has "Morality for the Standard," and this is clearly an inadequate foundation, as the Deists show by their notoriously immoral lives and their infamously deceptive discourse. If morality alone could provide us a guide for action, one would suppose that "while they recommend it [they] should practice it, and the Example should go along with the Doctrine." However, "the contrary [is] visible in most of their Works" (pp. 26–27). Woolston, for example, made a deceptive use of evidence. The author compares a passage from St. Hilary as Woolston employed it in the *Discourses* to the full text of the original passage. Hilary's own words contradict Woolston's interpretation of the passage. The author notes that there are numerous other instances he could cite to show that Woolston had misled his readers about the theological positions of the Fathers. Thus, Woolston, "this great Recommender of the *Golden Religion of Nature*, in his attacks upon Christianity, violates the first principles of Natural Religion, and makes a sacrifice of Common honesty to his Zeal against Revelation" (p. 29).

False Miracles and Natural Wonders

Christian writers argued from textual and circumstantial evidence to miracles and from miracles to divine endorsement of Jesus' doctrine. However, there were many well-attested Catholic and Pagan miracles that Protestants rejected. In addition, "prodigies" or strange events were taken by the common folk to be signs from God. How could the case for miracles be a limited case, one that reasonably excluded both "false" miracles and natural wonders?

Berkeley had argued the need to "consider the different sorts of proof that belong to different things" (p. 283). Christian writers repeatedly argued that the evidence for Christ's miracles met the standards for *probable* proofs. Moral certainty "suits past matters of fact, and is sufficient to make a candid and rational examiner easy in his assent," according to Doddridge (Doddridge 1758, p. 384n.). Leland found evidence "enough to satisfy any reasonable mind" supporting the New Testament miracles (Leland 1754, p. 61). For LeMoine, the evidence was "sufficient to satisfy a reasonable man, and even to oblige him to yield his assent" (p. 351). Burnet found the evidence for Christ's miracles to provide "as good rational ground of assurance of the truth of this record, as we can desire" (p. 198). The New Testament miracles are supported by "all the evidence in the world, which a matter of fact can have," according to Chapman (p. 136).

But some pagan and Catholic miracles satisfied this same standard of probability. The well-attested miracles alleged of the emperor Vespasian were frequently advanced by Deists, as were those currently being reported at the tomb of the Abbe Paris. In many cases, Deists argued, miracles which Protestant writers rejected were supported by evidence similar to that for biblical miracles.

Chubb added to this concern the problem that a miracle might be worked by an "invisible agent" to deceive us. God had allowed Satan or his demons to deceive people in some biblical narratives. Thus, "it is plain that God will suffer invisible agents to exert their power in serving what purposes they please" (Chubb 1741, p. 18). People deceive other people, and they control slaves. By analogy, why could not invisible agents do the same with us? Therefore, even if we were to witness a miracle, there is no way of confirming that it was wrought by God. In fact, were such deception not possible, God would be restricting the liberty to his rational creatures.

To solve such problems, Christian writers advanced criteria which a genuine miracle must satisfy. Some of these criteria were simple and straightforward, though several apologists developed elaborate tests to separate good from bad miracles. Warburton, writing in *An Enquiry into The Causes of Prodigies and Miracles* (1727), notes that there are many miracles recorded in ancient sources. It is also the case that the human mind has a capacity for "imposture" even to the point of "deceiving ourselves." Thus, superstition attends human history at every stage and persists in written histories. Warburton concedes these points to his opponents, as well as the fact that "natural Pride" is "a *second cause* of this Deluge of Prodigies in historic Composition" (pp. 4, 22).

Unlike other Christian writers, Warburton allowed that some pagan and Catholic miracles may be authentic. His criteria for determining a miracle's authenticity granted too much, according to his colleagues. "Are we then to condemn as fabulous and chimerical, all we meet with in profane History of prodigies and Miracles? By no means." And why not? Because some non-Christian miracles bear "the marks of Truth," including "Universal Consent in Testimony." Some have been performed "in favor of the common principles of Morality and Religion," which leave "no Room for an ambiguous meaning." Thus, miracles which attend "giving men Laws" should be allowed as possibly authentic, particularly when the laws themselves "carry with them the equal Marks of stupendous Wisdom and Power" (pp. 121, 123). Warburton's criteria were too broad for Christian apologetic purposes; the evidential function of Christ's miracles was lost if other miracles could be confirmed as genuine. Nevertheless, the notion of distinguishing criteria seemed a good solution, perhaps the only solution, to the the problem of rival miracles.

For most Christian writers, the simplest way of distinguishing true from false miracles was to consider the reasons for which the miracles were worked. Conybeare argued that authentic miracles are worked for "the natural good of the world." It is always essential that there be found some end "entirely worthy of God" attending a miracle (Conybeare 1732, pp. 438, 440). Burnet argued in his *Boyle Lectures* of 1736 that an essential characteristic of authentic miracles is that they be "beneficial to men" and tend "to some great and excellent purpose" (p. 191). God's "great and excellent purpose" in working the biblical miracles, one which could not easily be argued in connection with other miracles, was to confirm the truth of Christianity.

Similarly, Farmer argued that God will work a miracle "to attest a divine mission, and communicate some important instruction to his rational creatures" or to raise them "to a sublimer pitch of piety and virtue than they could otherwise attain." Authentic miracles "answer some extraordinary purpose of divine providence" (pp. 27, 71). Adams held that miracles are "credible in themselves" only when we can ascertain "a sufficient cause for willing them" (p. 40). Thus, "if virtue, and that knowledge which is necessary to it . . . were in danger of perishing out of the world," God could be expected to "send a righteous man to recall men to virtue." Such noble ends "will make miracles in every way credible" (p. 35). Similarly, LeMoine held that true miracles "must be wrought only upon extraordinarily important occasions, for wise ends, ends worthy of God" such as "the giving of a new revelation for the good of mankind, or some part of them." Expressing the perhaps overly hopeful sentiments of many Christian apologists on this point, LeMoine adds emphatically that "by this rule all the pretended miracles of heathens, and the Church of Rome, are easily shown to be false" (pp. 22–23, 24).

Chapman argued that the biblical miracles are reasonable when we consider "the very condition of that people" to whom God sent "his extraordinary messengers, endued with such miraculous powers." When God "favours mankind" with a "special revelation of his will and instructions from heaven in a way supernatural" it is because his people are at an "unhappy juncture" and are "miserably depraved and corrupted." When in this condition, people are "(humanly speaking) utterly incorrigible" without miraculous intervention by God (p. 89). Conybeare summarizes the usual Christian position in writing that when "we can assign an end worthy of a miracle; and shew, farther, that this is a proper means to obtain that end, it will be evident, that the working miracles is not inconsistent with wisdom." However, the "worthy end" is for all of these writers the same: "We assert then, that this is a sufficient end of working miracles, viz., to confirm the truth of a revelation" (Conybeare 1722, pp. 16, 17).

But there are many alleged revelations, distinguishable principally on the basis of their varying doctrine. Is not doctrine, then, the actual criterion for identifying true miracles, rather than vice versa? The issue of doctrine's place in distinguishing true from false miracles divided Christian writers. Some, like Leng, argued that "the doctrine intended to be proved by them" is to be considered in order to ensure that it is not "plainly unworthy of God" (p. 403). Thus it is imperative that "the nature of the doctrines which miracles are alleged to confirm, must be considered" (Conybeare 1732, p. 463). Similarly, Burnet affirmed that what contradicts "a belief of a God, and his goodness and truth" is not "capable of any proof." Thus "the reasonableness of the whole Christian revelation . . . a doctrine every way worthy of God" is its own proof, just as "at the same time we prove its divine authority from unquestionable miracles." This is the standard used in all cases, for "the nature of the evidence, and the nature of the thing to be proved" are always "both to be considered" (p. 195). But, surely we are in a rational conundrum at this point: The miracle proves the doctrine, which proves the miracle; each event is the only reasonable proof of the other.

LeMoine attempts to solve this problem by arguing that "many impositions and frauds may be committed under the pretence of a revelation made to one man, or to a particular set of men, it is true." However, it is easy "to discover them, and guard against them, because there is a standing rule to go by." And this is LeMoine's rule: Reason judges the truth of "the doctrine revealed," with "miracles to prove the divine mission of the publisher of it" (p. 134). Reason is, then, the final judge of whether a doctrine will be accepted. Is this not Deism? The problem in the Christian case remained unresolved.

Some Christian apologists, wishing to put to rest the persistent Deistic claim that miracles are claimed by all religions, developed elaborate criteria for distinguishing true from false miracles. Leng, for instance, held that authentic miracles satisfy "three conditions." First, "the effect produced" must be "something which is plain and obvious to the senses of the beholders." Second, the alleged miracle must be "supernatural," meaning that it will "exceed all natural human power known to us." Finally, the miracle will be "done for some evident end and design" (p. 388).

Leland's list of criteria is longer. Genuine miracles are "plainly above the power or art of man to perform." Second, they are "done not in a single instance, or in a very few instances," but consistently over "a course of years together." Third, such miracles are "wrought in professed attestation to the divine mission of the persons by whom . . . they were wrought." Fourth, authentic miracles cannot be worked "in secret or before a few only" but rather in "an open public manner." Finally, "the accounts of these miracles" must be "delivered by persons who themselves saw and knew" the miracle worker and who by their conduct "gave all the marks of disinterested probity and sincerity" (pp. 39–40).

Farmer's criteria are negative and intended to identify false miracles. False miracles are "destitute of every essential character of truth" and bear "the distinguishing characters of human imposture." Thus, they are "trifling, ludicrous and absurd in their own nature" and "manifestly calculated to answer some low or worldly purpose." They are also "related to incompetent witnesses." Moreover, false miracles have "never gained credit amongst any, but those whose ignorance and superstition exposed them to the grossest delusions" (p. 73).

But Farmer's criteria can be applied, by anyone wishing to argue the point, to the Christian miracles nearly as well as to any others. Annet, to cite the most obvious example, employs these same criteria in ridiculing the Resurrection and the Virgin Birth. Thus, the usefulness of these and all similar criteria outside of the community of believers was doubtful from the outset, in spite of the great effort expended in developing them.

Thomas Stackhouse in *A Fair State of the Controversy Between Mr. Woolston and His Adversaries* (1730) develops the most elaborate set of such criteria. A true miracle is first "possible," that is, not a contradiction in terms. It is also "probable," by which he evidently means not patently absurd or self-contradictory. The true miracle is, third, not below the "majesty of God"; nor is it, fourth, "inconsistent with his character." Fifth and sixth, such miracles are "performed openly before a sufficient number of competent witnesses" and "readily, without any previous forms or ceremonies, which make them look like incantation."

Seventh, authentic miracles are worked upon "proper and important occasions."

In addition, the miracle worker and his doctrine are required to meet eight tests. The worker must first be "a man of good report" and, second, in "perfect exercise of his reason and senses." Third, he must be "constant and uniform in the messages he delivers." Fourth, his doctrine should be "consistent with the principles of true reason and natural religion" and, fifth, "consistent with right notions and worship of God." Sixth, his doctrine is "consistent with former revelations" from God. Seventh, the miracle-worker's teaching must also tend to "recover men from their ignorance, to reform them from their vices." Finally, his doctrine must "advance the general welfare of societies, as well as every man's particular happiness in this life, and in his preparation for a better." With remarkable candor, Stackhouse writes, "and now to observe a little, how all these characters meet in the blessed Jesus" (pp. 33–34).

Clever forgeries of miracles by demons posed another version of the basic problem for apologists, and this odd issue was addressed in various ways. Farmer, for instance, argues that God, in allowing miracles at all, had to grant "created spirits" the capacity to disturb the "course and order of things which he has established." The principle of miraculous disturbance, strangely enough, actually "facilitates the proof of revelation," that is, by also making genuine confirmatory miracles a possibility. This leaves only "the easy task of proving the truth of the miracles of the gospel, in order to fully establish their divine original" (Farmer, p. vi). But Conybeare argues in *The Nature, Possibility and Certainty of Miracles* that "it is inconsistent" with God's "justice, his goodness, and his wisdom" to permit miracles "to be wrought by others" unless these same support divine doctrine. "God's goodness or justice" would not allow him "to delude mankind in the most important affair" (p. 25). Thus, the problem of the false miracle worked by a demon to deceive humans is not a problem at all, for God would not allow it.

In addition to the knotty problem of pagan, Catholic, demonic, and other "false" miracles, Christian writers occasionally had to engage the issue of natural "prodigies" which encouraged superstitions. The common people were inclined to find miraculous signs all around them. For instance, on Sunday, March 6, 1715, a bright light, probably a comet, appeared in the night skies over Britain, leading many to conclude that God was speaking to the nation. Was this a sign from God? Was judgment imminent? Was the light to be treated as a modern miracle? If the light was interpreted as a miracle, then the door was opened to labelling any number of natural anomalies miraculous and attributing to them various kinds of significance.

Rev. E. Smith interrupted his planned sermon for March 13 in order to address the problem of the light, which had exercised the members of his congregation. He selected the title: *The Superstition of Omens and Prodigies with the proper Reception, and Profitable Improvement*. The light raised the question of superstitious belief. Smith notes that "the strange *Appearance* we observed last week in the Firmament of Heaven . . . has left upon the Minds of most people such surprize, Doubt, suspicious Fear, and apprehension of some great prognosticated event" that Rev. Smith was compelled to engage the issue. His goals are to ease congregational anxiety, to remove "false superstitious Impressions," and to imprint "some due Improvement of solid Benefit, as the proper Influence of it upon our Hearts and Lives" (p. 1).

The problem of superstition is caused in part by the popular appetite for strange stories. Smith thus warns his parishioners not "to listen and inquire, with an insatiable Appetite to all presages" of future events. Moreover, "a Conscience of Guilt is another reason of inflaming our imaginations with the Fear of Evil, and the Dread of some approaching Punishment." We are also naturally "prone to admire such *visions* with a Degree of Astonishment" because of "Instinct," "the rarity and Seldomness of the object," and "From our Ignorance of the Causes" (pp. 4–5, 7).

On the other hand, Smith allows we are inclined by our very natures to admire the mighty works of God. However, he argues that in the age of the Church—the period between the deaths of the original apostles and the return of Christ—Christians should not demand and do not require the kinds of signs that we read about in the Old Testament. Though the Jews demanded signs and wonders before they would believe, "we *Christians* are enlighten'd, are refin'd with another, and far better Dispensation," which is, interestingly, "the still small Voice of Reason, strengthened, confirm'd, and perfected by the one of the distincter, the last, and all perfect *Revelation*" (p. 11).

Thus, Smith argues that Christians should in virtually all cases dismiss extraordinary events as having no religious significance. Reason and revelation have supplanted miraculous prodigies and apparitions as God's means of communication with his human creatures. Does this imply that Christ himself employed miracles because he mistrusted the reason of his audience? Are healings and other Christian miracles in the present age to be rejected as false? The position Smith outlines may solve the immediate problem of a congregation agog over a comet, but it also creates the problem of instilling a suspicion toward the miraculous generally.

Smith argues that Christians ought to attend to the "positive Ordinances" taught in scripture and to "the more Manly, Serene, and unfrighting Convictions of Reason . . . *and of a sound Mind*" rather than looking to natural wonders for guidance (p. 12). In fact, "the Priviledge of *Christianity* over *Heathenism*" is freedom from "the Bondage of Superstitious Fears," the kinds of fears which finding significance in the comet only reintroduces into the congregation. But Smith's position must elevate reason over miracle in the search for a means of combating the innate human love of wonders. Smith thus runs directly into the central dilemma of the Christian case for miracles: Miracles are necessary to prove revelation because reason was too weak to reach God on its own. However, the authenticity of miracles, and even of revelation, must be tested by that same reason.

Miracles and Doctrine

Christians typically took it for granted that genuine miracles stand as indisputable proof of the divine approval of doctrine. "Whatever revelation is attended with such miracles, as I have described divine miracles to be," wrote Leng, "must necessarily be a divine revelation" (pp. 420–421). Stackhouse affirmed that miracles are the "operation of God" and thus "an authentic and indisputable testimony that the persons entrusted with such power, were certainly sent and commissioned by God" (Stackhouse 1723, p. 25).

Deists probed the Orthodox case at this juncture. Chubb, Woolston, and others asked what possible connection existed between a miracle and a religious teaching. Surely this inference from miracle to doctrine was unwarranted. Deist challenges to this crucial Orthodox assumption made necessary a defense of the miracle-doctrine connection.

Christians argued first that Christ *intended* his miracles as signs of his own divinity and of the truth of his teachings. Leland reminded his readers that "Christ performed miracles not only to convince the people, but his disciples, that he was on a divine mission" (Leland 1744, pp. 14–15). But Christians also argued for the miracle-doctrine connection on the basis of the circumstances in which Jesus operated and the public to which he appealed. Miracles were, in fact, a kind of adaptation of God's discourse to a particular audience. Chapman argued in *Eusebius* that the urgent need for the gospel to be embraced quickly and by a variety of people made rational Jesus' use of miracles to establish his doctrine. This need could not be met by appealing to the excellence of doctrine alone, for "if every article of doctrine must be scanned and discussed minutely by every person of all ranks and conditions . . . what slow advances would be made by a divine revelation among such people, and how tedious and difficult a thing must their conversion become." Because the only instant proof of God's approval of doctrine is miracle, the miracle-doctrine connection was justified by the circumstantial need for such a proof. Chapman concludes that "miracles alone" are for some people the only "satisfying evidence of a divine mission" (pp. 91, 89).

LeMoine argued that the limited rational capacities of some audiences made miracles necessary. Many people are simply not capable of a "tedious inquiry" into diverse types of evidence. "Of what use then can be an argument which supposes so nice and so tedious an inquiry, and is perplexed with so many difficulties, especially to the generality of mankind, who want either capacity or leisure to enter into it?" Thus, a type of evidence is needed which transcends the varieties of rational capacities. This evidence is, for LeMoine, "an exertion of power superior to that of all created beings," that is, a miracle (pp. 130, 135).

Christian writers argued that miracles have a "natural" capacity for convincing the mind that God endorses a doctrine. They are, after all, God's own evidence, perfectly adapted by him to the purpose of persuading his human creatures. Doddridge asked whether it is "absolutely impossible" that God should "contrive such evidence of the truth of a revelation as should be sufficient to convince every honest inquirer who is capable of exercising reason in the common affairs of life?" He finds miracles to be "proofs so unparalleled, and so striking" as to render "long deduction or philosophical arguments" unnecessary to bring conviction (Doddridge 1743, 31–32, 16). Stackhouse argued that a miracle "pierces quite through the soul, strikes all the faculties at once, and by offering itself to our bodily senses, becomes an argument for the meanest capacity to judge of" (Stackhouse 1733, p. 50).

LeMoine emphasizes the crucial point that connection between miracles and doctrine is perfectly reasonable given the "natural" impact of miracles upon reason. Of course, these must be miracles that strike observers with "the thought that the finger of God is in them." Miracles intended "for a confirmation of a particular doctrine or message from heaven" will convince "upon the spot, and without great inquiry, those who see them, the greatest part of whom are not capable of entering into a minute and critical examination of their causes, reasons and ends" (pp. 24–25). Farmer as well held that miracles make "natural impressions" on the mind (pp. iv–v).

Christian respondents to Deism's case against miracles argued that reason's limitations made miracles necessary. God delivered a revelation to humankind precisely because reason, wounded in the Fall or clouded by sin, could not discover God on its own. That revelation, however, needed confirmation that it was, in fact, of divine origin. The evidence God provided was miracles. However, many religions claimed miracles, and miracle reports continued to be common in the eighteenth century. How was a pious reader, or even an impious skeptic, to know that the Christian miracles were alone divine evidences?

Apologists met this challenge by advancing criteria to guide the faithful in discerning true from false wonders. These criteria could be quite simple and few in number, or they could grow to lengthy lists of tests for both the miracle and the miracle-worker. The problem encountered by this rhetorical effort to shore up the claim to exclusive authenticity was that reason entered the arena again as final judge of miracles. If Christians did not face a direct contradiction on the issue of reason, they were at least in an unenviable spot rhetorically.

Something similar occurred on the question of whether even authenticated miracles could confirm a doctrine as divine. Deists challenged the idea. Christians argued the inherent reasonableness of immediately inferring divine intervention from the presence of a miracle virtually without rational scrutiny. In fact, miracles were "natural proofs" of God's activity. But again, were all apparent miracles to be accepted as from God and as thus confirming doctrine? Short of recommending a mystical solution to the problem on the order of some unaccountable inner awareness, reason must become part of the evaluative equation. And a reason that judges all religious claim was difficult to distinguish from the reason of Deism. Though Orthodoxy controlled the field temporarily through a combination of talent and authority, problems in its case for miracles would, with time and before less sympathetic audiences, become more apparent.

Chapter Nine

The Religious Rhetoric
of Jacob Ilive

I have read *The Book of Jasher* twice over, and I much approve of it, as
a piece of great antiquity and curiosity, but I cannot assent that it
should be made a part of the canon of scripture. Signed *Wickliffe*
From *The Book of Jasher*

This chapter explores the work of Jacob Ilive, a major figure in English Deism who is virtually unknown to the twentieth century. Despite
his invisibility, Ilive was one of the most daring and innovative of the
Deists and threatened traditional religious and political beliefs in England during the decades of the 1730s, 1740s, and 1750s. Ilive's bold
theological speculation and his ardent advocacy of freedom of the press
mark him as an important religious radical of the mid eighteenth century with considerable influence among London's mechanics class. Moreover, Ilive's particular theological speculation appears to have outlasted
Deism itself, being represented in a variety of rather powerful religious
movements even today. The perspectives that emerge from Ilive's rhetoric
are intriguing, often challenging traditional interpretations of the Deists.

Ilive's Life and Rhetoric

Jacob Ilive was born in Bristol in 1705. His father was a printer, and,
though he followed his father's trade, he claims to have developed many
of his religious views in conversation with his mother. He moved to
London, probably in the late 1720s, and went into business as a printer
and type founder. Ilive became well-known as a printer and is mentioned in Negus's list of printers.[1] He worked for a time with Mr. Cave
on *The Gentleman's Magazine* but quit to publish his own magazine under the same title between 1736 and 1738. Throughout the 1730s Ilive
was actively involved in the printers' guild in London.

Perhaps as a result of his involvement in the guild, Ilive became a Deist. An able and engaging writer and speaker, he gave frequent public lectures in London between 1730 and 1750 advocating his own exotic religious views. In keeping with established Deistic approaches to religious debate, Ilive ridiculed Christian history and doctrine while advocating a "religion of reason." Leaders of the Church, most notably Bishop Sherlock, sought to prevent both his expression of heterodox views and his publishing of the heretical views of other Deists. For answering an anti-Deistic tract by Bishop Sherlock in 1753, Ilive was tried and convicted for blasphemy, pilloried three times, and sentenced to a term in prison. A second legal action against him was initiated in 1757 while he was in prison, perhaps for a separate offense.

Ilive continued writing against Christianity after leaving prison and was active until his death in 1763. For more than thirty years Jacob Ilive was a tireless opponent of Christianity and proponent of a strange gnostic cosmology. He was also widely known for his advocacy of prison reform, having written a detailed account of the daily life of prisoners in English jails based on his own experiences.

Ilive's preferred rhetorical form in his early career as a polemicist was the public speech delivered in a guildhall, the speech subsequently being published and sold in printers' shops. His audiences consisted of guild members as well as others with skeptical leanings. Mechanics' guilds in London at this time provided a setting in which members of different social classes could mingle to discuss political and religious issues. As the guilds often operated as secret societies on the model of the Masons, they provided an ideal network for disseminating unconventional religious views. Printers played an especially important role in circulating heterodox literature in the first half of the century.[2]

Though Ilive advocated a religion of reason, his own theological views and rhetorical tactics tended toward gnosticism. He denied the resurrection of the physical body, affirmed the eternal preexistence of human souls, maintained that earth is hell, and argued that human beings are embodied fallen angels working their way through levels of spiritual achievement. Like most Deists, Ilive held that Christianity as practiced was a corruption of early, primitive, rational religious beliefs.

The Layman's Vindication

Perhaps the most striking feature of Ilive's rhetoric is the strange speculative theology he advanced in a series of lectures in London. The groundwork for these lectures is laid in Ilive's earliest and perhaps best-known publication, *The Layman's Vindication of the Christian Religion* (1730). Ilive sets out his doctrine of the preexistence of the soul and advocates a religion of reason. But he notes that "reason, in my sense is the pure intellect, or immortal soul, inhabiting or indwelling the body of man." In fact, "reason" for Ilive literally means a fallen angel imprisoned in a human body (pp. 4, 7). Ilive's doctrine of the immortal soul is, thus, a version of the ancient gnostic view that human souls have existed from eternity as uncreated spirit beings like God.[3]

Like other Deists, Ilive couched his heterodoxy in terms ambiguous enough to invite several interpretations, some of which were potentially orthodox. For instance, he writes that "Christianity tends to the perfection of our reasons" (*Layman's Vindication*, p. 25). Does this claim means that Christianity tends toward the improvement of the individual human mind? Or does it perhaps imply that God wishes people to exercise reason? The statement could even have meant to Ilive's audience that Christianity is rationally justifiable. But none of these meanings is what Ilive intended by the statement. His meaning is that Christianity assists the progress of the immortal soul (the fallen angelic being, "reason, in my sense") back to the divine state it once enjoyed. This, to Ilive, is "rational" progress: advancement through celestial levels to a state of reclaimed divinity.

Ilive's *Layman's Vindication* also sets out his views on creation, human nature, and the propagation and destiny of the human race. But another of Ilive's major themes is also tentatively advanced in *Layman's Vindication*, one that has received little attention as a characteristic of a Deism that publicly professed religious tolerance. Ilive, much like Annet, advanced a scathing criticism of Moses and the mosaic tradition that borders at points on anti-Semitism. Ilive calls in question the authenticity of the Pentateuch and cites a number of ancient authors who condemn the moral character of the Hebrews (p. 62ff.). Harsh treatment of the Jews was also a component of his later addresses to guild members.

The Joyner's Hall Oration: Ilive's Gnosticism

Ilive's *Oration Spoke at Joyner's Hall* was delivered in London on September 24, 1733. The oration, we learn from Ilive, was originally presented as a condition of the will of his mother, Jane Ilive, who apparently shared his fascination with exotic theology. He reveals in the preface to the published speech that he read his theological theories to his mother before going public with them, acknowledging a great debt to her for influencing his theological thought.

The *Oration Spoke at Joyner's Hall* is the clearest presentation of Ilive's gnosticism. Life on earth is merely part of a vast celestial scheme of spiritual and corporeal life on numerous other planets. Ilive founds this theory on Jesus' statement, "In my Father's house are many mansions," which Ilive takes as referring to other planets that human beings will eventually inhabit and rule, many of which are presently inhabited. Our own earth, "that Globe we now inhabit," is for Ilive, "Hell, i.e. the Place inferior to Heaven." Ilive's use of the term "inferior" suggests lower rank in the celestial hierarchy of habitable domains rather than a place of torment and punishment.

Earth, or Hell, was created for a very specific purpose, one strikingly at odds with the biblical account. Earth "was made for the reception of the Rebellious Angels," and thus "no new Order of Beings was created on Purpose to people it." Human beings are not special creations in God's image but rather are embodiments of eternally preexistent angelic souls. "The fallen Angels are in Prison, that is, embodied, so that Man is an apostate Angel and a Body" (p. 59).

Ilive's account closely parallels second- and third-century gnostic accounts of the demonization of the world. Pheme Perkins writes that "apocalyptic speculation within Gnosticism focuses on cosmological origins, the structure of the heavenly world, and the collapse of the world dominated by the evil angels." Ilive thus serves as a theological link between Christian and heretical writers of the early Christian period and later gnostic religions such as Mormonism, Theosophy, and Rosicrucianism. Ilive asserts, somewhat hopefully perhaps, that it is "undeniably and indisputably plain . . . that we are the very fallen Angels cloathed in Flesh, and that the Place we now inhabit, is Hell, and no other place" (pp. 40, 60).

This and related notions were not unknown to other Deists and may even have been embraced by some. In his "Letter to R. B." Charles Gildon writes of "the *Pythagoreans* and *Chaldeans*," who believed that human souls "were created in Heaven, and thence transmitted to the Bodies for punishment" and that as a result "we are Devils" (quoted in Berman 1983, p. 381). Charles Blount in his *Anima Mundi* of 1678 alludes to the gnostic theory that "the fall of those evil Angels" who assisted Lucifer in his rebellion "occasioned our Corporeal Creation." That is, human

bodies were created as places for "those wicked Spirits" to be imprisoned, the spirits thus becoming the humans' "souls." Demons were
placed in human bodies on earth "for expiating their guilt," and "our
Sublunary Orb" became "the only Hell" (pp. 63–64). Thus, there was in
Deism a long familiarity with early gnostic theories. Few besides Ilive
were willing publicly to announce adherence to such views, but this fact
does not by itself demonstrate that adherence was limited. Gnostic views
are, by definition, held in secret.

There is, as one might suspect, more to know about Ilive's narrative
account of the origins of the human race. As that story goes, Jesus, who
is not equal to the Father in divinity, was engaged in a great struggle
with Lucifer for control of Heaven. Lucifer lost this struggle, in which
he was joined by a host of angels. Lucifer and his evil angels were expelled from Heaven and sent to a place prepared less for their punishment than their reformation. That place, as it turns out, was earth. In
this new terrestrial place, the rebellious angels needed physical bodies
to survive, which God the Father created for them. The bodies created
are, in fact, our own bodies. As embodied fallen angels, all of the human
inhabitants of earth are working their way back to heavenly stature.
Again, this evolutionary spiritualism is fundamentally gnostic.[4]

Human bodies were created as "certain little Places of Confinement
for the reception of apostate Angels." God created human bodies as part
of a plan for "bringing back again the rebellious and apostate angels"
(Ilive, pp. 22–23, 25). Ilive believed that such a view solved a host of
knotty theological problems inherent to the Genesis account of creation.

This hypothesis of the Fallen Angels taking Flesh, being adopted as
truth, God in a literal Sense finished the Creation in six Days, and it is
more reasonable to believe that the fallen Angels are this Stock of
Souls, which they imagine to be created in that Period, than that such
a Number of new created Souls should then be made to actuate Bodies
not yet in Being, not otherwise than by the laws of procreation. (p. 27)

On Ilive's view, then, humans fell from the perfection of "heavenly
beings." Hell is less a place of punishment than of reformation, while
other planets are "Celestial Mansions" which human beings who make
adequate spiritual progress will eventually inhabit and dominate. Moreover, there are levels to the celestial order of things, and great advancement will be rewarded with assignment to more prominent planets.[5]

Derham's Astro-Theology

Ilive argued, then, that humans are preexistent spirit beings and that their destiny involves inhabiting and ruling other planets. Some of these ideas were derived from the work of William Derham, who published in 1715 a work entitled *Astro-Theology*. Derham was already famous for a remarkable book published in 1696 entitled *The Artificial Clockmaker*, in which he explained in lay terms how clocks are manufactured and calibrated so as to keep accurate time. But this book, like *Astro-Theology*, had a more important point to make. Derham implies that the universe itself is constructed like a gigantic mechanical device. The solar system is described in clockwork terms, though Derham does not go so far as to attribute such a design to God. He does, however, note that ancient authorities such as Cicero had posited a spirit moving the mechanisms of the universe. Such pantheism was common among Deists, particularly those influenced by John Toland, whose *Christianity Not Mysterious* appeared the same year as Derham's *Artificial Clockmaker* and whose *Pantheisticon* was published only a few years later in 1702. In *Astro-Theology*, which Ilive recommends enthusiastically to his readers, Derham extends the Copernican view regarding our own solar system into a theory that many other stars also are attended by planets. Using an enormous telescope developed by Huygen, which is reputed to have been 126 feet long, Derham claimed to have observed planets orbiting other stars. Thus, the universe is not made up only of "fix'd stars" but almost certainly contains innumerable planets. What is the purpose of so many planets if not that they should be inhabited like earth:

> Having thus represented the State of the *Universe* according to the *New System* of it, the usual Question is, what is the use of so many Planets as we see about the Sun, and so many as are imagined to be about the Fix'd Stars? To which the answer is, that they are *Worlds*, or places of *Habitation*, which is concluded from their being *habitable*, and well provided for habitation. (p. xlix)

Of course, Derham cannot have known that the planets he "observed" beyond our solar system were, in fact, planets, and he certainly cannot have known that these planets were habitable. He claims to have observed atmospheres surrounding the newly discovered planets, as well as physical features such as mountains, valleys, and seas. Some reports from astronomers, Derham claims, suggest that they have seen human-like beings moving about on these planets.

This theory of habitable planets fit exactly with Ilive's theological contentions. Derham writes that the new planets he has seen are "opaque Bodies as our Earth is, consisting in all probability of Land and Water, Hills and valleys, having atmosphere about them, and being enlightened, warmed and influenced by the Sun, whose yearly visits they receive as Seasons, and frequent Returns for days and nights" (p. 1). But announcing his "observations" to the public was not Derham's principal purpose in this work. His book is entitled *Astro-Theology*, and he, like Ilive, finds the planets to have theological significance. It is likely that some planets, comets, and stars are, like earth, hells. There is much more going on in the universe than we can know from our puny planet, which, Derham points out, is insignificant on a cosmic scale (pp. 218, 220).

The earth is not the center of the solar system and certainly is not the center of the universe. The universe is vast and populated, and human beings will one day explore and inhabit other worlds. Such notions opened up numerous possibilities for theological speculation. Who were the inhabitants of other planets? What functions were fulfilled by these other worlds? Were they places of torment or perhaps unimaginable paradises awaiting inhabitants? Could they be worlds which humans were someday destined to rule? Ilive did not shrink back from using Derham's "observations" as a starting point for developing his own fantastic theological schemes.

A Dialogue

The *Oration at Joyner's Hall* was sufficiently controversial to warrant rapid response from representatives of the Church and an immediate defense of its theology by Ilive. In *A Dialogue Between A Doctor of the Church of England and Mr. Jacob Ilive Upon the Subject of the Oration spoke at Joyner's-Hall,* Ilive acknowledges, with some understatement, that he has been criticized for advancing *"Heterodox Notions."* He welcomes "the Method of convincing me with Arguments" which is "so worthy of the Christian name," a reference to the Church's position on proper religious discourse. Argument is "the likeliest method to bring me to a publick Recantation" (p. 4). The *Dialogue* is flawed *as* dialogue in that the Doctor representing the Church consistently capitulates too quickly to Ilive's arguments.

The Church initially only threatened Ilive with prosecution, and the Doctor maintains that legal action is among the "proper Remedies" for serious cases of religious offense, "lest the Cause of Religion should suffer in the minds of the vulgar." The term "vulgar" had particular potency for many of Ilive's readers, who were themselves printers, masons, joyners, and chandlers. Ilive asks for a rhetorical battle, affirming that "I hope there are Men, who, without the Help of the secular Power, are capable of refuting my Notions, and so fully expose me to the Censure of the World." Nevertheless, the Doctor asks Ilive to recant of his *Oration* and of his theology, "for to be plain with you . . . the Doctrines contained in it are contrary to Truth, subversive of Christianity, destructive of Morality, reflective on the Clergy, and abusive of the *Mosaic* institution" (p. 4).

Ilive responds that morality is "destroyed already." Moreover, it is the great of society, including the clergy, who contribute to the decline of public morals:

What is it which corrupts the Morals of All? Is it not Balls, Plays, Masquerades, Operas, Ballads, Books of Love Intrigue, Fables, Histories of Thefts, Evil Conversation and bad Company, &c. the bad Examples of Great Men and the wicked lives of too many of our clergy, who by their actions declare, that they do not believe those grand Truths it is their Duty to teach? (pp. 15–16)

The bad example provided by society's leaders is "destructive of Morality" and is one of the principal "Causes of the Sinfulness of our Age; the Source of Infidelity, Atheism, Scepticism, and open Prophaneness." In addition, religious differences, superstitious practices, and intolerance all originated with "the Priests of all Ages and Nations [who] have by Art established Doctrines of their own Invention" (p. 22). The clergy have deceived by their "false Glosses of sacred Writ," including especially their invention of eternal punishment and other "*scarecrow Doctrines*" (p. 22).

Ilive's assault on "priestcraft" includes a harsh treatment of Moses, the father of all priestly deception. The good Doctor—the Church's defender—concedes, surprisingly, that Moses was a murderer, but the cleric demurs, "Though I cannot think it prudent to expose so great a Man" (p. 23). Ilive exploits this opening to advance his theories regarding Moses' crimes, deceptions, and errors. For instance, Jethro, his father-in-law, duped Moses with the trick of the burning bush. "But who inspired *Moses* at this time? *Jethro.* It was he that inchanted the Bush, and spoke out of it." This is "proved" by the fact that the voice told Moses to take his shoes off, Jethro knowing that Moses would walk no closer to the bush unshod, for there were many stones and thorns on the ground. Thus Jethro's identity could be concealed. To this account the Doctor responds with apparent understatement, "You have an odd way of representing Scripture" (pp. 24–26).

Moses, it turns out, learned deception from Jethro and magic from the sorcerers of Egypt. The Israelites' escape from Egypt is explained on this premise:

> Moses, wiser than the young King [Pharaoh], leads him a dance to-wards the Red Sea, where taking Advantage of the Reflux of the Wa-ters, attended with a strong easterly Wind, at stated times, which made a Path through this Part of the Sea, marches his [Moses'] Army through, Pharaoh with his Host mistaking the Time of the Flux of the Waters, and the Ceasing of the Wind, Marching in after them was drowned. (p. 27)

Moreover, Moses tricked the Israelite women into stealing from the Egyptian women, in part to precipitate a crisis in the face of which the Jews would be forced to leave Egypt. Ilive asks, in a manner which imitates Christian criteria for separating true from false miracles, "Why should those things, which cannot have God as their Author be represented to Us as his Acts?" Moses' alleged miracles were "the Effect of Knowledge *Moses* had gained among the Magi of Egypt." Even the great plagues were "wrought by Moses's Knowledge in the Magick Art" (pp. 26, 28). Blount also had claimed that Moses was "skill'd in all the *Aegyptian* Learning" (Blount 1678, p. 52).

But Ilive saves perhaps his most alarming allegation about Moses for last: He plotted the murder of all of the first-born children of the Egyptians and the theft of much Egyptian property to bring about the final departure of the Israelites who had developed a mighty army under the command of Caleb. "This Barbarity, the killing of the First-born of *Egypt*, gave Occasion to their final and total Departure. Thus they, by Murder and Theft, procured their Freedom." The Jews are thus not the chosen people of God but rather a murderous band of renegades under the leadership of the vicious general Caleb and the cunning sorcerer Moses. Moses and his men could be found that fateful night "killing the harmless babies while they sleep." Ilive suggests that a corrected version of Exodus "should read thus: And *Moses* said, About Midnight will I go out into the Midst of *Egypt,* and all the first-born in *Egypt* shall die. And the people smote all the First-born" (p. 32). The anti-Semitic cast of Ilive's argument was characteristic of much Deist rhetoric and may have influenced public attitudes toward Jews, who constituted a very small minority of the British population in the 1730s and 1740s.

God was not behind such unthinkable deeds. "What I contend for is this: that God was not the Author of these Murders and Magicks, which *Moses* attributed to him" (p. 33). All such machinations were Moses' own ideas, and he lied to the Israelites about their divine origins. In addition to destroying the character of Moses, Ilive intends to show that God does not contend for one people above others. Thus, the whole history of the Jews as a chosen people is a lie, and the Jewish religion a grievous oppression. Indeed, Ilive sums up by asserting that "the *Jewish* Religion," because it was of Mosaic origin, "was a grevious Yoke" (p. 34).

Moses, like other despots, some alive in Ilive's own day, found religion a useful tool in controlling the unthinking masses. The notion of a priesthood was especially helpful in this regard, as were mysteries, miracles, oracles, and powers. "If Gods, Oracles, Demons, had not been invented, there would never have been any Occasion, or use, for Priests." The same is true of the laws for which Moses is so famous. These laws, it turns out, were invented by Aaron and Jethro and foisted as a hoax on the people with smoke and mirrors. "This Lord might be *Jethro* or *Aaron.* Here they contrive the Wonder, and having established the Method of it, Moses came and called for the Elders of the People, and told them all the Words which the Lord [Jethro] commanded him." Moses, by means of the magic he had learned from the Egyptians, produced the smoke, thunder, and lightning that accompanied the giving of the law. The Doctor responds: "I am surprised you should attribute these Wonders to the *Black Art.*" Ilive answers, "Doctor, Pray, is it not in the power of Magicians to raise Artificial Storms and Tempests, Thunderings and Lightnings?" The Doctor answers meekly, "Yes." Ilive asks, "Did Moses understand Magick?" "He did." Thus ends the argument (pp. 44–45).

Oration at Trinity Hall

In another major address, the *Oration Spoke at Trinity Hall* on Monday, January 9, 1738, Ilive turned his sights on Christian doctrines that, he argued, had "through time, ignorance and design, denigrated so far from their original, that they have lost their primitive intention" (p. 7).[6] For instance, the apostle Paul had concocted the doctrine of the resurrection of the physical body of the believer in order to answer a pressing problem that had developed in the early church:

> The apostle St. *Paul,* having constantly insisted on Christ's immediate appearance in his arguments to the people to embrace Christianity, and it not coming to pass directly as he expected, flies to the invention of a new doctrine to support his cause. This was the doctrine of the resurrection of the same body. (p. 9)

Paul was a deceiver of the early church and was himself responsible for much of the corruption of pure religious doctrine. Ilive argued that Paul, like Moses, was of questionable character, willing to concoct wild doctrines to solve difficult problems. But this knife cuts both ways, for if the Pauline epistles already reflect a corrupted Christianity, what hope is there of finding earlier, uncorrupted sources in order to retrieve the genuine faith? In fact, Ilive intended to cast doubt on the whole body of biblical revelation and thus to clear the way for introducing "better" sources of truth.

So as not to be accused of outright heresy, Ilive quickly affirms that Christ himself *did* rise physically. This is likely a case of the "prudential lying" so common in Deistic tracts, however, for there is nothing in Ilive's theory that would allow for one to believe that Christ rose physically. Nevertheless, Ilive asserts that "There is certainly not a greater truth in the Christian Theology, than that our Lord did, after his crucifixion, within three days, assume his own body, the same numerical body that was wounded on the cross" (p. 15). Of course, this passage is ambiguous. What does it mean that Christ "assumed" his "numerical body"? Ilive's general argument against physical resurrection is founded on Paul's claim that "flesh and blood cannot inherit the Kingdom of heaven" (p. 14). This would apply equally to Christ's body as to anyone else's.

The Book of Jasher

In 1751 Ilive published perhaps the most peculiar and daring of all the works of Deism, *The Book of Jasher.* Ilive announced mysteriously that he soon would reveal a documentary discovery that would shake Christendom. The work he actually advanced was dismissed instantly by scholars as a forgery and is catalogued as such by the British Library.

Nevertheless, *The Book of Jasher* maintained a readership for most of a century, was republished in Bristol in 1829 with a solid recommendation from a Reverend C. D. Bond, and is still published and sold today by the Rosicrucians.

The Book of Jasher was purported to have been discovered and translated in the ninth century by St. Alcuin of England while on a pilgrimage to the Holy Land. It is, in fact, a highly inventive forgery that endorses Ilive's theology through an "uncorrupted" retelling of stories from Genesis. Ilive concocts an introductory narrative, attributed to Alcuin, which tells the history of the book's discovery and the intrigues associated with gaining permission to view and then to translate it. A lengthy commentary ascribed to ancient rabbinic writers also accompanies the text. *The Book of Jasher* relates the early history of the human race and of Israel. It is several times suggested by various commentators cited in the text that *Jasher* deserves to have been included in the canon of scripture but was excised by jealous priests whose positions were threatened by its pure historical accounts that condemned the priesthood.

The title of the original publication tells some of the story of the work: *The Book of Jasher with Testimonies and Notes explanatory of the Text Translated into English from the Hebrew by Alcuin of Britain, who went on a Pilgrimage into the Holy Land.* The text opens with a letter to an unnamed Earl about how the nobleman who is now making the book public found it by accident as it was being discarded along with many other old texts after an estate auction in the north of England. "Your Lordship's remark I must not here omit," writes the Nobleman, "that it was your opinion, *The Book of Jasher* ought to have been printed in the Bible before that of Joshua" (preface). Ilive even invents a note from John Wycliffe that reads: "I have read *The Book of Jasher* twice over, and I much approve of it, as a piece of great antiquity and curiosity, but I cannot assent that it should be made a part of the canon of scripture. Signed *Wickliffe*" (preface).

Though the great translator is alleged to have denied *Jasher* a place in the canon, Wycliffe nevertheless attests its authenticity and antiquity. A long introduction by Alcuin himself explains to the reader how he found the book. Ilive is a good storyteller with a sufficient command of the details of monastic life in the early middle ages to make his accounts plausible. Alcuin's narrative relates how an ancient sage of the Far East told Alcuin and his fellow travelers of a manuscript of *The Book of Jasher* "twice mentioned in the *Holy Bible*" (p. iv). Alcuin follows his instinct that there is something to the story. Repeated inquiries eventually bring him to the city of Ganza in Palestine, where the book is fabled to be kept in an ancient civic library. Alcuin and his friends stay in Ganza three years convincing, that is bribing, city officials to let them see and translate the ancient scroll.

Ilive adds captivating details to the story that enhance both its intrigue and credibility. Of the scroll itself he, or rather Alcuin, writes:

> *The Book of Jasher* is a great scroll, in width two feet three inches, and in length about nine foot. It is written in large characters, and exceeding beautiful. The paper on which it is wrote is for thickness the eight of an inch. To the touch it seems as soft as velvet, and to the eye as white as snow. (p. 5)

Jasher, the book's author, is reputedly a son of "Caleb who was general of the Hebrews, whilst Moses was with Jethro in Midian." Jasher, we are told, was an honest man, and his name confirms the point—it means "upright." Translating the scroll took Alcuin a year, and we even get to see Alcuin's notes about the variable translations possible of several troublesome Hebrew words. After completing the translation, Alcuin set out for England, though he stopped briefly in Rome on his return to inform the ninety-five-year-old pope of the historic discovery. When the pope heard the good news, he "then cried out"—somewhat cryptically— "I have lived to see the days of forgetfulness" (p. vi).

Alcuin's English "translation" is presented to the reader with chapter and verse divisions. This is a telling anachronism, for though it makes *Jasher* look like pages from the 1611 Authorized Version of the Bible, the actual verse and chapter breaks in the Bible were not inserted until more than two centuries after Alcuin's death. Moreover, the English of Ilive's *Jasher* imitates the early-seventeenth-century idiom of the Authorized Version rather than the ninth-century English of Alcuin.

Chapter 1 of *The Book of Jasher*, predictably, describes the creation of the earth, or, rather, its re-creation. We read, "So that the face of nature was formed a second time" (1:5). This claim, like others in the text, supports Ilive's view, articulated twenty years earlier in guildhall addresses, that the earth was created out of a protomatter as a place where fallen angels were sent for a period of reformation. The earth was not, therefore, a special creation for the habitation of another special creation— human beings.

Ilive employs narrative argument throughout the text, retelling biblical stories to support his own theological hypotheses and the Deist concept of an original and universal religion of reason. Thus there is no human fall into sin in Ilive's account of Adam and Eve. In fact, curiously, there is no mention of Eve in the creation account at all, though she appears later in the text. Then whence other human beings? Ilive puts into the mouth of one of his commentators this remarkable gloss on the creation story: "In process of time, the man [Adam] conceived, and he brought forth Cain" (p. 2).

Adam practiced a pure religion of reason. This original religion, according to a Deist theory that lacked documentary support until Ilive wrote *The Book of Jasher*, was later corrupted by priests, the first of whom was a son of Seth. A commentator explains how this transition from pure religion to superstition occurred:

> When Adam was dead, the days of whose life were nine hundred and thirty years. During all which time, the worship of the Creator, among the obedient sons of Adam, was spiritual and intellectual. After this period, the desponding son of Seth, since named Enos, invented the worship of the body. Hence arose the convention of the seventh day, the worshipping in groves, the use of symbols and of teraphim. (p. 3)

Another interesting contention concerns the relationship between Adam and Eve. As already noted, Adam bore Cain, though Eve may have born later children. Thus, Adam and Eve were biological equals. Further evidence of the equality of the first couple—and of their sinlessness—is set out in a passage which stands in stark contrast to the stories of Eve's creation from Adam's body, her temptation by the serpent, the couple's expulsion from the garden, and the divinely ordained asymmetrical relationship between the two discussed in Genesis:

> Adam was perfect in his generation, compleat in his stature; of the most extensive knowledge, walking uprightly, and eschewing evil. Eve was perfect in her generation, amiable, and lovely to look unto; of modest behaviour, of consumate chastity; beautiful, walking uprightly, and hating iniquity. Between these two there was not superiority, they were both made at one time, and they both had the same powers of knowledge. (p. 3)

Other Deists, notably Annet, also affirmed the essential equality of the sexes, but only Ilive attempted to build such a view into the creation story itself. The apostle Paul had appealed to the story of creation in Genesis to argue for the fundamentally different roles and responsibilities of men and women in the church.

Several other important stories are strategically altered to make the Deist case. Human history is not a tragic narrative of sin and treachery; such notions developed from stories corrupted in transmission over the centuries. For instance, Cain never murdered his brother Abel. Rather, Cain slew Abel's beast, and the story was related with the crucial error that one brother had killed the other. "From this act of Cain slaying the beast of Abel, it seemeth, arose that story recorded in the book of Moses, that Cain slew Abel" (p. 1). But if this fact was known to the ancients, why did they not correct the terribly erroneous story in Genesis? Noah is reported to have invented "a floating cave, a vehicle, a house to remain upon the surface of the waters" (p. 3). From this stirring account of human inventiveness, the Jews, whose chief talent seems to have been to get their own history wrong, derived the famous story of the deluge and the ark. Later, one of Noah's sons, displaying a genetic predisposition to nautical achievement, invented the sail, thus allowing the dissemination of human beings around the globe.

These stories of Noah and his offspring are important for several reasons, not the least of which is their power to help explain how corrupted versions of the original religion of Adam were spread throughout the ancient world. In fact, defending the ancient religion of reason and explaining the origin of revealed religions are the chief purposes of *The Book of Jasher.*

The rhetorical strategy of writing scripture anew provided Ilive the opportunity of answering a variety of questions and resolving numerous problems in the biblical accounts. For example, the story of Abraham being instructed by God to sacrifice his son Isaac has puzzled believers and skeptics alike for centuries. How could God make such a capricious and dangerous request of Abraham, particularly given the pain Abraham and Sarah had endured before the birth of Isaac? The Deists held that such stories encouraged superstition and led zealots to justify their own vicious motives by an appeal to God's.

In Ilive's retelling of the story, however, many of the difficulties of the original account are obviated. Abraham believes that he has been told by God to sacrifice his son. Returning home to relate the strange experience to his wife, Abraham is set straight by Sarah, who, in good Deistic fashion, employs reason alone to refute weak-minded delusion:

And Abraham removed from the plains of Mamre: and went and
dwelt between Kadesh and Shur. And Abraham was stricken in years:
and his mind failed him. And when Isaac was twenty-five years old,
Abraham heard a voice, saying: Take thy son, and slay him, and offer
him up a burnt offering in the land, wherein he was born. And Sarah
spake unto Abraham and said, the holy voice hath not so spoken: for
remember thou the words of that voice which said unto thee, I will
make thee a great nation. And Abraham repented of the evil he proposed to do unto his son, his only son, Isaac. (3:17–21)

In the notes to chapter 3 of *The Book of Jasher*, the commentator explains
regarding the story:

Tradition saith, that the Patriarch Abraham heard a voice as from
heaven, commanding him to slay his son Isaac, as he was in the field
alone by himself. Abraham returns to his wife Sarah disconsolate.
Sarah enquires the cause, and Abraham tells her, that a voice from
Heaven had said unto him, Take thy son, and slay him, and offer him
up a burnt-offering in the land wherein he was born. Upon this, Sarah, who was a woman of great wisdom and discernment expostu-
lated with Abraham, and convinced him that it could not be the voice
of God; and her argument was very conclusive: If the holy voice has
said, Of thee I will make a great nation, the holy voice cannot say
this, because if thou slayest thy son, how can the former be fulfilled?
(pp. 3–4)

Thus, simple logic triumphs over superstition, reason supersedes
revelation, and, interestingly, a woman corrects an addle-brained patriarch.

The notes in the commentary are of greater importance than the text
of *The Book of Jasher* because they clarify the intent of the sometimes
obscure text. These notes or commentaries are attributed to various rabbis and prophets of antiquity—Phineas, Othniel, Jazer, Tobias, and
Zadock—as well as to a lost rabbinical work entitled *Hur out of the Book
of Aaron*. Ilive accomplishes two rhetorical tasks by attributing the notes
to these sources. First, he makes Deist theology a continuation of an
ancient religious tradition which preceded Christianity and which was
the original, rational religion. Second, Ilive lends antique credibility to
the explanations of the text by making them the studied opinions of

religious experts from antiquity. Each of the rabbinical sources mentioned contributes his own brief "testimony" to endorse *The Book of Jasher*. However, one wonders how it was possible that *Jasher* survived well into the rabbinical era in direct contradiction to the Pentateuch without having raised concerns among the rabbis who apparently are never bothered by the inconsistencies between the two. It is also curious that one group of rabbis, those cited by Ilive, should escape the charge of priestcraft which was so freely levelled at other members of the rabbinate and pastorate. Perhaps the entire work is to be read as ironic imitation of the practice of writing religious documents to support one's theology. Thus, one set of "rabbis" is set to work to counteract a rival set. But such a reading undermines the apparently serious effort to present documentary proof for Deist premises.

The Book of Jasher addresses another important item on the Deist agenda—miracles. Miraculous events are explained naturalistically in *The Book of Jasher*. In Genesis, for example, Abraham has been told that he will be the "Father of many nations" and that his descendants will be "as the sands of the sea shore for number, and as the stars of the heavens." However, Abraham lives to an advanced age without an heir by his wife Sarah, who herself had lived well beyond childbearing age. "It had ceased to be with her," the Bible relates, "after the manner of women." Thus, any child born of these two people would involve a miracle, and Isaac's birth is, indeed, miraculous on the biblical account.

The Book of Jasher provides the reader a rather different telling of this story, one which explains much not only about how miracle stories originate but also about how strange tribal customs gain acceptance as divinely ordained religious practices. Ilive, then, advances a rudimentary psychology of religion. In *The Book of Jasher* we read this account:

> Now it came to pass: That Sarah Abraham's wife had not brought forth her first born. And Abraham complained, and said; Unto me thou has not given an heir: lo! The stranger born in my house shall rule after me. And Abraham heard a voice saying unto him, Circumcise the flesh of thy foreskin: for therefore art thou barren. And Abraham did so: and he went unto Sarah, and she conceived, and bore a son, and he called his name Isaac (note: the laugh). And Abraham was ninety and nine years old: when he circumcised the flesh of his foreskin. (3:12–16)

In this passage Ilive accomplishes several strategic purposes. He eliminates the miracle from the conception of Isaac and provides a remarkable but perfectly natural explanation of the event, save for the intervention of God himself into the problem's solution by a timely surgical instruction. Second, Ilive eliminates the possibility that God could have instructed Abraham to have all of his people circumcised, a barbaric and unreasonable command unfitting for a reasonable God. Third, in the seventeenth chapter of Genesis, God tells Abraham:

> This is my covenant, which you shall keep, between me and you and your descendants after you: Every male among you shall be circumcised. You shall be circumcised in the flesh of your foreskins, and it shall be a sign of the covenant between me and you. (17:11–12)

Thus, by eliminating circumcision as a special mark signifying a unique covenant between one nation and God, Ilive denies to the Jews the status of God's chosen people. This strategic maneuver also makes the crucial point that no one group of people could have special status before a rational God.

The Deists sought alternative explanations not only of religious developments but of social evolution as well. Concepts such as private property had developed alongside the corrupted forms of worship as priests and other deceivers set about to shape a world to benefit their own self-interest. Ilive builds into his narrative in *Jasher* an account of private ownership, human enmity, and religious intolerance. At the time of an ancient figure named Peleg, "it came to pass, that men first began to inclose lands." Peleg thus "enacted the laws of property," which gave the land rights to a limited set of families. Peleg became the "arbitrator" over land disputes, and "lands were given by him for cultivation." Peleg gathered to himself great power, and "infringers hence became culpable of his displeasure." As a result, the evils of "punishments, riches, pride, government, poverty, idleness, rebellion ensued."

Such enmity led to the first fragmenting of the great community of what Ilive calls "people friends," as their "different interests destroyed union" and "avarice arose." Human history was now set on its course of difference and strife:

> One from distance of place became strangers enemies to the other, contests and local vices sprung up. Leaders, rulers, teachers arose, new words and ideas took place, so that in process of time people

who understood one another heretofore could not converse; hence misunderstandings, misrepresentations, enmities, evil-speaking, war, &c. (p. 2)

Ilive, like other Deists, suffered official repression and was imprisoned for publishing his views. He laid the blame for such intolerance at the feet of the clerical and governmental hierarchies. In this passage about the ruler Peleg, Ilive maintains that private property, particularly in its capacity to allow one or a few people to write social rules, was the root of many human divisions. Religious intolerance and regional chauvinism were inextricably linked, and each was rooted in private ownership of lands and the boundary-making that such ownership necessitated. Thus, Ilive tacitly endorses a form of communism by denying the legitimacy of private property.

Ilive's reconstruction of biblical history may strike contemporary readers as anti-Semitic at some junctures. Such sentiments are thinly veiled in the story of Abraham as a confused old man who mistakenly thinks he hears voices telling him to sacrifice his only son. On the basis of this and related stories, according to *Jasher*, rests the entire history of the Jewish people who departed from the pristine religion of their earliest human ancestors.

But the account of Moses' leadership of the Jews makes Ilive's and the Deists' position clearer. Ilive's Moses is a cunning and murderous political leader who, as has been suggested, learned the secrets of both magic and political intrigue in the courts of the Pharaohs. In 5:14 of *The Book of Jasher*, Jasher records that "the child Moses grew and increased in stature: and was learned in all the magic of the Egyptians." This claim is crucial to explaining Moses' miracles. Ilive also alleges that Moses burned blasphemers and their families and committed various heinous atrocities against the Egyptians. Moses and the Jews are political opportunists who stop at nothing to accomplish their designs, including faking miracles, murdering innocent and defenseless people, and lying about messages from God.

Ilive closes *The Book of Jasher* with an imitation of the commandment contained in Revelation that the book must not be altered. "And Jasher said, this book which I have written, Ye shall neither add to nor diminish from: it is thine and thy sons to possess for ever" (p. xxxvii). The book concludes with various testimonies from priests and rabbis endorsing both Jasher and his book. These testimonials are ironic, for Ilive as a Deist would have rejected the testimony of both priests and rabbis as unreliable.

Later Publication of *Jasher*

In 1829 a reissue of *The Book of Jasher* was published in Bristol, edited by a Reverend C. D. Bond. *Jasher,* then, had maintained some kind of readership and influence for most of a century. Bond prefaces the work by commending its authenticity and its helpfulness to the spiritual seeker:

> Since 1751 the manuscript has been preserved with very great care, by a gentleman who lived to a very advanced age. On the event of his death, a friend to whom he had presented it, gave it to the present Editor, who, conceiving that so valuable a piece of antiquity should not be lost to men of literature and biblical students, has committed it to the press, not doubting but that the attention of the learned will be attracted to so singular a volume. (preface)

Bond notes that as editor he "cannot assert any thing from his own knowledge, beyond Alcuin's account, but," he adds, "*that* carries with it such an air of probability and truth, that he does not doubt its authenticity." Bond asserts that "some Account of this volume may be found in Alcuin's works, published in one volume, fol. in the year 1600 in Paris." But, he has apparently never seen this reference in Alcuin. "Should any gentleman possess a transcript of it, the Editor will be greatly obliged by any communication made to him, through the medium of the printer" (preface).

There are only two ways of explaining the reappearance and enthusiastic promotion of *The Book of Jasher* in the early nineteenth century. The first is that Bond was actually taken in by the work and, out of sincere concern for the advancement of theological thought, had it published and sold with the addition of some of his own notes. Unless Bond was a complete literary and theological naif, this possibility must be rejected.

The second explanation is more likely. Bond was, like Ilive and the Deists, a spiritual dabbler and adventurer who had an interest in speculative and exotic theological accounts. Bond tinkered with and augmented the notes to the original *Jasher,* which is important as Ilive tried to pass these off as also part of the original scroll. Bond may have been part of a secret religious movement which found in Jasher confirmation of its views.

Or perhaps each of these two hypotheses has something to offer. Bond may have willingly overlooked elements in the book that would raise the suspicion of any critical reader and hoped for some element of authenticity in *Jasher*. The book may have both intrigued him and helped him to propagate a set of heterodox views which were gaining some adherents both in England and America. It is interesting that Bond's reissue of *Jasher* in 1829 corresponds closely to the rise of Joseph Smith and the Mormons in America. The *Book of Mormon* was published in 1830, and there are numerous parallels between the cosmology of Smith and that of Ilive and Bond.

Bond argues for *Jasher* on the basis of "External and historical" as well as "internal proofs of its originality." But his evidences turn out to be uncritical acceptances of Ilive's original claims. Such "proofs" just as often work against the case for authenticity as for it. For instance, Bond notes as an historical proof that the *Book of Jasher* is mentioned twice in the Old Testament, in II Samuel 1:18 and in Joshua 10:13. But these references create two problems for *Jasher*'s authenticity. First, the *Book of Jasher* mentioned in the Bible is apparently a book of martial verse, while Ilive's work is an historical account. Second, Ilive's *Book of Jasher* contradicts much of the Pentateuch and so cannot have been a work revered by the authors of Joshua and II Samuel, who take the Pentateuch as historically accurate. Had these writers been aware of Ilive's work, they would certainly have rejected it out of hand as blasphemous and heretical.

Bond also takes some very peculiar "facts" as "proof" of *Jasher*'s authenticity. For instance, Bond somehow estimates the value of the gold with which Alcuin bribed the officials in Ganza at 500 pounds and adds, "which, at this distance of time, would have amounted to four times that sum." This great sum of money spent in acquiring a translation of *Jasher* Bond takes as proof of the book's authenticity. Bond also affirms at one point that "nothing can be produced to invalidate this authentic statement [regarding *Jasher*'s historicity], and, consequently, it merits our credence." This argument from ignorance, of course, does not prove the book's authenticity. Bond also takes the Wycliffe "testimony" about *Jasher* at face value, writing: "Its having been known to our first Reformers is evident from the testimony of that illustrious leader Wickliffe" (pp. iv, v). Would he then accept as having passed under Wycliffe's gaze any document to which anyone had signed the translator's name?

Bond asserts that the history in *Jasher* is written with "the simplicity and force of truth." And, he adds, the stories in *Jasher* "agree, in general, with the statements in the books of Moses, and where they differ, it appears that he relates one series of facts, which are not narrated by Moses, although likely to have occurred at the same time" (pp. v–vi). These comments are plainly false, for *The Book of Jasher* contradicts the Pentateuch in fundamental and undeniable ways on every question of substance it reports. The only way to explain Bond's great charity toward *Jasher* is that he was sympathetic with the religious agenda of the eighteenth-century Deists and was willing to imitate their rhetorical methods to advance that agenda. Thus, Deist speculative theology persisted well into the nineteenth century and may have a subsequent history with a different set of advocates throughout that century and even into the twentieth.

These contentions about Bond and his agenda gain support from some of his statements about the importance of *The Book of Jasher*. Bond writes that it is of utmost importance that this lost book teaches "the great doctrine of the immortality of the soul" (p. vi), that is, the preexistence of souls. This was one of Ilive's most fervently advocated views, defended in several of his works and setting him sharply at odds with the Church. On this view, human souls are uncreated and, like God himself, eternal in both directions. Thus, for instance, Adam and Eve would have existed eternally prior to their "creation," which for Ilive is merely their embodiment. Human beings, like God, are uncreated. If there is any doubt about what Bond and Ilive mean, Bond quotes the opening chapter of *Jasher* to the effect that "JEHOVAH appeared in Eden, and created man, and made him to be an image of his own eternity" (p. vi). In characteristic fashion, Ilive's ambiguity leaves him a means of escape while still insinuating his views. The "image" of God that Adam and Eve bear is "eternity," while their "creation" is only the shaping of bodies as containers for their preexistent souls, or, rather, fallen angels.

Bond notes with detachment that "the fall of man, the promise of the woman's seed, and the early predictions of a deliverer, are not mentioned by Jasher" (p. vii). The editor explains this simply as a problem of two accounts, one in Genesis, the other in *Jasher*. He adds, however, that *Jasher* is "simply a work of record, and not of revelation or prediction" and that Jasher knew that other stories were already recorded by Moses. The problem with Bond's explanation of the differences between the two is that Jasher's accounts both ignore and contradict these crucial elements in the Genesis story of Creation and Fall. The Fall is not an ancillary component in the Pentateuch that can be discounted or ignored. Of course, without a Fall there is no need of a promise of redemption or of a messianic redeemer. Deists held that all of these aspects of the Judeo-Christian tradition are later fabrications by priests to enslave the faithful. Thus, Ilive's desire to retell these stories so as to exclude special creation of humans, sin and a fall from grace, and the promise of a special redemption of the human race by God is not surprising. Nor is Bond's willingness to dismiss as trivial their exclusion from the documentary history of Israel.

Most of the rest of Bond's edition of *The Book of Jasher* looks much as the original, with the exception that the "testimonies" from Jazer, Ben Zaddi, Zadock, Othniel, Phineas, and Ezra are left out of the opening pages. Perhaps these were too clearly concoctions by Ilive. Bond may not have wished to risk exposing the project on the basis of a large number of superfluous and overly enthusiastic ancient endorsements.

The other important difference between Bond's edition and the original is Bond's free tampering with the notes which follow *Jasher* and which were supposed to have been part of the original scroll which was translated by Alcuin himself. Where Ilive is clearly unorthodox in his notes, Bond excises passages. Most of Ilive's notes on chapter 1, those dealing with the strange account of Creation, Adam and Eve's relationship, Noah, and other important stories, Bond omits. A careless or gullible reader might have missed Ilive's implied argument against principal theological tenets of Christianity in the narrative of *Jasher*, but even an obtuse reader could not fail to detect the unorthodox nature of the commentary which "explained" the text. Thus, Bond does not merely reproduce *Jasher*, he improves it.

Bond also adds notes where recent advances in archaeology or other sciences have tended to confirm the account in *Jasher*. Thus to the notes from chapters 7 through 11 Bond adds many of his own observations and the comments of various early-nineteenth-century scholars. How widely read Bond's edition was is not known, though its appearance means that *The Book of Jasher* and its strange theology of "reason" and "nature" lived on well after Ilive.

Jacob Ilive's persistent challenges to Christian orthodoxy provoked religious and civil authorities sufficiently to bring about his arrest and trial for blasphemy. He was tried in 1753 (though not for *Jasher*), convicted, pilloried, and sent to prison for three years. Surviving prison, he continued writing and lecturing. He was again arrested and tried in 1757.[7]

Ilive explored new, or perhaps ancient, spiritual territory, unhindered by the traditional limitations of Christian theology, arriving at conclusions that have prompted historians to ignore or dismiss him.

Nevertheless, a complete interpretation of the Deist controversy must account for Ilive and the clandestine world of London's guilds and secret societies.

Ilive is important as a proponent of several notions that must be seen as part of the religious radicalism of the first half of the eighteenth century. Biblical criticism developed out of the works of Spinoza, Reimarus, Woolston, Lessing, and others in Germany, England, and France. Miracles were called in question by Annet, Tindal, and Hume. Pantheism was advocated by Blount, Toland, and Voltaire. Hobbes and Locke suggested new political directions, Bayle and Diderot new approaches to knowledge generally. Less often is Deism associated with extraterrestrialism, gnosticism, and anti-Semitism. But these commitments often mark junctions in the labyrinth known as "the modern mind," and each suggested directions for the subsequent intellectual history of the West.

Chapter Ten

Conclusion

I think it is not doing justice to the Deity, to call it, in the gross, the *revealed will* and *word of God*. . . . The Bible is such a composition as that the most *opposite* tenets are extracted from it. . . . It has been the *groundwork* of most of the *heresies* and *schisms* that have taken place in *Christendom*, and has occasioned a great *confusion*.

Thomas Chubb, *Posthumous Works*

Deism threatened British Christianity between 1680 and 1760. A rising tide of skepticism, heresy, blasphemy, and atheism swept the realm as the foundational presuppositions of Christianity were assaulted. Talented and persistent writers like Toland, Shaftesbury, Tindal, Collins, Woolston, Annet, Chubb, and Ilive argued against the need for revelation, miracles, and priests. Christian writers like Berkeley, Butler, Sherlock, Stackhouse, Gibson, and Law defended Christian verities against the attack.

Deism claimed to provide the foundation of a new religion of reason and nature. God obeyed the dictates of reason, and nature pursued its course in the grip of immutable law. Ordinary human reason had access to all of the truth necessary to present or future happiness. Revelation was at best a republication of natural and universal truth and was more likely a collection of meaningless fables, lies, and superstitions. Any revelation departing from "the religion of reason" was simply false. Miracles, mysteries, and prophecies were all irrational. Great rhetorical energy was focused on pressing the case against miracles, which opposed common experience and supported irrational doctrines.

The Deists wrote for an audience of urban, literate working people with only tentative ties to the Church. Before this audience, Deists advanced a radical criticism of received religious truths while exploring new spiritual domains. Christian apologists defended the rationality of revealed religion and argued vigorously for the unique truthfulness of a Christianity confirmed by miracles. But the seeds of doubt had been sown.

The Deist controversy was no minor difference of opinion among writers who were all in basic agreement on the foundational tenets of traditional monotheism. Rather, the opposition in views between Deist and Christian was fundamental and comprehensive. Deists advocated pantheism, atheism, unitarianism, or gnosticism in answer to trinitarian monotheism. Deists argued for a preexistent and uniform nature following immutable laws, while Christians responded with a created nature fully under the control of a sovereign God who miraculously disrupted its normal course on occasion. Deism proposed a potent human reason which discovers accurate religious truth unassisted by revelation, while Orthodoxy countered with a weak and fallen reason which only in great and dangerous pride saw itself as autonomous and sufficient. Deists viewed revelation as a "a tissue of lies and fables," while Christians found scripture a divine gift to which reason must submit. Deists developed a method of reading biblical texts through the lens of critical ridicule, while officers of the Church warned their flocks to approach the scriptures with reverence and humility.

Deist Method: Foundation of a Critical Case

The Deists' critical goal of undermining revelation required the invention of a critical method. The sources of Deistic method are found in writers ranging from Cicero in the rhetorical tradition to Spinoza in the philosophical to Simon in the theological. But to English Deists must go the credit for developing biblical criticism of the type that later characterized critical explorations in Germany, Britain, and America.

Foundational to this method was the "test of ridicule" which "separates [an object] from its artificial connections, and exposes it naked with all its native improprieties" (Home, p. 205). Collins, Woolston, Morgan, Annet, and other Deists employed ridicule, along with complementary methods such as natural and allegorical interpretations of miracles, a study of historical contexts for the biblical documents, and a search for textual inconsistencies and ambiguities in and among accounts. The Deists propagated their corrosive approach to the Bible among a popular audience by employing a variety of distinctive rhetorical tactics, including—in addition to argument—ridicule, lying, disguise, profanity, insult, selection, and forgery. They experimented with historical criticism, naturalistic explanations of miracles, comparative religious studies, and allegorical schemes of interpretation. Their purposes in developing a critical approach to the Christian scriptures were strategic rather than scholarly and destructive rather than apologetic. The Deists' method was invented out of the need for a tool for dismantling the biblical texts, particularly miracle narratives, as part of a grand project of forging a case against the notions of revelation and religious privilege.

Woolston is particularly significant in this regard. He employed ridicule extensively with Christian miracles to "clear the way" for allegory, that is, to eliminate the possibility of a literal reading. He then advanced allegorical interpretations, drawn from Origen and other of the Church Fathers, to provide the "true spiritual meaning" of the New Testament miracles. Woolston's refusal to allow any historical merit to Christ's miracles marks him as one of the first modern biblical critics. Annet can also be identified as an early practitioner of modern biblical criticism. Emanuel Hirsch has written that "he is the originator of scientific criticism of the Easter stories and thereby gave impetus to the field of New Testament studies" (quoted in C. Brown 1985, p. 45). Annet identified logical holes in accounts, highlighted inconsistencies among parallel accounts of an event such as the Resurrection, and mocked what he labelled "absurdities" in texts.

Their principal target throughout the long controversy was the Bible, the foundation of the Christian faith but also of British government. "If there are any propositions in the Bible which when rightly understood are plainly repugnant to the Nature or Truth of things," wrote Chubb, "all such Propositions must be allow'd to be *false.*" And since there is much repugnant to reason in the Bible, as he read it, "therefore it would justly be *excluded* from being the *Rule* of *Truth* in any Point whatever" (Chubb 1727, p. 7). The New Testament books plainly *"were not* written by *divine inspiration* according to the vulgar use of that expression" (p. 5). The Bible is merely a book, and as such, is filled with historical and theological errors. The English Deists' initial development of biblical criticism is an important chapter in the history of the critical enterprise whose most famous representatives include Lessing, Strauss, and Schleiermacher.

Christian advocates argued forcefully that reason does not lead to universally recognized religious premises. Thus, the central tenet of Deism—the existence of a universal religion of reason—was, on its face, false. Deists tried to answer this charge with an appeal to priestcraft, the conspiracy of religious leaders to mislead humanity on spiritual matters as part of a grab for power. But the priestcraft hypothesis seemed an insufficient explanation of religious diversity and condemned virtually all religions but Deism itself. Eventually the Deists were left defending the untenable position that all religions in the history of the world, except a fabled and inaccessible "primitive religion of reason," were false due to the machinations of priests. The true religion of reason had lain largely hidden from human view until the seventeenth century, when it was rediscovered in England by a small group of religious thinkers. But this primitive religion was reputed by these same thinkers to be universally accessible to unaided human reason. The failure of the priestcraft hypothesis to account for human religious experience, and the vulnerability of the argument about reason's sufficiency, meant that Deism as a religious philosophy could not survive the criticism of skilled advocates like Berkeley, Butler, or Law.

This is not to say, however, that Deism's critical project of calling in question the status of the Christian scriptures failed as well; it did not. "The deistic arguments may have been answered for the time being adequately by the Orthodox," writes Melinsky, "but the questioning of the literal infallibility of the Bible on rational grounds was going to have alarming consequences in a century's time" (p. 48). Roland Stromberg adds that "deism never died," for "the critical spirit endured; so did the search for a moral order independent of any special or miraculous revelation" (p. 68) [1] Thus, its critical project remains, along with the theory of freedom of expression, as English Deism's lasting legacy.

Critical and Constructive Elements of Christian Rhetoric

The defense of revelation and miracle involved both critical and constructive strategies. Christian writers argued critically from the rhetorical manner, theological tenets, and character of the Deists. Each of these three approaches also fed legal efforts to silence the Deists. First, linguistic, stylistic, and tactical qualities of their rhetoric provided a basis for arguing that the Deists' discourse was frequently blasphemous. Second, Deist theology which elevated reason, denigrated revelation, and neutralized Christ himself as a source of theological truth provided a second major line of argument for Orthodox writers. Finally, Christian apologists sought to marginalize the Deists by portraying them as social pariahs, subhuman aberrations, animals, and monsters. Such characterization, coupled with the arguments from language and theology, prepared the way for unusually harsh treatment of some Deists by the authorities. The trials of Woolston, Annet, and Ilive were all successful in securing verdicts of guilt. The view of the Deists reflected in the rhetoric of powerful figures such as Addison and Berkeley encouraged both social rejection and legal censure and might conceivably have provided grounds for even harsher measures. "A solemn judicial Death is too great an honour for an Atheist," wrote one contributor to the *Spectator* in 1712 (quoted in Berman 1975, p. 91n.).

The constructive side of the Christian case rested on answering Deist criticism of scripture with the method of evidentialism. Apologists engaged in a careful judicial sifting of biblical and historical evidence for Christian miracles. Evidentialism of the type displayed in Sherlock's *Tryal*, Berkeley's *Alciphron*, and the anonymous *Miracles of Jesus Vindicated* was widely adopted by Orthodox apologists.

Evidentialism accomplished two strategic tasks for Orthodoxy. First, it answered Deist ridicule, which did not appear to allow serious consideration of evidence. By carefully setting out all of the textual and circumstantial evidence supporting miracles, Orthodox apologists clearly hoped to discredit their opponents' mocking treatment of the available proof. Second, evidentialism highlighted the strengths of the biblical evidence for miracles. That evidence was weak when construed as isolated miracle accounts taken apart from their narrative context. Much of the same evidence was considerably stronger when taken cumulatively as generally consistent accounts drawn from several independent sources. Evidentialism was so successful that it has never been abandoned by Christian apologists.

Orthodox treatments of the evidence for miracles were, however, optimistic. Later, less sympathetic critics and audiences would arrive at strikingly different conclusions regarding the same evidence. Law, who scrupulously avoided evidentialism in favor of a fideistic defense of miracles, was prescient in this regard.

Evidentialism rested on the debatable claims that miracles are simple historical events and that testimony is a particularly powerful form of evidence. Annet and others challenged both ideas, requiring for miracles "more than common proof" and arguing that testimony is often fallible (Annet, *Resurrection of Jesus Considered*, p. 9). The authenticity of the Christian miracles relied on the validity of the ancient documentary testimony contained in the New Testament. Thus, Christian writers sought to enhance the rational status of testimony by arguing that we often accept such evidence in opposition to experience. But we also are aware of testimony's frequent failure as evidence. Moreover, circumstances, such as the desire to establish a prophet as "on a divine mission," often render testimony's falsehood more likely than it would otherwise be. Biblical testimony was potentially fallible in various ways that Deists were happy to rehearse. Moreover, Christian advocates were also plagued by the question of false miracles and moved to meet this challenge by advancing elaborate criteria to distinguish true from false miracles. Deists noted in response that some Catholic and pagan miracles could be established on evidential grounds that satisfied Christians' criteria. The tension in Christian apologetic on this point was never satisfactorily resolved.

The claim that miracles are "simple historical events" also appeared to ignore their significance as religious events intended to inspire faith. Even in the New Testament, miracles are not presented as *merely* historical events but as sacred interventions of divinity into the daily lives of people. Miracles thus strike a responsive chord deep within the human soul. To treat miracles as principally or exclusively historical occurrences diminishes their significance as *religious* phenomena. M. A. H. Melinksy points out that "the evidentialists supposed the truth of a miracle could be established by purely objective criteria, without need for any religious intuition. This landed them in an impossible position because they observed only half of the definition of a miracle" (p. 52).

Alternatives to the evidentialist case were sought but never achieved popularity with Christian writers. William Law defended miracles in a manner not subject to the dangers of evidentialism. Jesus' miracles are clear and indisputable signs of his divinity and are encountered directly and mystically. "Guilty, disordered reason" has a limited role in judging divine truth. Authentic miracles impress the soul indubitably. True miracles are thus God's own self-validating evidence, in the face of which reason merely capitulates. But Law appeared to have demolished reason in the process of developing his case, and thus his argument was considered dangerous by other Christian writers.

Behind the entire constructive case for Christianity lurked the daunting problem of reason's relationship to revelation. Christian writers faced a delicate rhetorical problem in answering the Deists on the question of reason, as Law's failed efforts proved. If, as the Deists affirmed, reason is capable of discovering religious truth, then revelation is superfluous. This position was, of course, unacceptable to Christians. But if reason were held to be impotent as regards religious truth, one is thrown back on mysticism. "The dictates of reason," wrote a Christian respondent to Chubb, "become dim, and almost imperceptible thro' *vice* and the abuse of the humane faculties" (*An Answer to Mr. Chubb's book Entitled The True*

Gospel of Jesus Christ, p. 97).[2] Thus, revelation was necessary to our present and future happiness. But, this position necessitated discrediting reason, making Christianity a religion for the thoughtless. Rendering reason the judge of miracles and doctrine, however, brought Christianity too close to Deism. No satisfactory resolution of this issue was achieved by Orthodox apologists in the Deist controversy.

The Popular Audience, Free Expression, and Rhetorical Triumph

Radical British Deism was a popular religious and rhetorical movement. Deists like Woolston, Annet, Toland, Chubb, and Ilive wrote for a literate though not well-educated urban audience. Annet and Ilive operated in the clandestine world of London's mechanics guilds, where each disseminated his views to a popular audience. Toland's explorations of ancient religions, Ilive's gnostic theology, Chubb's caustic criticisms of revelation, and Woolston's ridicule and allegorizing of miracles are all strategies of popularization which brought theological debate to a broad public. Each strategy is an adaptation of discourse to an emerging reading public which was interested in questioning the established authority of a clergy that often seemed out of touch with the realities of the laboring classes.

The strategies of popularization threatened the Church by suggesting that theological issues were not resolved by reference to authority. Thus the very popularity of Deist biblical criticism earned its authors censure, including prosecution. As a result, Deists became ardent proponents and theorists of free expression, especially religious expression. Their influence in this regard has not been fully appreciated. The Deists' assault on Christian revelation spawned an important controversy regarding freedom of expression focused on the Church's right to prosecute blasphemers. Deists also argued forcefully for religious tolerance and for an end to prosecution for religious crimes. The persuasive impact of their case on this and related points was felt as far away as the American colonies. Clark writes that "the correlation between Deism and anti-monarchical politics was to survive and indeed culminate in 1776 in the most effective of all Deist political tracts, *Common Sense*" (Clark 1994, p. 38).

Orthodox writers succeeded temporarily in shoring up the rational foundations of revelation in the face of the Deist assault. They also successfully defended Christianity's claim to being England's proper social and political foundation. This success was due to the talents of writers like Butler and Sherlock, to the political power of figures like Gibson, and to the sheer number of Christian apologists active in the early eighteenth century. A ceaseless barrage of tracts, sermons, pamphlets, and books presented the Christian case, often with skill and intelligence, for more than half a century. In addition, penning a telling rebuttal of a well-known Deist such as Tindal could mean a cleric's advancement within the Church. Thus, dozens of ambitious apologists of varying talents sought to enhance their careers by answering "atheists and infidels." For every Deist willing to attack revelation, there were five clerical apologists willing vigorously to defend it. Of course, the rhetorical success of Christian writers was assisted by several social facts of eighteenth-century Britain: The majority of the British public still accepted Christian cosmology, the Church still commanded considerable power to prosecute authors and printers for blasphemy, and printers faced no penalties for publishing Christian books and tracts. But the Deists' determination in pursuing the battle against such odds, coupled with their considerable rhetorical acumen, resulted in some diminution of clerical power. No longer could the appeal to authority carry quite the same weight, no longer was the language of veneration the only vocabulary for discussing the Bible, and no longer was theological debate the domain only of trained specialists. The contours of the English religious mind had been altered in a few highly significant ways.

Like the Sophists of Plato's day, English Deists applied the acid of rational criticism to the eternal verities of a great society and in so doing threatened many things valuable, stable, and defining about it. Like the Sophists, the Deists' impact has often been either underestimated or misunderstood due to the presence on their historical stage of more talented actors. And, like the rhetoric of Plato's rivals, Deist discourse has shaped the modern, urban, pluralistic society in fundamental and lasting ways, while to the mimetic work of others has often gone the credit.

Notes

Chapter 1: The Social and Religious Context of the Deist Controversy

1. See also Levy, pp. 316–30; Holmes, p. 192.
2. See also William Stephens, p. viii.
3. The Blasphemy Act remains in effect to this day.
4. Harvard Houghton Library, FMS 1090 (1–3), no. 1. Locke and Collins were very close friends. Locke wrote to Collins on October 4, 1704, "I have the hope to see and embrace you again. . . . You and I have other satisfactions together than eating and drinking, and yet there is no fault in expressing one's wellcome to a friend in a good dish of meat" (Harvard Houghton Library, FMS 1090 [1–3], no. 3).
5. Blount was "more negative than Herbrt of Cherbury, and bitterly anti-clerical, he rejected miracles, particularly with regard to the birth of Christ, and treated many leading biblical characters simply as impostors" (Hurlbutt, p. 70).
6. "This century saw the first rules of criticism (Mabillon), the introduction of methodological doubt (Descartes), the restriction of biblical authority by science and history, and the growing triumph of reason over revelation. The scriptures were more and more treated like ordinary historical documents. The process of objectification had begun" (Krentz, p. 16).
7. On Toland's life and works, see Sullivan, *John Toland and the Deist Controversy.* On Deist doctrine and influence, see Byrne, *Natural Religion and the Nature of Religion;* Reventlow, *The Authority of the Bible and the Rise of the Modern Mind;* and C. Brown, *Jesus in European Protestant Thought,* pp. 29–55.
8. See the account in Holmes, chapter 9.
9. For discussions of the scope and significance of this controversy, see Burns, *The Great Debate on Miracles,* pp. 9–18; C. Brown, *Miracles and the Critical Mind,* pp. 47–78; Trench, *Notes on the Miracles of Our Lord,* p. 70.
10. Just how widespread Deism was in the first half of the century is a matter of some dispute. That it was well entrenched in major cities seems certain, and J. M. Robertson holds that by 1710 "some form of rationalism inconsistent with

Christianity would have been found to be nearly as common as Orthodoxy" (p. 717). However, Roland Stromberg writes, "There are abundant indications that the countryside remained far less touched by currents of free-thought" (p. 4). Moreover, Philip Doddridge wrote in 1726 that "an atheist or a deist is a monstrous kind of creature, which in the country we only know by report" (quoted in Stromberg, p. 4n.).

11. On the nature of the ancient skeptical tradition, see Annas and Barnes, *The Modes of Skepticism*. On more recent treatments of skepticism, see Ferreira, *Scepticism and Reasonable Doubt*. See also Strawson, *Scepticism and Naturalism: Some Varieties*.

12. See, for example, *An Apology for the Writings of Walter Mayle, Esq.*

13. For background, see Becker, *The Heavenly City of the Eighteenth Century Philosophers*; Brown, *Miracles and the Critical Mind*; Burns; Cassirer, *The Philosophy of the Enlightenment*; Cragg, *Reason and Authority*; Craig, *The Historical Argument for the Resurrection of Jesus During the Deist Controversy*; Flew, *Hume's Philosophy of Belief*; Keller and Keller, *Miracles in Dispute*; Lewis, *Miracles*; Melinsky, *Healing Miracles*; Wood, ed., *Miracles*; Stephens, *English Thought in the Eighteenth Century*, volume 1; Sullivan; Tennant, *Miracle and its Philosophical Presuppositions*; Willey, *The Eighteenth Century Background*.

14. See also the response to Fleetwood by Hoadley.

15. This work is frequently referred to under the abbreviation used here; however, the full title reveals more clearly Collins's concern with specific issues of the miracles controversy, especially the proper uses of testimonial evidence. That title is *An Essay Concerning the Use of Reason in Propositions the Evidence Whereof Depends Upon Human Testimony*.

16. Bentley, *Remarks Upon a late Discourse of Free Thinking*; Hoadley, *Queries Recommended to the Authors of the late Discourse of Free Thinking*; Hare, *The Clergyman's Thanks to Philentherus*; see also *An Answer to the Discourse on Free Thinking*.

17. Besides the original edition of 1729, the work was reissued in 1733, 1735, 1739, 1748, 1765, 1788, and 1794. As late as 1838 the Presbyterian Board of Education was still printing a revised version of the *Tryal*.

18. Each of these titles is attributed to Annet in the catalogues of the British Library, though Annet's name does not appear on the title page of any.

19. It is now a conventional treatment of Hume's essay to affirm that it revived a dead or dying debate. There does not seem to be much evidence to support such a view, however. Dodwell was still receiving answers in 1748 and later, and Annet and Chubb were doing much to popularize the attack on miracles. Thus, Hume published at a time when there was intense interest in miracles, and the controversy still raged.

20. It is interesting that Hume, though he is now the most famous contributor to the miracles controversy, did not elicit nearly the number of responses to "Of Miracles" that were elicited by works such as Woolston's *Discourses* or Tindal's

Christianity as Old as Creation. In fact, judged simply by the number of eighteenth-century responses, Hume's essay was only moderately controversial. Even Dodwell's satire provoked more sustained attack.

Chapter 2: Characteristics of British Deism

1. Jacob, *The Radical Enlightenment: Pantheists, Freemasons and Republicans* and *Living the Enlightenment: Freemasonry and Politics in Eighteenth-Century Europe;* Evans, *Pantheisticon;* Sullivan, *John Toland and the Deist Controversy;* Levy, *Blasphemy;* Buckley, *At the Origins of Modern Atheism.* Kerry S. Walter has traced the development of Deism in America in *The American Deists.*

2. That the traditional view of the Deists persists is evident in David Christie-Murray's treatment of the Deists in *A History of Heresy,* chapter 17.

3. See her *Radical Enlightenment* and *Living the Enlightenment.*

4. *The Works of John Dryden,* edited by Sir Walter Scott, volume 10, p. 38.

5. Peter Gay has a similar assessment. To the Deists the Bible was concocted of "insidious lies" and "ludicrous romances" (p. 379).

6. See Sullivan, chapters 6–8.

7. See the entry in the *Dictionary of National Biography* on Woolston.

8. The report on Collins comes from J. H. Monck's *Life of Bentley* (London, 1830).

9. F. R. Tennant writes as well that "in course of time . . . suspicion concentrated on the miracles" (pp. 6–7).

10. See responses such as Hewlett, *Miracles real Evidences of a Divine Revelation.*

11. The full citation reads: "That testimony cannot be credible which relates incredible things; therefore the relaters of such have not an equal right to be believed, as those that relate any other historical facts . . . I ought to have extraordinary evidence, to induce me to believe extraordinary things, that are supernatural, which cannot be so credible as ordinary things which are natural." Middleton demands that believers in miracles "must refer us to instances which tally with their testimonies, and experimentally prove the truth of them. . . . These answerers must show how those testimonies are verified by facts" (pp. xxviii, xxxi).

12. Cameron treats Spinoza's method in chapter 1, "Prologue, the Legacy of Benedict de Spinoza." Chapter 2 is entitled "The Nineteenth-Century Ferment." The Deist contribution to the debate is essentially ignored by Cameron.

13. In his study *The Rise of Biblical Criticism in America, 1800–1870,* Jerry Wayne Brown doesn't mention the English Deists as he briefly traces historical developments from Origen to Edward Everett and George Bancroft at Harvard in the early nineteenth century (pp. 1–9). R. K. Harrison, B. K. Waltke, D. Guthrie, and G. D. Fee skip from Astruc's development of some of the principles of literary criticism of the Bible, directly to the late-eighteenth-, early-nineteenth-century biblical scholar J. G. Eichhorn (1752–1827) in their brief history of critical theory

in *Biblical Criticism: Historical, Literary and Textual*, p. 21. The Deists also have no role to play in the development of *The Logic of Gospel Criticism*, as far as Humphrey Palmer can see, though the book offers an interesting and entertaining discussion of some of the intellectual history of biblical criticism.

14. Merton Christensen, among others, has challenged this view, arguing that biblical criticism of the scholarly German type was practiced in England much earlier than the middle of the nineteenth century.

15. See the Reimarus entry in the *New International Dictionary*; see also C. Brown, *Jesus in European Protestant Thought*, p. 2.

16. See C. Brown 1985, pp. 16–36; Gay, *The Englightenment: An Interpretation*, pp. 381–82.

17. Ong reveals the origins of medieval "methods" in the medical theories of Galen.

18. See also McLachlan, *Socianism in Seventeenth Century England*, pp. 325–27.

19. The other works included *Histoire critique du texte du Nouveau Testament* (1689), *Histoire Critique des versions du Nuveaux Testament* (1693), and *Histoire critique des principaux commentaires du Nuveaux Textamente* (1693).

Chapter 3: The Rhetoric of Subterfuge and Characterization

1. For general studies of the miracles controversy see Burns, *The Great Debate on Miracles*, and Craig, *The Historical Argument for the Resurrection of Jesus During the Deist Controversy*.

2. Theologians and philosophers still recognize the significance of miracles such as the Resurrection to the integrity of Christianity. Antony Flew has recently written: "[The Resurrection] is the very heart and essence of the Gospel message that the second person of the Trinity became man: that he was born of woman, if not necessarily of a virgin; that he preached the word of his Father in the Galilee; that he was crucified, dead and buried; *and that He rose again on the third day*" (*Of Miracles: David Hume*, p. 7)—emphasis in original.

3. Books discussing ridicule include Browne, *A Fit Rebuke to a Ludicrous Infidel*; Bulkley, *A Vindication of My Lord Shaftesbury, on the Subject of Ridicule*; Collins, *A Discourse Concerning Ridicule and Irony*; Cooper, *Characteristics*; Hutcheson, *Reflections upon Laughter, and Remarks upon the Fable of the Bees*; Morris, *An Essay Toward Fixing the True Standards of Wit, Humour, Raillery, Satire, and Ridicule*; Ramsay, *An Essay on Ridicule*; Whitehead, *An Essay on Ridicule*. Periodical discussions of ridicule include Addison, *The Spectator*, no. 445; "The Force of Ridicule in Writing," in *The Orators Miscellany* 639 (October 7, 1738); "An Oration on Grave Conundrums, and Serious Buffoons," in *The Orators Miscellany*, no. 1 (London, 1731), p. 5; *The Weekly Oracle or Universal Library* (London, 1737), p. 7.

Essays and lectures on ridicule include James Beattie, "On Laughter, and Ludicrous Composition," in *Essays* (Edinburgh: 1776), p. 693; John Brown, *Essays on the Characteristicks*, second edition (London, 1751), p. 105; "Christianity Standing the Test of Ridicule," in *The Theological Repository*, ed. Joseph Priestley, third edition, no. 2 (London, 1759); Benjamin Ibbot, *Boyle Lectures* (1727), pp. 228–29; William Preston, "Essay on Ridicule, Wit and Humour," in *The Transactions of the Royal Irish Academy* no. 2 (1788).

4. See Grean, *Shaftesbury's Philosophy of Religion and Ethics*, chapter 8; Reventlow, *The Authority of the Bible*, pp. 308–21; Cameron, *Biblical Higher Criticism*, chapter 1; Krentz, *The History of Critical Method*, pp. 16–22; C. Brown, *Jesus*, pp. 203–7.

5. See Aldridge, "Shaftesbury and the Test of Truth"; Templeman, "Warburton and Brown Continue the Battle over Ridicule"; Hughes, *The Sense of the Ridiculous*; Tave, *The Amiable Humorist*; Gilmore, *The Eighteenth-Century Controversy over Ridicule as a Test of Truth: A Reconsideration.*

6. Redwood writes: "Where it would take many volumes to determine inconclusively the larger questions concerning the nature of creation or the accuracy of the biblical account, it was possible to make fun of God's cosmos as described by the theologians and philosophers, in the space of five minutes of theatre jests, or in the odd quip in the tavern or coffee house" (p. 14).

7. See Bullitt, *Jonathan Swift and the Anatomy of Satire*, especially chapters 1 and 3.

8. For a helpful treatment of the problem of hasty interpretation of miracle accounts, see Laramer, *Water into Wine?*, pp. 115–19.

9. See also Bullitt, p. 20.

10. On class and language in eighteenth-century Britain, see McIntosh, *Common and Courtly Language.*

11. On "movements up and down the ladder of society" in eighteenth-century England, see Speck, *Society and Literature in England, 1700–1760*, pp. 94–115.

12. See Thompson, *Whigs and Hunters: The Origins of the Black Act*; "Eighteenth-Century English Society: Class Struggle Without Class?," p. 139; "Patrician Society, Plebian Culture."

13. On insinuation in other writers of the period, specifically Thomas Hobbes and Edward Gibbon, see Berman's "Some Light on the Hidden Hobbes" and "Deliberate Parapraxes."

14. On the social significance of lying in seventeenth-century England, see Shapin, *A Social History of Truth.*

15. See Novak, "DeFoe, the Occult, and the Deist Offensive"; Sullivan, *John Toland and the Deist Controversy*; Jacob, *The Radical Enlightenment.*

16. On the social milieu of Grub Street see, Pat Rogers, *Grub Street.*

17. On Addison's distinction between true and false wit, see Sitter, "About Wit."

Chapter 4: The Rhetorical Career of Thomas Woolston

1. See the Woolston entry in the *Dictionary of National Biography*.

2. See Grant and Tracy, *A Short History of the Interpretation of the Bible*, chapter 6; Williams, *The Descent of the Dove*, p. 39.

3. See McDonald, *Mystical Bedlam*, especially chapter 4, "Popular Stereotypes of Insanity."

4. Michel Foucault also notes the dilemmatic nature of attitudes toward the insane in the Christian West: "From the depths of the Middle Ages, a man was mad if his speech could not be said to form part of the common discourse of men. His words were considered null and void, without truth or significance, worthless as evidence . . . And yet, in contrast to all others, his words were credited with strange powers, of revealing some hidden truth, of predicting the future, of revealing, in all their naivete, what the wise were unable to perceive." (p. 217).

5. For example, *An Answer to Aristobulus's two Letters to Dr. Bennett* is attributed to "A Country Curate" but was likely written by Woolston.

6. See Reventlow, *The Authority of the Bible and the Rise of the Modern Mind*, p. 611n.159. Woolston's works and trial were followed in France and the American colonies and later were discussed in Germany.

7. Swift, "Verses on the Death of Dr. Swift," p. 564. Also quoted in Burns, *The Great Debate on Miracles*, p. 10. Swift attacked Woolston in a note, writing that "Woolston was a Clergyman, but for want of Bread, hath in several Treatises, in the most blasphemous Manner, attempted to turn Our Saviour and his Miracles into Ridicule. He is much caressed by many great Courtiers, and by all the Infidels, and his Books read generally by the Court Ladies" (p. 564).

8. The *Second Discourse* is dedicated to Edward, Bishop of Lichfield; the *Third Discouse* to Richard, Bishop of St. David's; the *Fourth* to Francis, Bishop of St. Asaph; the *Fifth* to Thomas, Bishop of Bangor; and the *Sixth* to John, Bishop of Oxford.

9. The *First* and *Second Discourses* were published in 1727; the *Third, Fourth,* and *Fifth* in 1728; and the *Sixth* in 1729.

10. On ridicule as a critical method in the miracles debate, see Herrick, "Miracles and Method."

11. Levy notes that "the Jews constituted a special case" as regards blasphemy under British law. "They enjoyed freedom of religion . . . although they enjoyed no other civil rights." They also were not punishable under the Blasphemy Act for religious beliefs directly associated with Judaism, and in fact, "Protestant England never prosecuted a Jew for blasphemy . . ." (1981, 319–20). Woolston may have been making a statement about the inconsistency of blasphemy legislation by his use of the persona of the Rabbi.

12. Blasphemy had been defined by English legal scholars as "injuring God with contumelious words" or "to detract from God the honour due to him, or to attribute any evil to him" (Levy 1981 p. 329).

13. This remarkably popular work went through continuous editions until at least 1823—almost a century after it first appeared. No skeptic even attempted to answer Sherlock until Annet, fifteen years later in 1744.

14. Among the dozens of other replies are Harris's answer to Woolston's *Fifth Discourse, The Reasonableness of Believing in Christ; Two Sermons Preached at Salters Hall, May 21 and 28, 1728*, and Stebbing, *A Defense of the Scripture History*.

15. It is not certain that Woolston did not himself write this tract, however.

16. The prosecution was drawing on a "judicial decision of 1676 that held that because Christianity was part of the law, to blaspheme it was a crime against the state" (Levy 1981 p. 333).

17. See C. Brown 1984, pp. 50, 103–36.

18. Middleton's work was so popular that Hume complained it eclipsed his first *Enquiry*, which appeared the same year—1749.

19. See the Woolston entry in the *Dictionary of National Biography*; see also Reventlow, p. 412.

20. See C. Brown 1985, chapters 1 and 2.

Chapter 5: Tolerance, Expression, and Prosecution

1. Hefelbower cites Bury, *History of Freedom of Thought*, p. 59.

2. See also Tilly, *The Power, Vertue, and Influence of Christ's Resurrection*, p. 3.

Chapter 6: Peter Annet

1. Biographical material from Twyman, *Peter Annet, 1693–1769*.

2. Annet's treatment of the life of Paul was popular enough to have been translated into French. See *Critical Examination of the Life of St. Paul*, translated from the French of Boulanger (London: R. Carlile, 1823).

3. The third edition of this work appeared in 1744 and was printed by M. Cooper, the first edition having been printed "for the author." Annet writes that "the second edition is spurious and erroneous" (3d ed., title page).

4. See Delepierre, *Des Livres Condamnes au feu en Angleterre*. Portion attached to *The Records of the Court of King's-Bench, at Westminster* (London: 1763). Periodicals that were sanctioned in the 1760s included *The Daily Journal, The Daily Post, The Declarations of the Pretender, Ascanius, The Alchemist*, and *The Genuine Journal*, among dozens of others. Most of these are described in official documents as "libels," with many described as "blasphemous."

5. See Conway, *Life of Thomas Paine*, volume 2, p. 194.

Chapter 7: Reason, Revelation, and Miracle

1. Among the few works on Law are Grainger, W. *Law and the Life of the Spirit*; Cropper, *Sparks Among the Stubble*; Green, *John Wesley and William Law*; and Hobhouse, *William Law and Eighteenth-Century Quakerism*.

2. Stephen adds: "Law's assaults upon Hoadly [in the Bangorian controversy], Mandeville [author of *The Fable of the Bees*], and Tindal [in *Christianity as Old as Creation*] could only have failed to place him in the front rank because they diverged from the popular theories."

3. Referring to Law's interest in the works of the German cobbler-mystic Jacob Boehme, Madan writes: "For by these very means one of the brightest stars in the firmament of the church (Oh! lamentable and heart breaking sight) falling from the heaven of Christianity into the sink and complication of Paganism, Quakerism and Socinianism, mixed up with Chymistry, and astrology, by a possest cobler" (pp. x, xi).

4. See also Mossner, *Bishop Butler and the Age of Reason*. Stromberg writes that Law "rejected reason the most boldly" (p. 101).

Chapter 8: Miracles and Method in Christian Apologetic

1. Melinsky suggests that the Orthodox tendency to treat miracles strictly as historical events ignores an important dimension of the miracle—its nature as a religious sign: "The [Orthodox] evidentialists supposed the truth of a miracle could be established by purely objective criteria, without need for any religious intuition. This landed them in an impossible position because they observed only half of the definition of a miracle" (p. 52).

Chapter 9: The Religious Rhetoric of Jacob Ilive

1. Ilive is also mentioned in More's *Dissertation upon English Typographical Founders*, p. 647.

2. Margaret Jacob has shown the close relationship between some Masonic lodges and the printers operating around St. Paul's in Ilive's day. See *The Radical Enlightenment*, chapter 4, "The Origins of European Freemasonry."

3. On gnosticism's influence in medieval Europe and later, see Legman, *The Guilt of the Knights Templar*. On a similar tradition associated with the Jewish Cabala, see *The Anatomy of God*, trans. Roy A. Rosenberg (New York: Ktav Publishing House, 1973) and Leo Schaya, *The Universal Meaning of the Kabbalah* (London: Allen and Unwin, 1971).

4. See Geddes MacGregor, *Gnosis* (Wheaton, Ill.: The Theosophical Publishing House, 1979), p. 144.

5. Theologies involving the preexistence of human souls and spiritual evolution toward divinity were not unknown in other Deist writers. Asgill wrote in 1730 that humans will eventually ascend to "even the same State as Christ arisen from the Dead. From whence they are called the Sons of God." (pp. 22, 278ff.)

6. This is an answer to Felton's *True Discourses*.

7. The order for this second arrest being issued on April 28, while Ilive was already a prisoner: "These are, in his Majesty's Name, to authorize and require you, to receive into your Custody the body of *Jacob Ilive*, now a Prisoner in Clerkwell Bridewell, and to keep him safe and close 'till he shall be delivered in due Course of Law, and for, &.c. Given at Whitehall, April 28, 1757, in the thirtieth Year of his Majesty's Reign" (*Copies Taken from the Records of the Court of King's Bench, at Westminster* no. xxvi [London, 1763]).

Chapter 10: Conclusion

1. See also Waldman, "Origins of the Doctrine of Reasonable Doubt."
2. See also Fleming, *Remarks on Mr. Thomas Chubb's Vindication.*

Bibliography

Primary Sources

A. B., *A Letter to Mr. Woolston*. London: J. Roberts, 1729.

An Account of the Trial of Thomas Woolston, B.D., Sometime Fellow of Sidney College in Cambridge. London: T. Read, 1729.

Adams, William. *Essay on Mr. Hume's Essay*. London, 1752.

Addison, Joseph. *The Evidences of the Christian Religion*. London: J. Tonson, 1730.

Anderson, James. *The Constitutions of the Freemasons*. London, 1723.

Annet, Peter. *The Conception of Jesus Considered as the Foundation of the Christian Religion*. London, 1744.

———. *Critical Examination of the Life of St. Paul. Translated from the French of Boulanger*. London: R. Carlile, 1823.

———. *Deism Fairly Stated*. London: W. Webb, c. 1746.

———. *Examen Critique*. London & Amsterdam: M. M. Rey, 1770.

———. *Free Inquirer*. 1761. Rpt. London: R. Carlile, 1826.

———. *The History and Character of St. Paul, Examined: in a Letter to Theophilus, a Christian Friend . . . in a Letter to Gilbert West, Esq.* London: F. Page, n.d.

———. *The History of Joseph Consider'd: or, The Moral Philosopher Vindicated Against Mr. Chandler's Defense of the Prime Ministry of Joseph, by Mercius Philalethes*. London: M. Cooper, 1744.

———. *The History of the Man After God's Own Heart*. London: R. Freeman, 1761.

———. *Judging for Ourselves; or Free Thinking The Great Duty of Religion*. London: T. Cox, c. 1739.

———. *Lectures Corrected and Revised*. London: J. Smith, n.d.

———. *The Miraculous Conception: or, The Divinity of Christ*. N.d. reprint London: R. Carlile, 1819.

———. *The Resurrection Defenders Stripped of all Defense*. London, 1745.

———. *The Resurrection of Jesus Considered by a Moral Philosopher in answer to The Tryal of the Witnesses*. London, n.d.

———. *The Resurrection of Jesus Considered in Answer to The Tryal of The Witnesses*. 3d ed. London: M. Cooper, 1744.

———. *The Resurrection of Jesus Demonstrated to Have No Proof*. London: J. Jackman, n.d.

———. *The Resurrection Reconsidered*. London: M. Cooper, 1744.

————. *Social Bliss Considered in Marriage and Divorce; Cohabiting Unmarried, and Public Whoring.* London: R. Rose, 1749.

————. *Supernaturals Examined.* London: F. Page, 1747.

An Answer to Aristobul's Two Letters to Dr. Bennet. By a Country Curate. London: M. Smith, 1721.

An Answer to Mr. Chubb's book Entitled The True Gospel of Jesus Christ. London, 1739.

An Answer to the Discourse on Free Thinking. London, 1713.

An Answer to the Jewish Rabbi's Two Letters Against Christ's Resurrection. London: J. Stephen, 1729.

An Apology for the Writings of Walter Mayle, Esq. London, 1727.

Asgill upon Woolston. London: W. Innys, 1715.

Assheton, William. *An Admonition to a Deist.* London, 1685.

Bentley, Richard. *Remarks Upon a Late Discourse of Free Thinking.* London, 1713.

Berkeley, George. *Alciphron or the Minute Philosopher* [1732]. London: Thomas Nelson, 1950. Vol. 3 of *The Complete Works of George Berkeley* (1948–1957).

Blasphema Detestanda: Or a Caution Against the Diabolism of Arius. Exon: Nathaniel Thorn, 1719.

Bliss, Anthony. *Observations on Mr. Chubb's Discourse Concerning Reason.* London: S. Wilmot, 1741.

Blount, Charles. *Anima Mundi.* London, 1678.

————. *The Deist: A Satyr on the Parsons: To the Tune of Old Simon the King* (unpublished MS, c. 1686). British Library MS Harley 7315.

————. *Miracles no Violation.* London, 1683.

————. *The Oracles of Reason.* London, 1693.

Bowles, Thomas. *The Gradual Advances, and Different Periods of Divine Revelation . . . in Opposition to the Infidelity of Mr. Woolston.* Oxford: L. Lichfield, 1729.

Bowman, William. *A Defense of our Savior's Miracle of Cursing the Fig Tree in Answer to Mr. Woolston's Discourse Thereon.* London: S. Austen, 1721.

Brown, John. *Essays on the Characteristics.* London: C. Davis, 1751.

Browne, Simon. *A Fit Rebuke to a Ludicrous Infidel in some Remarks on Mr. Woolston's Fifth Discourse.* London: R. Ford, 1732.

Browne, Thomas. *The Works of Sir Thomas Browne.* London, 1857.

Bulkley, Charles. *A Vindication of My Lord Shaftesbury, on the Subject of Ridicule.* London, 1751.

Burnet, Gilbert. *A Defense of Natural and Revealed Religion.* London: A. Bettesworth, 1737.

Butler, Joseph. *The Analogy of Religion* [1736]. London: Bell and Darby, 1864.

Campbell, George. *The Philosophy of Rhetoric* [1776]. Carbondale: Southern Illinois University Press, 1967.

Castellio, Sebastian. *De l'Art de Douter (De Arte Dubitandi)* trans. C. Baudouin. Geneva, 1953.

Chandler, Edward. *A Defense of Christianity from the Prophecies.* London: J. Knapton, 1725.

Chandler, Samuel. *A Vindication of the Antiquity and Authenticity of Daniel's Prophecies.* London: Gray, 1728.

———. *The Witnesses of the Resurrection of Jesus Christ Re-examined.* London: J. Noon, n.d.

Chapman, John. *Eusebius.* 2 volumes. Cambridge: W. Thurlbourn, 1739; London, 1741.

Chubb, Thomas. *Collection of Tracts.* London, 1730.

———. *A Discourse Concerning Persecution in Three Tracts.* London, 1727.

———. *A Discourse Concerning Reason with Regard to Religion and Divine Reason.* London: T. Cox, 1731.

———. *Discourse on Miracles.* London: T. Cox, 1741.

———. *An Enquiry Concerning the Books of the New Testament in Four Tracts.* London: T. Cox, 1727.

———. *An Enquiry into the Grounds and Reasons.* London, 1732.

———. *Four Letters to a Friend.* London: R. Ford, 1725.

———. *The Posthumous Works.* 2 volumes. London: R. Baldwin, 1748.

———. *The True Gospel of Jesus Christ Vindicated.* London, 1739.

Cicero. *De Oratore.* Trans. E. W. Sutton, H. Rackham. London: Heinemann, 1967.

Collins, Anthony. *A Discourse Concerning Ridicule and Irony in Writing, In a letter to the Rev. Dr. Nathaniel Marshall.* London: J. Brother, 1729.

———. *A Discourse of Free Thinking* [1713]. New York: Garland, 1978.

———. *A Discourse of the Grounds and Reasons of the Christian Religion.* London, 1724.

———. *An Essay Concerning the Use of Reason in Propositions The Evidence whereof depends on Testimony.* London, 1707.

Conybeare, John. *A Defense of Revealed Religion.* London, 1732.

———. *The Mysteries of the Christian Religion Credible.* Oxford: L. Lichfield, 1723.

———. *The Nature, Possibility and Certainty of Miracles.* Oxford, 1722.

Cooper, Anthony Ashley, Lord Shaftesbury. *Characteristics of Men, Manners, Opinions, Times.* London, 1711.

———. *Letter Concerning Enthusiasm.* London: J. Morphew, 1708.

Copies Taken from the Records of the Court of King's Bench, at Westminster. No. xxvi. London, 1763.

Craig, Mungo. *A Satyr Against Atheistical Deism.* Edinburgh: Robert Hutchinson, 1696.

A Defense of the Scripture History . . . In Answer to Mr. Woolston's Fifth Discourse on the Saviour's Miracles. London: E. Symon, 1733.

DeFoe, Daniel. *The Free Masons; an Hudibrastic POEM.* London: A. Moore, 1723.

———. *The Perjur'd Free Mason Detected.* London: T. Warner, 1730.

———. *The Secrets of the invisible World Disclosed or, a Universal History of Apparitions.* London: J. Clarke, 1729.

———. *A System of Magic or, a History of the Black Art.* London: J. Roberts, 1727.

———. *Robinson Crusoe* [1719-1720]. New York: Houghton Mifflin, 1909.

Deism Revealed or, the Attack on Christianity Candidly Reviewed. 2 vols. London: A. Millar, 1751.

Delepierre, Octava. *Des Livres Condamnés au feu en Angleterre.* N.p., n.d. (1763?).

Derham, William. *The Artificial Clockmaker.* London: J. Knapton, 1696.

——. *Astro-theology, or a Demonstration of the Being and Attributes of God from a survey of the Heavens.* London: W. Innys, 1715.

A Dialogue Between Mr. Grounds and Schemes & C. and Tom Woolston. London: J. Roberts, 1729.

Discourse Sur Les Miracles De Jesus Christ, Traduits de L'Anglois de Woolston. Trans. Baron d'Holbach [?]. Amsterdam, 1769.

Doddridge, Philip. *A Letter to the Author of Christianity Not Founded on Argument.* London, 1742.

——. *Perspicuity and Solidity of Those Evidences of Christianity . . . in a Letter.* London, 1742.

——. *A Second Letter to the author of a Pamphlet intitled Christianity not Founded on Argument.* London: M. Fenner, 1743.

——. *A Third Letter.* London: M. Fenner, 1743.

Dodwell, Henry. *Christianity Not Founded on Argument.* London: T. Cooper, 1741.

Douglas, John. *The Criterion.* London, 1754.

Dryden, John. *Works of John Dryden.* Ed. Sir Walter Scott. London, 1808.

Edgcumbe, James. "Two Sermons Preach'd before the University of Oxford at St. Mary's Church on Sunday, October 27, 1734, and Monday February 2, 1735–6." Published as *Human Reason an Insufficient Guide in Matters of Religion and Morality.* London, 1736.

Entwick, John. *The Evidence of Christianity.* London: J. Pete, 1729.

The Evidence of the Resurrection Clear'd from the Exception of a late Pamphlet entitled, The Resurrection of Jesus Consider'd by a Moral Philosopher. London, 1744.

Farmer, Hugh. *A Dissertation on the Miracles.* London: Cadell, 1771.

Fleetwood, William. *An Essay Upon Miracles.* London: C. Harper, 1701.

Fleming, C. *Remarks on Mr. Thomas Chubb's Vindication of his True Gospel of Jesus Christ.* London, 1739.

For God or the Devil. London, 1728.

A Friendly Admonition to Mr. Chubb. London: R. Ford, 1727.

Gibson, Edmund. *The Bishop of London's Pastoral Letter to the People of his Diocese.* London: Samuel Buckley, 1728.

——. *Pastoral Letter,* 3d ed. London: Samuel Buckley, 1728.

The Gradual Advances, and Different Periods of Divine Revelation . . . in Opposition to the Infidelity of Mr. Woolston. Oxford: L. Lichfield, 1729.

H. F., *A Modest Address to the Wicked Authors of the Present Age.* London, 1765.

Hallett, Joseph. *The Consistent Christian—Being a Confutation of the Errors advanced in Mr. Chubb's late Book: entitled, The True Gospel of Jesus Christ Asserted.* London: J. Noon, 1738.

Hare, Francis. *The Clergyman's Thanks to Philentherus*. London, 1713.

Harris, William. *The Reasonableness of Believing in Christ; Two Sermons Preached at Salters Hall, May 21 and 28, 1728*. London: R. Ford, 1729.

Hewlett, Ebenezer. *Miracles real Evidences of a Divine Revelation . . . In answer to Mr. Chubb's Discourse on Miracles*. London, 1741.

Hoadley, Benjamin. *A Letter to Mr. Fleetwood*. London, 1702.

———. *Queries Recommended to the Authors of the late Discourse of Free Thinking*. London, 1713.

Homes, Henry, Lord Kames. *Elements of Criticism* [1762]. New York: Barnes and Burr, 1865.

Hume, David. *Enquiry Concerning Human Nature* [1748]. Oxford: Oxford University Press, 1936.

Hutcheson, Francis. *Reflections upon Laughter, and Remarks upon the Fable of the Bees*. London, 1750.

Ibbot, Benjamin. *A Course of Sermons*. London: J. Wyatt, 1729.

Ilive, Jacob. *The Book of Jasher*. London, 1751.

———. *The Book of Jasher*. Ed. C. D. Bond. Bristol, 1829.

———. *The Layman's Vindication of the Christian Religion*. London, 1730.

———. *The Oration Spoke at Joyner's Hall*. London, 1733.

———. *The Oration Spoke at Trinity Hall in Aldersgate Street: on Monday, January 9, 1738*. London: J. Wilford, 1738.

———. *The Speech of Mr. Jacob Ilive to His brethren the Master-Printers on the great Utility of the Art of Printing, at a General meeting, Wednesday, the 18th of July, 1750*. London, 1750.

Jones, Jonathan. *Liberty Vindicated Being a Defense of Mr. Woolston's Discourses on the Miracles of our Savior*. London: R. Walker, 1730.

Lardner, Nathaniel. *A Vindication of Three of our Blessed Savior's Miracles*. London: T. Sanders, 1729.

Law, William. *The Case of Reason* [1731]. In *Works of William Law*. Setley, England, 1892, vol. 3.

Leland, John. *Remarks on a Late Pamphlet Entitled Christianity Not Founded on Argument*. London: R. Hett, 1754.

———. *A Second Letter*. London, 1744.

———. *A View of the Principal Deistical Writers*. 2 volumes. London: Benjamin Dodd, 1757.

LeMoine, Abraham. *Treatise on Miracles*. London: J. Nourse, 1747.

Leng, John. *Natural Obligations to Believe the Principles of Religion and Divine Revelation*. London: R. Knapock, 1719.

Leslie, Charles. *The Charge of Socinianism against Dr. Tillotson Considered*. London, 1708.

Lewis, Richard. *The Robin Hood Society*. London: E. Withers and W. Reeve, 1756.

Luther, Martin. *D. Martin Luther's Werke*. Weimar: H. Bohlau, 1883–1848.

Madan, M. *A Full and Complete answer to the Capital Errors Contained in the Writings of the Late Rev. Law*. London: Edward Dilly, 1763.

Manning, Gillian. "The Deist: A Satyr on the Parsons," *The Seventeenth Century* 8 (Spring 1993): 149–60.

Mason, John. *A Plain and Modest Plea*. London, 1743.

Middleton, Conyers. *A Free Inquiry Into the Miraculous Powers*. London, 1748.

———. *The Miscellaneous Works of Conyers Middleton*. London: R. Manby, 1755.

Miracles of Jesus Vindicated. London, 1729.

Montaigne, Michel de. "Apologie de Raimond Sebond." In *Les Essais de Michel de Montaigne*, volume 2. Ed. Pierre Villey. Paris, 1922.

Monthly Chronicle for March, 1729. London: A. Ward, 1729.

Monthly Chronicle for May, 1728. London: A. Ward, 1728.

Morgan, Thomas. *The Moral Philosopher* [1738]. New York: Garland Publishing, 1977.

———. *The Moral Philosopher, v.II*. London, 1739.

———. *The Moral Philosopher, v. III*. London: T. Cox, 1740.

Morris, Corbyn. *An Essay Toward Fixing the True Standards of Wit, Humor, Raillery, Satire, and Ridicule*. London, 1744.

The New Aryan Reproved. London: T. Childe, 1711.

Pastoral Politicks. London: J. Huggonson, 1742.

Piozzi, Hester Lynch. *British Synonymy* [1794]. Menston, U.K.: Scholar Press, 1968.

Port-Royal Logic, 8th ed. Trans. T. S. Baynes. Edinburgh: W. Blackwood and Sons, 1880.

Powell, William Samuel. *Discourses on Various Subjects*. London, c. 1770.

Price, Richard. *Four Dissertations*. London, 1768.

Prideaux, Humphrey. *The True Nature of Imposture Fully Displayed*. London: William Rogers, 1697.

Ramsay, Allan. *An Essay on Ridicule*. London, 1753.

Randolph, Herbert. *Legal Punishments Consider'd. A Sermon Preached at the Assizes held at Rochester before the Honourable Mr. Justice Denton, On Wed. March the 12th, 1728/9*. London: Wm. Innys, 1729.

Ray, T. *A Vindication of our Saviour's Miracles in Answer to Mr. Tho. Woolston*. London: J. Marshall, 1729.

Reasons for not Proceeding Against Mr. Whiston by the Court of Delegates. London, 1713.

Reid, William H. *The Rise and Dissolution of Infidel Societies*. London, 1800.

Rutherforth, Thomas. *The Credibility of Miracles Defended*. Cambridge, 1751.

Sacheverell, Henry. *The Dangers of False Brethren*. London, 1709.

Saul et David. London: R. Freeman, 1771.

Shaftesbury's Ghost Conjur'd. London, 1738.

Sherlock, Thomas. *The Tryal of the Witnesses to the Resurrection of Jesus*. London, 1729.

Skelton, Philip. *Ophiomaches: or Deism Revealed.* 2 vols. London, 1749.

Smalbroke, Richard. *Sermon Preached to the Societies for Reformation of Manners on Wednesday, January 10, 1727.* London: J. Dwoning, 1728.

————. *A Vindication of the Miracles of our Blessed Saviour, in which Mr. Woolston's Discourses on Them are Particularly Examined.* 2 vols. London: J. and J. Knapton, 1729.

Smith, E. *The Superstition of Omens and Prodigies with the proper Reception, and profitable Improvement. A Divinity Lecture upon the Surprising Phenomenon of Light, March 6, 1715, on the Sunday after.* London, 1715.

Some Authentic Memoirs of the Life of Colonel Ch— — —s. London, 1730.

A Speech Delivered by an Indian Chief. London, 1753.

Spinoza, Benedict. *The Chief Works of Spinoza.* 2 volumes. Trans. R. H. M. Elwes. New York: Dover, 1961.

Stackhouse, Thomas. *Defense of the Christian Religion.* London, 1733.

————. *A Defense of the Christian Religion from the Several Objections of Modern Antiscripturists.* London: E. Symon, 1723.

————. *A Fair State of the Controversy Between Mr. Woolston and His Adversaries.* London, 1730.

Stebbing, Henry. *A Defense of the Scripture History.* London: John Pemberton, 1729.

Stephens, William. *An Account of the Growth of Deism in England.* Ed. James Force. Los Angeles: Augustan Reprint Society, Clark Memorial Library, U.C.L.A. no. 261, 1990.

Stilton, W. *A View of the Life of King David.* London, n.d.

Swift, Jonathan. *Mr. C— — — —n's Discourse of Free-Thinking Put into plain English, by way of Abstract for use of the Poor.* London: J. Morphew, 1713.

————. "Verses on the Death of Dr. Swift." *The Poems of Jonathan Swift.* 2d ed. Edited by Harold Williams. Oxford: Clarendon Press, 1958.

Tilly, William. *The Power, Vertue, and Influence of Christ's Resurrection; and the Excellence of Knowing that above and beyond all other Knowledge.* Oxford: L. Lichfield, 1718.

————. *A Preservative Against the Growing Infidelity and Apostasy of the Present Age.* London: J. Roberts, 1729.

Tindal, Matthew. *An Address to the Inhabitants of the Two Great Cities of London and Westminster in Relation to a Pastoral Letter, Said to be Written by the Bishop of London.* London: J. Peale, 1729.

————. *Christianity as Old as Creation.* London, 1730.

Toland, John. *Christianity Not Mysterious.* London, 1696.

————. *Letters to Serena.* London: Bernard Lintot, 1704.

————. *Vindicus Liberius: or Mr. Toland's Defense of Himself.* London, 1702.

Tom of Bedlam's Short Letter to his Cozin Tom W—lst—n. London, 1728.

The Two First Books, of Philostratus, Concerning the Life of Apolloniun Tyaneus. London, 1680.

The Vanity of Free Thinking. London: J. Morphew, 1713.

Wade, George. *Two Discourses. The First an Appeal to the Miracles of Jesus as Proofs of his Messiahship, The Second a Demonstration of the Truth and Certainty of Resurrection from the Dead.* London: G. Strahan, 1729.

Warburton, William. *A Critical and Philosophical Enquiry into the Causes of Prodigies and Miracles, as related by Historians.* London: T. Corbett, 1727.

———. *Divine Legation of Moses.* London: F. Gyles, 1738.

Waugh, John. *A Charge Delivered to the Clergy of the Diocese of Carlisle. May 26, 1747.* London: E. Owen, 1747.

Whitehead, William. *An Essay on Ridicule.* London: R. Dodsley, 1743.

Woolaston, William. *The Religion of Nature Delineated.* London, 1722.

Woolston, Thomas. *Four Free Gifts to the Clergy.* London, 1722–1724.

———. *Letter to Dr. Bennett.* London, 1721.

———. *An Old Apology for the Christian Religion.* Cambridge, 1705.

———. *Origens Ademanti Renati Epistola ad Doctores Whitebeium, Waterlandium, Whistlium.* London: J. Roberts, 1720.

———. *Six Discourses on the Miracles of Our Savior* [1727–1729]. New York: Garland Publishing, 1979.

———. *A Third Discourse on the Miracles of our Savior.* London, 1728.

———. *Woolston's Works.* London: J. Roberts, 1733.

Secondary Sources

Aldridge, Alfred O. "Shaftesbury and the Test of Truth," *Proceedings of the Modern Language Association* 60 (1945): 129–56.

The Anatomy of God. Trans. R. A. Rosenberg. New York: Ktav, 1973.

Annas, Julia, and Jonathan Barnes. *The Modes of Skepticism.* Cambridge: Cambridge University Press, 1985.

Becker, Carl. *The Heavenly City of the Eighteenth Century Philosophers* [1932]. New Haven: Yale University Press, 1961.

Berman, David. "Anthony Collins and the Question of Atheism in the Early Part of the Eighteenth Century," *Proceedings of the Royal Irish Academy* 75, no. 5 (1975): 85–102.

———. "Censorship and the Displacement of Irreligion." *Journal of the History of Philosophy* 27 (October 1989): 601–4.

———. "David Hume and the Suppression of Atheism," *Journal of the History of Philosophy* 21 (July 1983): 375–87.

———. "Deism, Immortality, and the Art of Theological Lying," in *Deism, Masonry, and the Enlightenment.* Ed. J. A. Leo Lamay. Newark: University of Delaware Press, 1987. 61–78.

———. "Deliberate Parapraxes," *International Review of Psycho-Analysis* 15 (1988): 381–84.

———. "Disclaimers as Offence Mechanisms in Charles Blount and John Toland," in *Atheism from the Reformation to the Enlightenment*. Ed. Michael Hunter and David Wootton. Oxford: Clarendon Press, 1992. 255–72.

———. *A History of Atheism in Britain: from Hobbes to Russell*. London: Croom Helm, 1988.

———. "Some Light on the Hidden Hobbes," *Topoi* 5 (September 1986): 197–99.

Billig, Michael. *Arguing and Thinking*. Cambridge: Cambridge University Press, 1987.

Black, Jeremy. "The Challenge of Autocracy," *Studi Settecenteschi* 3–4 (1982–83): 107–18.

Brown, Colin. *Jesus in European Protestant Thought*. Durham, N.C.: Labyrinth Press, 1985.

———. *Miracles and the Critical Mind*. Grand Rapids, Mich.: Eerdmans, 1984.

Brown, Harold O. J. *Heresies*. Garden City, N.Y.: Doubleday, 1984.

Brown, Jerry Wayne. *The Rise of Biblical Criticism in America, 1800–1870*. Middleton, Conn.: Wesleyan University Press, 1969.

Buckley, George T. *Atheism in the English Renaissance* [1932]. New York: Russell and Russell, 1965.

Buckley, Michael J. *At the Origins of Modern Atheism*. New Haven: Yale University Press, 1987.

Bullitt, John M. *Jonathan Swift and the Anatomy of Satire*. Cambridge, Mass.: Harvard University Press, 1953.

Burns, R. M. "David Hume and the Miracles Controversy." Ph.D. dissertation. Princeton University, 1971.

———. *The Great Debate on Miracles*. Lewisberg, Penn.: Bucknell University Press, 1981.

Bury, J. B. *History of Freedom of Thought*. London, 1913.

Bushell, Thomas L. *The Sage of Salisbury: Thomas Chubb 1679–1747*. New York: Philosophical Library, 1967.

Byrne, Peter. *Natural Religion and the Nature of Religion*. London: Routledge, 1989.

Cameron, Nigel M. de S. *Biblical Higher Criticism and the Defense of Infallibilism in 19th Century Britain*. Lewiston, N.Y.: Edwin Mellen, 1987.

Cassirer, Ernest. *The Philosophy of the Enlightenment*. Boston: Beacon, 1965.

Chandler, Thomas B. *Life of Samuel Johnson*. New York, 1824.

Christensen, Merton. "Taylor of Norwich and the Higher Criticism," *The Journal of the History of Ideas* (1959): 179–94.

Christie-Murray, David. *A History of Heresy*. Oxford: Oxford University Press, 1989.

Clark, J. C. D. *English Society: 1688–1832*. Cambridge: Cambridge University Press, 1985.

———. *The Language of Liberty 1688–1832*. Cambridge: Cambridge University Press, 1994.

Colie, Rosalie Littel. *Light and Enlightenment*. Cambridge: Cambridge University Press, 1957.

Conway, Monroe D. *Life of Thomas Paine*. London: Putnams, 1892.

Cropper, Margaret. *Sparks Among the Stubble*. London: Longmans, Green, 1955.

Cragg, G. R. *Reason and Authority*. Cambridge: Cambridge University Press, 1964.

Craig, William Lane. *The Historical Argument for the Resurrection of Jesus During the Deist Controversy*. Lewiston, N.Y.: Edwin Mellen, 1985.

DeWar, James. *The Unlocked Secret: Freemasonry Examined*. London: Kimber, 1966.

Edwards, David. *Christian England*. Grand Rapids, Mich.: Eerdmans, 1984.

Emerson, Roger. "Latitudinarianism and the English Deists," in *Deism, Masonry and the Enlightenment*. Ed. Leo J. LeMay. Newark: University of Delaware Press, 1986. 19–48.

Evans, Robert Rees. *Pantheisticon: The Career of John Toland*. New York: Lang, 1990.

Ferreira, M. Jamie. *Skepticism and Reasonable Doubt*. Oxford: Clarendon Press, 1986.

Fine, Gary Allen. "Humorous Interaction and the Social Construction of Meaning," *Studies in Symbolic Interaction* (1984): 85–87.

Fisher, Walter R. *Human Communication as Narration*. Columbia: University of South Carolina Press, 1987.

Flew, Antony. *Hume's Philosophy of Belief*. London: Routledge and Kegan Paul, 1961.

———. *Of Miracles: David Hume*. La Salle, Ill.: Open Court, 1985.

Foucault, Michel. *The Archaeology of Knowledge*. New York: Random House, 1972.

Gasciogne, John. *Cambridge in the Age of the Enlightenment*. Cambridge: Cambridge University Press, 1989.

Gay, Peter. *The Enlightenment: An Interpretation, The Rise of Modern Paganism*. New York: Knopf, 1967.

Gilmore, Thomas. *The Eighteenth-Century Controversy over Ridicule as a Test of Truth: A Reconsideration*. Atlanta: University of Georgia Press, 1970.

Grainger, Muriel. *W. Law and the Life of the Spirit*. Shorne, England: Ridgeway House, n.d.

Grant, Robert M. *Heresy and Criticism*. Louisville, Ky.: John Knox Press, 1993.

Grant, Robert M., and David Tracy. *A Short History of the Interpretation of the Bible*, 2d ed. Philadelphia: Fortress, 1984.

Grean, Stanley. *Shaftesbury's Philosophy of Religion and Ethics*. Athens: Ohio University Press, 1967.

Green, J. Brazier. *John Wesley and William Law*. London: Epworth, 1945.

Harrison, R. K., B. K. Waltke, D. Guthrie, and G. D. Fee. *Biblical Criticism: Historical, Literary and Textual*. Grand Rapids: Zondervan, 1978.

Harvey, Rev. S. *The Mysticism of William Law*. London: SPCK, 1914.

Hefelbower, S. G. *The Relation of John Locke to English Deism*. Chicago: University of Chicago Press, 1918.

Herrick, James A. "Miracles and Method," *Quarterly Journal of Speech* 75 (August 1989): 321–34.

Holmes, Geoffrey. *Politics, Religion and Society in England 1679–1742.* London: Hambledon, 1986.

Hobhouse, Stephen. *William Law and Eighteenth-Century Quakerism.* London: Allen and Unwin, 1927.

Howell, Wilbur Samuel. *Logic and Rhetoric in England: 1500–1700.* New York: Russell and Russell, 1961.

Hughes, Richard. *The Sense of the Ridiculous: Ridicule as a Rhetorical Device in the Poetry of Dryden and Pope.* Unpublished Ph.D. dissertation. University of Wisconsin, 1954.

Hurlbutt, Robert. *Hume, Newton and the Design Argument.* Lincoln: University of Nebraska Press, 1965. 69, 70.

Hutcheson, Harold. *Lord Herbert of Cherbury's De Religione Laici.* New Haven: Yale University Press, 1944.

Jacob, Margaret. *Living the Enlightenment: Freemasonry and Politics in Eighteenth-Century Europe.* New York: Oxford Press, 1991.

———. *The Radical Enlightenment: Pantheists, Freemasons and Republicans.* London: Allen and Unwin, 1981.

Keller, Ernst and Marie-Louise. *Miracles in Dispute.* Philadelphia: Fortress, 1969.

Kneale, William and Martha. *Development of Logic.* Oxford: Clarendon Press, 1975.

Kreiser, Robert. *Miracles, Convulsions, and Ecclesiastical Politics in Early Eighteenth-Century Paris.* Princeton: Princeton University Press, 1978.

Krentz, Edgar. *The History of Critical Method.* Philadelphia: Fortress, 1975.

Laramer, Robert A. *Water Into Wine?* Montreal: McGill / Queen's University Press, 1988.

Legman, G. *The Guilt of the Knights Templar.* New York: Basic Books, 1966.

Levy, Leonard. *Blasphemy: Verbal Offense Against God from Moses to Salman Rushdie.* New York: Alfred A. Knopf, 1993.

———. *Treason Against God: A History of the Crime of Blasphemy.* New York: Schocken Books, 1981.

Lewis, C. S. *Miracles.* New York: Macmillan, 1978.

Lovejoy, A. O. *The Great Chain of Being.* Cambridge, Mass.: Harvard University Press, 1950.

MacGregor, Geddes. *Gnosis.* Wheaton, Ill.: Theosophical Publishing House, 1979.

Manent, Pierre. *An Intellectual History of Liberalism.* Princeton: Princeton University Press, 1994.

The Margins of Orthodoxy. Ed. Roger D. Lund. Cambridge: Cambridge University Press, 1995.

McDonald, Michael. *Mystical Bedlam.* Cambridge: Cambridge University Press, 1981.

McIntosh, Carey. *Common and Courtly Language: The Stylistics of Class in Eighteenth-Century English Literature.* Philadelphia: University of Pennsylvania Press, 1986.

McLachlan, H. *Socinianism in Seventeenth Century England*. Oxford: Oxford University Press, 1951.

Melinsky, M. A. H. *Healing Miracles*. London: A. R. Mowbray, 1968.

Monck, J. H. *Life of Bentley*. London, 1830.

Morais, Herbert. *Deism in Eighteenth-Century America*. New York: Russell and Russell, 1960.

Morrison, Samuel E. *Freedom in Contemporary Society*. Boston: Little, Brown, 1956.

Mossner, Ernest C. *Bishop Butler and the Age of Reason*. New York: MacMillan, 1936.

Murphy, Paul. *The Meaning of Freedom of Speech*. Westport, Conn.: Greenwood, 1972.

The New Cambridge Modern History. 14 vols. Cambridge: Cambridge University Press, 1970.

Novak, Maximillian E. "Defoe, the Occult, and the Deist Offensive during the Reign of George I," in *Deism, Masonry, and the Enlightenment: Essays Honoring Alfred Owen Aldridge*. Ed. J. A. Leo Lemay. Newark: University of Delaware Press, 1986. 93–108.

O'Higgins, James, S.J. *Anthony Collins: The Man and His Works*. The Hague: Martinus Nijhoff, 1970.

Ong, Walter J. *Method and the Decay of Dialogue*. Cambridge, Mass.: Harvard University Press, 1958.

Orwell, George. *Collected Essays, Journals and Letters*. Ed. Sonia Orwell and Ian Angus. 4 vols. London: Secker and Warburg, 1968.

Palmer, Humphery. *The Logic of Gospel Criticism*. London: Macmillan, 1968.

Palmer, Jerry. *The Logic of the Absurd*. London: British Film Institute, 1987.

Perelman, Chaim, and L. Olbrechts-Tyteca. *The New Rhetoric*. Notre Dame: University of Notre Dame Press, 1969.

Perkins, Pheme. *Gnosticism and the New Testament*. Minneapolis: Fortress, 1993.

Plumb, J. H. *The Origins of Political Stability: England 1675–1724*. Boston: Houghton Mifflin, 1967.

Popkin, Richard. *The History of Skepticism from Erasmus to Spinoza*. Berkeley: University of California Press, 1979.

Porter, Roy. *English Society in the Eighteenth Century*. New York: Penguin Books, 1983.

Pound, Roscoe. *The Development of Constitutional Guarantees of Liberty*. New Haven: Yale University Press, 1957.

Rack, Henry D. *Reasonable Enthusiast: John Wesley and the Rise of Methodism*. Nashville: Abingdon, 1993.

Randall, J. H. *The Making of the Modern Mind*, 2d ed. New York: Houghton Mifflin, 1940.

Redwood, John. *Reason, Ridicule and Religion*. Cambridge: Harvard University Press, 1976.

Reventlow, Henning Graf. *The Authority of the Bible and the Rise of the Modern Mind.* Philadelphia: Fortress Press, 1985.

Richetti, John. "Representing an Underclass: Servants and Proletarians in Fielding and Smollett," in *The New Eighteenth Century: Theory, Politics, English Literature.* Ed. Felicity Nussbaum and Laura Brown. New York: Methuen, 1987. 84–98.

Robertson, J. M. *A Short History of Free Thought.* London: Watts, 1915.

Rogers, Pat. *Grub Street.* London: Methuen, 1972.

Rosen, George. *Madness in Society.* Chicago: University of Chicago Press, 1968.

Sambrook, James. *The Eighteenth Century: The Intellectual and Cultural Context of English Literature, 1700–1789.* New York: Longman, 1986.

Schaya, Leo. *The Universal Meaning of the Kabbalah.* London: Allen and Unwin, 1971.

Schmitt, C. B. "The Rediscovery of Ancient Skepticism in Modern Times," in *The Skeptical Tradition.* Berkeley: University of California Press, 1983.

Shapin, Steven. *A Social History of Truth: Civility and Science in Seventeenth-Century England.* Chicago: University of Chicago Press, 1994.

Sitter, John. "About Wit," in *Rhetorics of Order/Ordering Rhetorics.* Ed. J. Douglas Canfield and J. Paul Hunter. Newark: University of Delaware Press, 1989.

Smith, Craig. *Freedom of Expression and Partisan Politics.* Columbia: University of South Carolina Press, 1989.

Speck, W. A. *Society and Literature in England, 1700–1760.* Dublin: Gill and Macmillan, 1983.

Spragens, Thomas. *Reason and Democracy.* Durham, N.C.: Duke University Press, 1990.

Stephen, Leslie. *English Thought in the Eighteenth Century* [1876]. 2 vols. New York: Harcourt, Brace and World, 1976.

Strawson, P. F. *Skepticism and Naturalism: Some Varieties.* New York: Columbia University Press, 1985.

Stromberg, Roland. *Religious Liberalism in Eighteenth-Century England.* Oxford: Oxford University Press, 1954.

Sullivan, Robert. *John Toland and the Deist Controversy.* Cambridge: Harvard University Press, 1985.

Tave, Stuart M. *The Amiable Humorist.* Chicago: University of Chicago Press, 1960.

Templeman, William Darby. "Warburton and Brown Continue the Battle over Ridicule," *Huntington Library Quarterly* (1953): 17–36.

Tennant, F. R. *Miracle and its Philosophical Presuppositions.* Cambridge: Cambridge University Press, 1925.

Thompson, E. P. "Eighteenth-Century English Society: Class Struggle Without Class?," *Social History* 3 (May 1978): 133–65.

———. "Patrician Society, Plebian Culture," *Journal of Social History* 7 (1974): 382–405.

————. *Whigs and Hunters: The Origins of the Black Act.* New York: Pantheon Books, 1975.

Thrower, James. *A Short History of Western Atheism.* London: Pemberton Books, 1971.

Torrey, Norman V. *Voltaire and the English Deists.* New Haven: Yale University Press, 1930.

Trapnell, William. *Thomas Woolston: Deist and Madman?* Bristol: Thoemess, 1993.

Trench, Richard C. *Notes on the Miracles of our Lord.* New York: Appleton, 1854.

Twyman, Ella. *Peter Annet, 1693–1769.* London: Pioneer Press, 1938.

Waldman, Theodore. "Origins of the Doctrine of Reasonable Doubt," *Journal of the History of Ideas* 20 (1959): 299–316

Walter, Kerry S. *The American Deists.* Lawrence: University of Kansas Press, 1992.

Watts, Michael R. *Dissenters.* Oxford: Clarendon Press, 1978.

Wiley, Basil. *The Eighteenth Century Background* [1940]. Boston: Beacon, 1961.

Williams, Charles. *The Descent of the Dove* [1939]. Rpt. Grand Rapids, Mich.: Eerdmans, 1979.

Wood, G. F. "The Evidential Use of Miracles," in *Miracles.* Ed. G. F. Wood. London: Mowbray, 1965.

Yolton, John. *John Locke: An Introduction.* Oxford: Blackwell, 1985.

————. *Thinking Matter.* Minneapolis: University of Minnesota Press, 1983.

Index